A·N·N·U·A·L E·D·I·T·I·O·N·S

International Business
03/04

Twelfth Edition

EDITOR

Fred Maidment
Western Connecticut State University

Dr. Fred Maidment is associate professor of management at Western Connecticut State University in Danbury, Connecticut. He received his bachelor's degree from New York University and his master's degree from the Bernard M. Baruch College of the City University of New York. In 1983 he received his doctorate from the University of South Carolina. He resides in Connecticut with his wife.

McGraw-Hill/Dushkin
530 Old Whitfield Street, Guilford, Connecticut 06437

Visit us on the Internet
http://www.dushkin.com

Credits

1. **The War on Terrorism**
   Unit photo—United Nations photo by John Isaac.
2. **The Nature of International Business**
   Unit photo—© 2003 by PhotoDisc, Inc.
3. **The International Environment: Organizations and Monetary Systems**
   Unit photo—TRW Inc. photo.
4. **Foreign Environment**
   Unit photo—AP Photo by Greg Baker.
5. **How Management Deals With Environmental Forces**
   Unit photo—Courtesy of Christine Asenjo.

Copyright

Cataloging in Publication Data
Main entry under title: Annual Editions: International Business. 2003/2004.
1. Management—Periodicals. I. Maidment, Fred, *comp*. II. Title: International Business.
ISBN 0–07–254849–5   658'.05   ISSN 1091–1731

© 2003 by McGraw-Hill/Dushkin, Guilford, CT 06437, A Division of The McGraw-Hill Companies.

Copyright law prohibits the reproduction, storage, or transmission in any form by any means of any portion of this publication without the express written permission of McGraw-Hill/Dushkin, and of the copyright holder (if different) of the part of the publication to be reproduced. The Guidelines for Classroom Copying endorsed by Congress explicitly state that unauthorized copying may not be used to create, to replace, or to substitute for anthologies, compilations, or collective works.

Annual Editions® is a Registered Trademark of McGraw-Hill/Dushkin, A Division of The McGraw-Hill Companies.

Twelfth Edition

Cover image © 2003 PhotoDisc, Inc.
Printed in the United States of America   1234567890BAHBAH543   Printed on Recycled Paper

Editors/Advisory Board

Members of the Advisory Board are instrumental in the final selection of articles for each edition of ANNUAL EDITIONS. Their review of articles for content, level, currentness, and appropriateness provides critical direction to the editor and staff. We think that you will find their careful consideration well reflected in this volume.

EDITOR

Fred Maidment
Western Connecticut State University

ADVISORY BOARD

Riad A. Ajami
University of North Carolina

Syed Tariq Anwar
West Texas A & M University

Jeffrey Arpan
University of South Carolina

Robert T. Aubey
University of Wisconsin, Madison

Marca M. Bear
University of Tampa

Eldon H. Bernstein
Lynn University

Martin S. Bressler
Houston Baptist University

Charles R. Chittle
Bowling Green State University

Kerry Cooper
Texas A & M University

John D. Daniels
University of Miami

Frank L. DuBois
American University

Erwin F. Erhardt
Thomas More College

Basil J. Janavaras
Minnesota State University–Mankato

Paul R. Johnson
Bond University

Paul E. Jursa
College of Charleston

Michael J. Kuryla
Broome Community College

Joseph A. LeMay
Ramapo College of New Jersey

Patricia M. Manninen
North Shore Community College

Wendell H. McCulloch, Jr.
California State University, Long Beach

Kevin M. McNeilly
Miami University

Lucie Pfaff
College of Mt. St. Vincent

Keramat Poorsoltan
Frostburg State University

Betty Jane Punnett
University of the West Indies

John E. Richardson
Pepperdine University

Belay Seyoum
Nova Southeastern University

Angelo Tarallo
Ramapo College of New Jersey

Arienne Turner
Fullerton College

Staff

EDITORIAL STAFF

Ian A. Nielsen, Publisher
Roberta Monaco, Senior Developmental Editor
Dorothy Fink, Associate Developmental Editor
Iain Martin, Associate Developmental Editor
Addie Raucci, Senior Administrative Editor
Robin Zarnetske, Permissions Editor
Marie Lazauskas, Permissions Assistant
Diane Barker, Proofreader
Lisa Holmes-Doebrick, Senior Program Coordinator

TECHNOLOGY STAFF

Richard Tietjen, Senior Publishing Technologist
Jonathan Stowe, Executive Director of eContent
Marcuss Oslander, Sponsoring Editor of eContent
Christopher Santos, Senior eContent Developer
Janice Ward, Software Support Analyst
Angela Mule, eContent Developer
Michael McConnell, eContent Developer
Ciro Parente, Editorial Assistant
Joe Offredi, Technology Developmental Editor

PRODUCTION STAFF

Brenda S. Filley, Director of Production
Charles Vitelli, Designer
Mike Campell, Production Coordinator
Laura Levine, Graphics
Tom Goddard, Graphics
Eldis Lima, Graphics
Nancy Norton, Graphics
Juliana Arbo, Typesetting Supervisor
Karen Roberts, Typesetter
Jocelyn Proto, Typesetter
Cynthia Powers, Typesetter
Cathy Kuziel, Typesetter
Larry Killian, Copier Coordinator

To the Reader

In publishing ANNUAL EDITIONS we recognize the enormous role played by the magazines, newspapers, and journals of the public press in providing current, first-rate educational information in a broad spectrum of interest areas. Many of these articles are appropriate for students, researchers, and professionals seeking accurate, current material to help bridge the gap between principles and theories and the real world. These articles, however, become more useful for study when those of lasting value are carefully collected, organized, indexed, and reproduced in a low-cost format, which provides easy and permanent access when the material is needed. That is the role played by ANNUAL EDITIONS.

When the first edition of *Annual Editions: International Business* was being compiled, the world, then as now, was extremely unstable. Power in the Soviet Union was very much in question, and hard-liners had conducted a coup against the reform government. On August 19, 1991, Russian president Boris Yeltsin jumped on a tank outside the Russian parliament building and denounced the coup leaders, galvanizing the people to take back their government. On that same day, I was writing the introductory essay for the section of the first edition of this book that included articles on the Soviet Union. In fact, I was typing the essay at the very moment when the news bulletin reporting Yeltsin's act came over the radio. Needless to say, I had to rewrite the essay.

Today, we are entering another era of instability. On September 11, 2001, the United States was savagely and brutally attacked by terrorists at the World Trade Center in New York and the Pentagon in Washington, and further acts of terror were thwarted by the bravery and resolve of passengers on an airliner over the hills of Pennsylvania. This act of terrorism was the first real attack by a foreign power against the homeland of the United States since the War of 1812, nearly 190 years ago.

At this writing, the only thing that is clear is that the Taliban and Al Qaeda are on the run and that Afghanistan has been liberated from one of the world's most repressive regimes. But the future remains unclear and where the war on terror will lead is still to be determined. One thing is certain, however: the world changed when that airliner tore into the north tower of the World Trade Center. How it changed and what the world will be like in the future remains to be seen. Students of business administration and, indeed, all people involved in business need to be aware of this new international environment. They need to recognize the opportunities and the problems associated with doing business outside of their home markets. They need to understand that the same types of opportunities await all who engage in business.

Business must respond to this change in the environment by keeping an open mind about the opportunities available to it on a global basis. The articles that have been chosen for *Annual Editions: International Business 03/04* comprise a cross section of the current literature on the subject. The collection addresses the various aspects of international business, with emphasis on the foundations and environment of international trade and on how corpo-

rations respond to and deal with this environment. To this editor, the general tone of the articles seemed to be growing more optimistic over the past several years, but now, with the terrorist attacks on the United States, there may have been a change. Now there seems to be some apprehension in the literature. Some people are asking questions about the benefits of international trade. They are questioning the workings of such organizations as the WTO, IMF, and the World Bank. The disruption of trade meetings in Seattle has shown that many people are less than convinced of the benefits of world trade. This trend has been borne out in the twelfth edition of *Annual Editions: International Business.* The problem is that not everyone has benefited. In fact, there are great numbers of people who have not benefited at all and, indeed, are in worse shape. But most of the literature seems to be more hopeful and less bleak and foreboding than it was at the start of the 1990s, and it will be interesting to see if this trend can be maintained. There is, for now, more talk about opportunity and success and less talk about problems and failure, in spite of the terrorist attacks.

This edition of *Annual Editions: International Business 03/04* contains a number of features designed to make it useful for people interested in international business. These features include a *topic guide* for locating articles on specific subjects and a *table of contents* with abstracts that summarize each article and draw attention to key words in bold italics. This edition also contains *World Wide Web* sites that can be used to further explore the topics.

We would like to know what you think about our book. Please take a few minutes to complete and return the postage-paid *article rating form* in the back of the volume. We need your advice and assistance to help to improve future editions of *Annual Editions: International Business.*

Fred Maidment

Fred Maidment
Editor

Contents

UNIT 1
The War on Terrorism

Four articles consider how terrorism has impacted on the international business community.

modern cargo handling

UNIT 2
The Nature of International Business

Seven selections describe the dynamics of today's international business community with special attention to international trade and investment.

The concepts in bold italics are developed in the article. For further expansion, please refer to the Topic Guide and the Index.

UNIT 3
The International Environment: Organizations and Monetary Systems

Seven articles examine international organizations, the international monetary system, and the finance of international business.

The concepts in bold italics are developed in the article. For further expansion, please refer to the Topic Guide and the Index.

UNIT 4
Foreign Environment

Sixteen selections discuss how international markets are influenced by the common pressures of financing, the economy, sociocultural dynamics, politics, the legal system, labor relations, and other forces.

The concepts in bold italics are developed in the article. For further expansion, please refer to the Topic Guide and the Index.

The concepts in bold italics are developed in the article. For further expansion, please refer to the Topic Guide and the Index.

UNIT 5
How Management Deals With Environmental Forces

Twenty articles discuss challenging aspects of managing in the international business community.

The concepts in bold italics are developed in the article. For further expansion, please refer to the Topic Guide and the Index.

The concepts in bold italics are developed in the article. For further expansion, please refer to the Topic Guide and the Index.

The concepts in bold italics are developed in the article. For further expansion, please refer to the Topic Guide and the Index.

Topic Guide

This topic guide suggests how the selections in this book relate to the subjects covered in your course. You may want to use the topics listed on these pages to search the Web more easily.

On the following pages a number of Web sites have been gathered specifically for this book. They are arranged to reflect the units of this *Annual Edition.* You can link to these sites by going to the DUSHKIN ONLINE support site at *http://www.dushkin.com/online/.*

ALL THE ARTICLES THAT RELATE TO EACH TOPIC ARE LISTED BELOW THE BOLD-FACED TERM.

Accounting
2. Rebuilding Afghanistan: A Multi-Billion Dollar Plan
3. Money's Costing More
14. The Deficit That Just About Everyone Overlooks
15. The Sacking of Argentina: The IMF Deserves to Be Blamed, but So Does the Country's Willing Political Class
16. Failure of the Fund: Rethinking the IMF Response
17. Accounting Challenges Overseas
18. What the New Currency Means to the European Economy
19. Economics Focus: Big MacCurrencies
25. Free Markets and Poverty
29. Government: Progress Against Corruption
34. International Alliance Negotiations: Legal Issues for General Managers
51. Reforming Globalization

Advertising
8. Europeans Covet U.S.
20. Nike's Voice Looms Large
24. The Gains and Pains of Free Trade
27. Hype at the End of the Tunnel
34. International Alliance Negotiations: Legal Issues for General Managers
35. Putting Branding on the Map: Branding a Country Has Outgrown Its Corporate Roots to Develop Positioning Insights That are World Class
36. Does Globalization Have Staying Power?
37. International Growth Patterns Remain Strong

Brands
5. International Trade: Globalization vs. Protectionism
6. American Corporations: The New Sovereigns
8. Europeans Covet U.S.
10. Smart Globalization
11. Integrating Multinational Firms into International Economics
19. Economics Focus: Big MacCurrencies
20. Nike's Voice Looms Large
21. Social Accountability in Central America: Not Just Ethical, But Economical
27. Hype at the End of the Tunnel
35. Putting Branding on the Map: Branding a Country Has Outgrown Its Corporate Roots to Develop Positioning Insights That are World Class
36. Does Globalization Have Staying Power?
37. International Growth Patterns Remain Strong

Competition
5. International Trade: Globalization vs. Protectionism
6. American Corporations: The New Sovereigns
8. Europeans Covet U.S.
9. Free Trade Bush's Way
10. Smart Globalization
11. Integrating Multinational Firms into International Economics
13. Free Trade Area of the Americas: NAFTA Marches South
24. The Gains and Pains of Free Trade
25. Free Markets and Poverty
27. Hype at the End of the Tunnel
32. The Highest Court You've Never Heard Of
33. The World According to Monti
34. International Alliance Negotiations: Legal Issues for General Managers

35. Putting Branding on the Map: Branding a Country Has Outgrown Its Corporate Roots to Develop Positioning Insights That are World Class
36. Does Globalization Have Staying Power?
37. International Growth Patterns Remain Strong
39. AAEI Conference Highlights: What Does China's Entry Into the WTO Mean for U.S. Exporters?
47. Has Strategy Changed?

Consumer behavior
5. International Trade: Globalization vs. Protectionism
8. Europeans Covet U.S.
10. Smart Globalization
13. Free Trade Area of the Americas: NAFTA Marches South
18. What the New Currency Means to the European Economy
19. Economics Focus: Big MacCurrencies
20. Nike's Voice Looms Large
22. Ascension Years
23. The Non-Performing Country
24. The Gains and Pains of Free Trade
25. Free Markets and Poverty
27. Hype at the End of the Tunnel
30. Serving Up the Commons: A Guest Essay
35. Putting Branding on the Map: Branding a Country Has Outgrown Its Corporate Roots to Develop Positioning Insights That are World Class
36. Does Globalization Have Staying Power?
37. International Growth Patterns Remain Strong
39. AAEI Conference Highlights: What Does China's Entry Into the WTO Mean for U.S. Exporters?
51. Reforming Globalization

Corporate culture
1. New Realities of Globalization
4. Going Global Can Bring on a World of Challenges
6. American Corporations: The New Sovereigns
7. 2001's Most Influential People in World Trade
10. Smart Globalization
16. Failure of the Fund: Rethinking the IMF Response
18. What the New Currency Means to the European Economy
20. Nike's Voice Looms Large
21. Social Accountability in Central America: Not Just Ethical, But Economical
23. The Non-Performing Country
24. The Gains and Pains of Free Trade
25. Free Markets and Poverty
26. Empires Without Umpires
29. Government: Progress Against Corruption
30. Serving Up the Commons: A Guest Essay
34. International Alliance Negotiations: Legal Issues for General Managers
36. Does Globalization Have Staying Power?
37. International Growth Patterns Remain Strong
44. Comrades Are on the March Again
46. The Incredible Shrinking World
47. Has Strategy Changed?
48. Personnel Demands Attention Overseas
49. Safe Haven
50. International HR Manager
51. Reforming Globalization
53. Globalisation's Misguided Assumptions
54. Heavy Surf and Tsunamis

World Wide Web Sites

The following World Wide Web sites have been carefully researched and selected to support the articles found in this reader. The easiest way to access these selected sites is to go to our DUSHKIN ONLINE support site at *http://www.dushkin.com/online/*.

AE: International Business 03/04

The following sites were available at the time of publication. Visit our Web site—we update DUSHKIN ONLINE regularly to reflect any changes.

General Sources

Information Institute: Law About...Pages
http://www.law.cornell.edu/topical.html

Explore this site's searchable index to learn about a myriad of international legal subjects. Organized by topic, it provides usefulsummaries with links to key primary source material and off-Net references.

Internet Resources for International Economics & Business
http://dylee.keel.econ.ship.edu/econ/

Dr. Daniel Lee of the College of Business at Shippensburg University maintains this site, which lists Internet resources related to economics and business in general, references, and specific international business topics such as international development.

North American Free Trade Association (NAFTA)
http://www.nafta-sec-alena.org

NAFTA's stated objective is "to provide accurate and timely information to U.S. exporters experiencing market access barriers in Canada or Mexico."

Office.com
http://www.individual.com

This site from Individual, Inc., provides daily business briefings and more in-depth stories related to such fields as computing and media, banking and finance, health care, insurance, and transportation and distribution.

Sales & Marketing Executive International (SME)
http://www.smei.org

Visit this home page of the worldwide association SME. Through this "Digital Resource Mall" you can access research and useful articles on sales and management. You can even listen in as marketing leaders discuss their latest strategies and ideas.

STAT-USA
http://www.stat-usa.gov/stat-usa.html

A service of the U.S.Department of Commerce, this essential site presents daily economic news; a myriad of links to databases, statistical releases, and selected publications; and general information on export and international trade as well as business leads and procurement opportunities.

World Trade Centers Association (WTCA)
http://www.wtca.org

WTCA On-Line presents this site as a news and information service. Members can access the *Dun & Bradstreet Exporters' Encyclopaedia* and other valuable sources, and guests to the site can also gain entry to interesting trade-related information.

UNIT 1: The War on Terrorism

CIA - The War on Terrorism
http://www.cia.gov/terrorism/

This site is created by the CIA covering news and events inside the intelligence community in the war on terror. It offers a list of lectures and addresses, plus testimony on terrorism.

America's War Against Terrorism
http://www.lib.umich.edu/govdocs/usterror.html

The University of Michigan created this Web page to gather links and resources covering all aspects of the attacks of September 11, 2001.

Alternative Resources on the U.S. "War Against Terrorism"
http://www.pitt.edu/~ttwiss/irtf/Alternative.html

A Web site created by International Responsibilities Task Force of the American Library Association's Social Responsibilities Round Table, listing numerous alternate sources of commentary and analysis on the war against terror.

UNIT 2: The Nature of International Business

Center for International Business Education and Research
http://www.cob.ohio-state.edu/ciberweb/

Surf this site for information about international business/trade organizations and emerging markets, and for news links to related topics.

Institute of International Bankers (IBB)
http://www.iib.org

Examine this site for information on the Institute of International Bankers, IBB events, and publications in order to become familiar with trends in international banking. The site also features regulatory compliance issues relating to the Year 2000 date change.

International Labour Organization (ILO)
http://www.ilo.org

ILO's home page leads to links that describe the goals of the organization and summarizes international labor standards and human rights. Its official UN Web site locator can point you to many other useful resources.

Lex Mercatoria: International Trade Law Monitor
http://lexmercatoria.net

Access a number of resources related to international trade from this site, including data on the European Union and the International Monetary Fund. Among its many links, it addresses such topics as Principles of International Commercial Contracts and UN Arbitration Laws.

Resources for Economists on the Internet
http://rfe.org

This site and its links are essential reading for those interested in learning about the Organization for Economic Cooperation and Development, the World Bank, the International Monetary Fund, and other important international organizations.

www.dushkin.com/online/

We highly recommend that you review our Web site for expanded information and our other product lines. We are continually updating and adding links to our Web site in order to offer you the most usable and useful information that will support and expand the value of your Annual Editions. You can reach us at: *http://www.dushkin.com/annualeditions/.*

UNIT 1
The War on Terrorism

Unit Selections

1. **New Realities of Globalization**, Michael Cherkasky
2. **Rebuilding Afghanistan: A Multi-Billion Dollar Plan**, Josh Martin
3. **Money's Costing More**, Mel Mandell
4. **Going Global Can Bring on a World of Challenges**, Tom Witkowski

Key Points to Consider

- Do you think that the attacks on September 11 changed the way people do business? If so, how?

- What do you think the cost will eventually be for the war on terror? How long do you think it will last?

- Are there any additional considerations that a company might have before going global? What might they be?

 **Links: www.dushkin.com/online/**
These sites are annotated in the World Wide Web pages.

CIA - The War on Terrorism
  http://www.cia.gov/terrorism/
America's War Against Terrorism
  http://www.lib.umich.edu/govdocs/usterror.html
Alternative Resources on the U.S. "War Against Terrorism"
  http://www.pitt.edu/~ttwiss/irtf/Alternative.html

The war on terror has changed the perspective of every American, indeed, every citizen in the Western world. On September 11, 2001, it would not be an exaggeration to say that the world changed. That day was one of those demarcation days that happen in history. Much like December 7, 1941, September 11, 2001, will always be marked as the day the United States began a war against those who would attempt to force Americans and Western civilization to change their way of life to a darker and less free world than we enjoy today.

This war, however, is different from other wars the United States has waged in the past. This war is not against a particular nation, although certainly nations are on the opposing side. Indeed, they have been identified as an "Axis of Evil" that includes Iraq, Iran, and North Korea. This war is against an idea, an idea that has attempted to hijack a great religion, and to some extent succeeded. An idea that would seek to limit the potential of

the human race by restricting the free inquiry of civilization into the mysteries and wonders of the universe. An idea that would take the women of the world and force them to live in ignorance and poverty; an idea that must be banished from the face of the Earth.

What began on September 11 is still being sorted out by Western society, and the "New Realities of Globalization" have yet to be fully determined. There are, however, some things that are now clear:

1. The war on terror is going to be a long and difficult conflict. The enemy is using the very ideals of freedom and liberty in Western civilization to work against the West.

2. The cost of this war is going to be great. That cost will not only include the direct cost of waging the war, in guns, resources, and people's lives, but indirect costs as well. The cost of "Rebuilding Afghanistan: A Multi-Billion Dollar Plan," is only the beginning of what is certain to be the cost of rebuilding the places where the direct conflict of this war is certain to occur. The bill for rebuilding Afghanistan will be followed by the bill for other countries that are certain to come under the weight of American and allied arms. This war will not be over when it is over. The end of the conflict will only be the end of the beginning of what is needed to ensure that terrorists do not rise again.

3. It is going to cost more to do the same things that businesses have always done. Security measures are going to be needed and put in place to protect employees and others. The federal government of the United States has taken over the security system of the airports in the coun-

try, but that is only the beginning. Security is now going to be a priority for every organization. Whether that organization is in what was the shadow of the World Trade Center or surrounded by corn fields in the rural Midwest, security will now have a much higher priority than in the past, and that means that more money is going to be spent on it. In addition, there is the simple fact that "Money's Costing More." The additional risk factors that came into play after September 11 have driven the cost of money up.

4. Organizations that do business outside their home country are facing greater problems than they have in the past, and that is going to require new ways of looking at and new ways to handle those situations. "Going Global Can Bring on a World of Challenges" as everyone who has ever done it knows, but now those challenges have increased and become more difficult and even more deadly than they were in the past.

Organizations that engaged in international business must recognize that the world changed on September 11. On that day it became a more difficult and more frightening place in which to live. To a certain extent, the terrorists did succeed in that they changed the rules under which people must now conduct their lives. But, those lives must continue to be conducted. Precautions need to be taken, of course, but people cannot allow terrorists to dictate what they do and how they do it. To do so would mean that the terrorists will have scored the victory they had hoped for, and that the Western countries and peoples would then be held hostage to be dealt with by a terrorist's whim.

NEW REALITIES OF GLOBALIZATION

TERRORISM AIMS TO CREATE FEARS AND PARALYZE US. LEADERS MUST COMBAT TERROR BY MAKING SURE WE UNDERSTAND IT, THEN BY MITIGATING IT, ADJUSTING TO IT AND MOVING ON

MICHAEL CHERKASKY

To understand the security issues after September 11, we need to understand what happened over the last 20 years that led to an Islamic terrorist war on America. I'll start in 1981, when the Cold War threatened nuclear annihilation and 40 percent of the world—over 2 billion people—under Communist control were unavailable to you for sales and production.

Over the next 20 years, we conquered the world and created a Pax Americana. This 20-year invasion drummed out local markets and created economic interdependence; as Thomas Friedman said, what goes on on the trading floor in Thailand affects what goes on on Wall Street.

The troops of our invasion, our corporations, brought forth American culture. Indeed, our culture conquered the world, and many people do not like that. Islamic fundamentalists, for one, feel attacked. Their young with any affluence, have been Americanized. Their culture could not withstand our onslaught, and they have fought back with violence. To them, and I am in no way justifying it, it is cultural genocide.

"CEOs must talk short- and long-term risk and prioritize the dangers. Identify current problems and develop solutions that are easily implemented or critical. You need control of access, you need smart cards, and you need to do background checks. You need guards. And you need executive protection."

We should have seen it build. [See timeline, tracing the rise of the current wave of terrorism.]

Today we find ourselves with a catastrophic failure of intelligence, of law enforcement and the military. We may be the overwhelming military superpower, but Americans and American corporations face enormous risk throughout the world. We are in a real war, where there are no rules, no courts. It is worldwide, and the enemy will choose some battlefields. It will be long term because

they are patient—they started preparing for the African embassy bombings in 1994.

I hear politicians saying, "We can't give in, we can't change the American way of life. They win if we do that." That's naive. It has been changing for 20 years, and we haven't realized it.

So what are the necessary steps to secure corporate America now? Corporations must mitigate risk. Those at most risk are industries viewed as propagating our culture: the entertainment industry; the media industry and any high-profile, multinational company.

CEOs must talk short- and long-term risk and prioritize the dangers. Identify current problems and develop solutions that are easily implemented or critical. Do classic triage. You need control of access, you need smart cards, and you need to do background checks. You need guards. And you need executive protection. Before, targets were soldiers and governments. Today executives are targets. We are the people who spread the culture.

TIMELINE *for current wave of terrorism*

1981

October 6, 1981 Islamic Jihad assassinates Egyptian President Anwar Sadat. (Intelligence doesn't understand significance.)

1988

1988 Al-Qaeda founded as umbrella group for terrorism. Individual proposals funded by bin Laden.

1990

November 5, 1990 Rabbi Meir Kahane shot to death by Arab named Nosair. Judged as murder case; files of Arabic documents, tape recordings not translated.

1993

February 26, 1993 Bombing of WTC. Six people die in attempt to kill 25,000. Joint terrorist task force translates Nosair files, learns about hate cells, Sheik Rahman and Islamic Jihad, bin Laden and Al-queda. Learns of plans to destroy America, blow up tall buildings in the "great Satan" America.

October 3, 1993 Ambush in Mogadishu, Somalia. America soldiers killed (linked to bin Laden).

1994

December 26, 1994 AirFrance plane hijacked in Algeria; was intended to crash into Eiffel Tower.

1998

August 7, 1998 Bombings of U.S. embassies in Kenya and Tanzania (linked to bin Laden).

1999

December 14, 1999 Arrest prevents millennium bombing in U.S.

2000

October 12, 2000 Attack on USS Cole (linked to bin Laden).

2001

September 11, 2001 World Trade Center and Pentagon attacks.

The anthrax we're seeing is weapons-grade. We must protect our ventilation systems. At least put a lock on the door. You need new mail protocol and new travel protocol. Long term, you need comprehensive crisis plan assessment and implementation—security systems, architectural modifications. Bombs are the real threat; they worked for them in Russia.

How do we win? By maintaining security without substantial compromise of traditional American freedoms. Think of a graph where on one side is individual freedom and on the other side is security. If you have total individual freedom you have anarchy, no laws. On the other, you have total security, but no freedom—totalitarianism. We must have a thoughtful discussion about where on that graph we need to be. We cannot have greater security without giving up something.

Nationally, we need leadership that's willing to have a dialogue about liberty and security, about what cost we're willing to bear. We need to use our technology—it's the difference-maker for us. We need a national identification system. And patience.

1942 brought a horrible tragedy when we put the Japanese in camps. Were our fathers or our grandfathers worse people than we? Do you think we won't do that if more of our kids get killed? Do the things today that will keep us from doing those horrible, unacceptable things tomorrow.

Michael Cherkasky is President and CEO of Kroll.

From *Chief Executive*, January 2002, pp. C10–C12. © 2002 by Chief Executive.

CURRENT AFFAIRS

REBUILDING AFGHANISTAN: A MULTI-BILLION $ PLAN

*The $1.7 billion Afghanistan aid package pledged in Tokyo in late January is only the beginning. The actual cost of putting the war-torn country back on its feet may well exceed $20 billion. **Josh Martin** reports.*

When Afghanistan's Prime Minister, Hamid Karzai, visited the US in late January, he took time out to meet with Afghan students. "Work hard, study hard," he told them. Then he added, with a grin, "Make money and bring it to Afghanistan."

Afghanistan needs to build or rebuild just about everything that defines a human society

Afghanistan needs a lot of money. It needs the money to build or rebuild just about everything that defines a human society: decades of war have all but levelled the country's infrastructure: the central bank was looted in the last days of the ousted Taliban regime and government employees have not been paid for months. The country needs schools, roads, hospitals and communication systems.

The challenge of Afghanistan's development ranges from reconstruction of the infrastructure to the delivery of social services and the creation of an environment which will allow the private sector to flourish productively.

Because of the country's geo-political importance, an unprecedented multilateral aid package has been assembled, with 25 donor nations contributing to it. Donations ranged from the European Union's pledge of $500 million, down to $5 million from Turkey.

Every little bit helps. The reconstruction plan now underway, developed by the World Bank, the UN Development Programme and the Asian Development Bank, carries a base price tag of $14.7 billion, spread out over a 10-year period.

It was developed at the insistence of the Steering Group for the Reconstruction of Afghanistan, whose members include the European Union, Japan, Saudi Arabia and the United States.

It is a remarkable plan. Few details have been given about the rules for spending the aid money since it was unveiled at a Tokyo summit meeting in January. Moreover, the reconstruction plan does not carry the conventional stipulation that the recipient country is required to use aid it receives to buy goods from companies in donor countries.

World Bank President, James Wolfensohn, points out that the top priority of the Steering Committee members was to get a programme in operation: "The important thing is to get things moving forward in an atmosphere of uncertainty."

AFGHANISTAN AT A GLANCE

Despite its vast mineral resources, and its geographic position astride key regional trading routes, Afghanistan remains one of the poorest countries on earth. According to the United Nations data, per capita income is less than $200 per year.

Virtually all indicators show a country which, leaving aside the damages of war, will need substantial foreign aid in order to reach even the minimal living standards of any of its neighbours. It is a terrible indictment of a decade of misrule, first by competing warlords, and then by the Taliban.

Consider these figures: infant mortality is 15 per cent; life expectancy at birth remains less than 45 years; less than 30 per cent of the 27 million Afghanis are able to read and write. All normal government operations—including tax collection—are minimal or non-existent. The mainstay of the economy, agriculture, has been undermined both by arbitrary policies of the Taliban regime, as well as by the absence of a reliable transportation system to bring goods to market. The country lacks all but the most rudimentary road and communication networks.

Yet Afghanistan has significant natural resources which can be used to underwrite an economic recovery. It has large proven reserves of oil and natural gas, as well as coal, copper, iron and lead. The formation of a new government around Prime Minister Karzai has revived hopes of building a multi-

billion dollar oil and gas pipeline through the country, to bring Central Asian energy products to Pakistani ports.

There is also great potential in the agriculture sector. Although only 12 per cent of the land is arable, it can be highly productive, yielding wheat, fruit and nuts, as well as opium.

Until the Taliban announced an eradication campaign two years ago, opium had been the country's largest single cash crop, and its most lucrative export. Throughout the 1990s, Afghanistan had the dubious distinction of being the world's largest producer of the narcotic. Both government and press reports indicate that, following the collapse of the Taliban, many farmers have replanted poppies.

This situation is likely to anger many of the countries that have contributed to the multi-billion dollar reconstruction package. A key challenge to Prime Minister Karzai and his successors will be to convince farmers to return to legitimate agricultural production. But to do that, the government must guarantee access to markets and a pricing structure that would make legitimate agriculture economically viable.

Many experts believe any progress in reviving the Afghan economy will depend on neutralising the country's warlords and restoring the rule of law. It is no wonder, then, that Prime Minister Karzai wants not only international financial aid, but the long-term presence of a peace-keeping force, to give his government room to build the country anew.

Some aid experts believe accounting safeguards, to ensure the aid is spent wisely, should temper the urgency. Both the US and the former Soviet Union have had ample experience of Afghanistan's rapacious warlords, into whose hands untold billions of aid dollars flowed—and disappeared—in earlier times.

"We all know that it's going to be tough to make sure that the money gets to the place that it should go," Wolfensohn says. "But I think with a proper transparent system, with a lot of auditing, with accounting, there's a fair chance that we'll get most of the money to where it's supposed to be."

The fact that so much was collected, helps give the interim Afghan government a stability it previously lacked

With $2.6 billion already collected— far more than the $1.7 billion initial needs assessment prepared by the World

Bank—the Steering Committee's reconstruction plan can commence.

The fact that so much was collected, helps give the interim Afghan government a stability it previously lacked. One supports the other: the funds give Prime Minister Hamid Karzai breathing space, and Karzai's continued presence creates a more stable environment in which to carry out reconstruction.

While the speed with which the world community assembled funds is promising, the political situation in Afghanistan remains far from settled. The Taliban and their followers may be defeated, but the country's myriad warlords still have great power (and a vast array of weapons garnered from both US and Soviet regimes). The current regime, cobbled together late last year after negotiations in Germany, which resulted in the Berlin Agreement, is under great pressure to show results. Until the country's traditional, quasi-parliamentary Loya Jirga assembles later this year to name a legitimate government, Karzai can only hold

power if he is seen within the country as an indispensable player. The best way to achieve that would be by bringing in the money needed to rebuild the country.

Karzai's chief economic adviser, Torek R Farhadi, bluntly points out that the prime minister's election campaign will hinge on a simple pitch: "He's the guy bringing back the billions."

The Steering Committee's $1.7 billion initial needs budget is expected to start flowing soon. A significant portion will be needed to cover the country's recurrent costs, as the interim government is unlikely to be able to collect taxes in the foreseeable future.

The World Bank estimates that simply paying civil servants the arrears of the salaries they are owed will cost $250 million

It is estimated the country will need about $1.8 billion to cover recurrent costs during next 30 months, including the sal-

THE GLOBAL COST OF TERROR

How much does terror cost? While donor nations line up to foot the $15 to $20 billion bill for reconstructing Afghanistan, many continue to suffer the economic consequences of the terrorism that once emanated from that country.

When Al Qaeda operatives succeeded in blowing up New York's World Trade Centre buildings last September, it is unlikely that they calculated just how high a price the world would pay. As the twin towers collapsed, global financial markets went into free fall. In the first full week of trading after the incident, those markets lost almost 10 per cent of their nominal value. Few have fully recovered since. Whole industries were devastated, especially air transport and international tourism.

The Al Qaeda, along with their Taliban hosts, have been swept from power in Afghanistan in one of the costliest global policing operations. But the economic impact of their actions is still being felt.

Ironically, the Arab world has suffered disproportionately from an act that was purportedly meant to strike a blow on its behalf. Tourism receipts in the Middle East have all but disappeared. Investment levels have plunged. Non-oil trade has been weakened, hurt by recession in the West, a decline in available trade finance, and sharply rising insurance rates.

In some cases, no firm cost estimates can be made. For example, many western companies have scaled back their overseas direct investment plans, in order to put their money in local—safer—havens. The absence of such investments will have a direct impact on the economic growth rates of many emerging market countries in the Middle East. Egypt, Morocco, and Turkey have all seen sharp drops in overseas investor commitments since 11 September.

But some figures are definite: the cost of the World Trade Centre, the economic losses of airlines, the decline in equity values, and the increase in military budgets. Here is a breakdown of the measurable global costs so far:

CATEGORY	COST/LOSS ($ BILLION)
Real property (including lost value):	$12.0
Insurance:	20.0
US equity markets:	1,000.0
Global equity markets:	500.0
International tourism:	60.0
Air transport:	40.0
Military response:	110.0
Total cost (to date):	$1,742.0

Source: US State Department; UNDP; JAM Research.

aries of civil servants who lost their jobs during the Taliban era and whom the interim government now plans to re-hire. The World Bank estimates that simply paying civil servants the arrears of the salaries they are owed will cost $250 million (based on 170,000 eligible employees, including many female civil servants, summarily dismissed when the Taliban regime was established).

The reconstruction plan now underway calls for more than just day-to-day maintenance. It will significantly impact on all aspects of Afghan economic and social life. In brief, its key elements include:

• **Security**—10 year cost: $1.7 billion. Funds will be used to build up a national security force to offset the power now wielded by regional warlords. Separately, funds would be allocated to continue demining the countryside (the Initial Needs Assessment report grimly notes that "Afghanistan is the most mine—and unexploded ordinance—affected country in the world"), and to controlling illegal drug production (the country is presently the source of 80 per cent of the world's opium poppy production).

• **Governance and Economic Management**—10 year cost: $1.9 billion. Funds would be used to pay for day-to-day government operations, restoration of private sector development and for the re-establishment of a legal system. Funds would also be used to re-establish a central bank and finance ministry, with a regulatory framework "creating a sound investment climate aimed at the re-emergence of an efficient and thriving private sector."

The reconstruction plan calls for a complete re-integration of women into the country's social fabric

The reconstruction plan calls for a complete re-integration of women into the country's social fabric. One of the first areas where this will be seen is in the country's civil service which, the World Bank notes, had been 43 per cent female prior to the Taliban regime assuming power.

• **Social Protection, Health and Education**—10 year cost: $2.6 billion. The reconstruction plan calls for the creation of a major public works programme, to serve the dual purpose of building the national infrastructure while providing "social protection" for women, refugees, war disabled and orphans. The plan also calls for a dramatic campaign to re-open schools, with an emphasis on getting school-age girls back to school. Not least, the programme aims to revive and improve the public health delivery system.

• **Infrastructure**—10 year cost: $6.9 billion. The largest single expenditure envisaged in the reconstruction plan, is aimed at rebuilding ground transport, civil aviation, water and sanitation systems, and telecommunications.

• **Agriculture and Natural Resources Management**—10 Year cost: $1.4 billion. Much of this cost represents the restoration of war-damaged irrigation systems and the development of a natural resource management system.

Many experts believe the success of the reconstruction plan depends not only on the inflow of aid dollars, but the speed with which the Afghan government can restore a civil society based on the rule of law. "There has to be a 'rule-of-law' culture in place," says Raj Bhala, associate

dean of international and comparative law at George Washington University. "Businessmen and investors will want to see the rule of law well established before they start making investments."

It is essential that a peaceful and stable Afghanistan be built

Bhala believes that if the political will is there, an effective national legal system can be operational within three years. But this assumes first that Karzai will resist getting involved in tribal conflicts (a difficult task, given the country's long history of tribal politics). And it assumes that Karzai will amass sufficient central political power to deflect attempts by regional warlords to dominate the national economy.

Realistically, many experts say, the plan's 10-year cost figure will soon need to be revised upwards. For example, the cost of restoring the agricultural sector will also have to include significant financial inducements to farmers who would otherwise devote their land to opium production.

The biggest revision will probably be needed in the telecommunications sector. The current plan allocates only $120 million in donor assistance, anticipating that the real capital investments needed to build a national grid (estimated at upwards of $2 billion) would be financed by the private sector.

The World Bank itself cites a high case 10 year cost figure of $18.1 billion. But given the additional infrastructure costs, unlikely to be taken up by private sector investors, many experts now see the total required aid package reaching $20 billion.

Whether donor nations will be able to meet the challenge remains to be seen.

Japan's Prime Minister, Junichiro Koizumi, speaking for many if not all donors, believes it is not a matter of choice. "In order to eradicate terrorism, we must eliminate conditions that allow terrorism to take root," he says. "To do so, it is essential that a peaceful and stable Afghanistan be built. This cannot be done in one or two years."

AFGHANISTAN ECONOMIC OUTLOOK

Impact of the Reconstruction Plan

Indicator	2003	2006	2009
Population (Millions):	27	29	31
GDP annual growth (%):	15	10	7
Per capita GDP:	$200	271	326
GDP ($ billions):	$5.0	7.6	10.1

Sources: UNDP; World Bank; JAM Research.

From *The Middle East*, March 2002, pp. 5-8. © 2002 by The Middle East Journal.

BANKING, FINANCE, & TRADE SERVICES

Money's Costing More

AMONG TERRORISM'S MANY EFFECTS ARE INCREASED CREDIT INSURANCE RATES

BY MEL MANDELL

The September 11th terrorist attacks on New York are impacting the U.S. economy in some not-so-obvious ways. For instance, the cost of credit insurance is rising. Why? Because insurers and reinsurers must cover so many billions of dollars in property damage. This means that carriers of credit insurance will also be charged more by reinsurers. And this comes at a time when overseas economies are weakening, so that remote customers may not be in as strong a position to pay their bills, so demand for credit insurance is rising.

The war against terrorism can also cause carriers to refuse to underwrite orders from certain beleaguered nations. Not that there's anything new about unavailability of coverage for orders from nations not distressed by terrorism. Argentina qualifies right now, according to Joe Ketzner, executive vice president of Euler American Credit Indemnity.

Then there's the long-term problem of dicey financial-reporting practices. For instance, like private carriers, the U.S. government's Export-Import Bank requires exporters to obtain pertinent documentation such as financial statements from overseas buyers. However, Piper Starr, a vice president of the Washington, D.C.-based bank, notes there are certain nations where the quality of financial reporting is questionable (see the "Country Limitation Schedule" on the bank's web site at *www.exim.gov*).

The financial statement requirement has become more rigorous lately, according to Ken Horne, a senior vice president with MMC Enterprise Risk, one of the many divisions of Marsh & McLennan Companies, the giant insurance broker. "In a rapidly changing environment, current financial information is a must."

Some Good News

There's a ray of hope in the increasingly gloomy situation: sales that companies have learned to garner via the Internet can be covered under their general credit-insurance policies. Ketzner of Euler reports his firm, which has been insuring Internet transactions since 1993, is currently insuring about $5 billion worth annually now that "more-traditional suppliers are going after them." B2B sales are quite unlike conventional transactions. As Ketzner explains, "a single customer may order from dozens of suppliers at the same time."

If an exporter can't obtain credit insurance or bear the higher rates it could turn to that major alternative, the letter of credit. Problem is, letters of credit are burdensome for buyers. As Horne puts it, "Customers used to purchasing on unsecured terms of payment will resist any effort to require letters of credit."

Typically, credit underwriters cover all of a client's orders or a broad category of orders under policies that are renewed annually; letters of credit require dealing with orders one by one.

If private carriers won't underwrite or appear to charge rates too much, what about obtaining coverage from the ExIm Bank, known as "the insurer of last resort?" In creating the bank, Congress specifically enjoined it not to compete with private carriers. That's why most of the U.S. exporters served by the bank are smaller outfits. However, the bank may underwrite a high-risk situation for a larger entity that can't obtain coverage from the private sector, Starr says. During the fiscal year ended September 30, 2001, the bank covered $2.27 billion worth of U.S. exports.

U.S. exporters have to make a real effort to obtain private coverage before turning to the ExIm Bank. And the bank doesn't write blank checks. Like the private carriers, it first requires clients to assess the creditworthiness of overseas customers. This primary source is supplemented, including reliance on "the recognized credit-reporting agencies." That's why Starr says the ExIm Bank enjoys an enviable record in terms of defaults.

One more *caveat*: the ExIm Bank won't get involved if overseas customers question the quality of the goods delivered or has other complaints. Of course, this could simply be a ploy to delay payment. Fortunately, this rarely happens, according to Christopher Short, vice president of CNA Credit, who adds, "In the case of a nuisance complaint, we would file suit to establish the legality of the claim. While some debtors do make frivolous complaints, it isn't a common occurrence (far less than 1 percent of claims), and all it takes to establish the claim is proof that the client indeed adhered to the terms of the sales contract."

The ExIm Bank is making it easier for its clients to obtain payment if an overseas customer fails to pay. The often lengthy repayment process can now be initiated electronically, although pertinent documents must ultimately be delivered in original paper form.

Collections Services, Too

The private carriers are also responding to defaults by offering "professional collection services." And a company doesn't have to be a client of CNA Credit to use its collection services, which are now a standalone offering, Short says.

We're in the midst of a war on terrorism, the U.S. and other economies are in recession—Japan is in worse shape, and credit insurance may be more costly. But don't despair. According to Short, there has been just a slight increase in defaults to date and a minor increase in reliance on buyer-burdening letters of credit. In other words keep on seeking business overseas, especially via the Internet.

Mel Mandell is an international business writer and consultant based in New York.

From *World Trade*, April 1, 2002, pp. 58-61. © 2002 by Business News Publishing Company.

Going global can bring on a world of challenges

BY TOM WITKOWSKI
JOURNAL STAFF

The changed world political landscape and a war in Afghanistan have added logistical complications for local technology companies with engineering centers in other parts of the world—particularly Asia—but the labor savings still make the offshore model attractive for the long term.

Cost-conscious business customers are demanding even more the lower prices that the offshore model allows, given the uncertainties in the economy since the Sept. 11 attacks, business executives said. Westborough-based eRunway Inc. has seen its business increase in recent weeks because it does much of its work in Hydrabad, India, and Colombo, Sri Lanka, where labor costs are lower.

Even with travel complications and worries about political conflicts, the cheaper labor in those countries and others makes the risks worth it, experts said.

Still, those travel limitations can negatively effect business in the short term. One local company's plans to expand its offshore business are delayed because its investment bankers will not fly to India right now. But that company is still intent on locating part of its operation in India.

'Uncertain future'

"As people brace for a very uncertain future, precipitated by what happened on Sept. 11, it's incumbent on them to figure out how to spread that business dollar even farther," said Kris Canekeratne, chief executive officer of privately held software developer eRunway. Customers have shut down their own engineering facilities in this country and outsourced the work to eRunway to save money, he said. Since Sept. 11, eRunway has signed nine new customers, he said. In the same period of time before Sept. 11, the company signed five new customers.

"There's a lot of benefit, if you need to cut your burn rate, to have development done elsewhere," said Erel Margalit, managing partner with Jerusalem Venture Partners LP, a venture capital firm with offices in New York and Jerusalem. Many companies Margalit has invested in have locations in this country and in Israel and other parts of the world.

One company he has worked with has a large facility in India, and that is helping the company be successful, he said.

"This company is selling like crazy, and the cost of development is so low," Margalit said.

An important factor is management's being informed about not only the area of the world, but also the region of a country, where the work is being done, he said.

"You can't be guessing about it; you've got to know it," he said.

Rethinking the ties

Still, many U.S.-based companies are being forced to reconsider strong financial or developmental ties to a facility halfway around the world. Keane Inc. of Boston, an information technology consultancy, has operated an offshore development center in Canada and wants to buy a company in India to convert into its India-based development center.

But Keane hit a snag because its bankers "will not issue a ticket to India for its staff right now," said Larry Vale, Keane's vice president of external communications. Keane cannot get the bankers to visit the prospective purchases to do its pre-loan due diligence.

"That's a negative for the future sales perspective," he said, adding that flying clients to an engineering center was often needed to give the client confidence in the outsourcing model.

Ease of travel between corporate headquarters in the United States and sites in India made the offshore model a lucrative and relatively hassle-free way of doing business. But that has changed.

"One of the key parts of the sales perspective is they took people over for site visits. I do not know anyone flying right now to India," said Vale. The long-term impact is still unknown, but for now, there are mixed signals, he said.

"The Asian and Indian companies are stating they're continuing to sign deals," said Vale. Then again, those deals could have a sales cycle as long as a year and have been too far along in September not to sign the contract, he suggested. Keane's plans are on hold, but the strategy has not changed, and an operation in India will eventually be part of Keane's offerings, he said.

Videoconferencing offers alternative

Canekeratne's company has always relied more on video conferences than client trips to India, the CEO said. eRunway's customers need not worry about flying to India or Sri Lanka, because eRunway stresses it is a Massachusetts-based company, even though its 400 engineers are in Asia, and it will bring its teams to the customer sites if necessary.

"Customers come here, and they spend half their meetings with the entire project team without having to travel," said Canekeratne. "We manage all of the projects out of the U.S. All of the assets and the intellectual property created on a daily basis is in repositories and secure right here in the U.S.," he said.

Executives at eRunway are also seeing a transition in its clients, who are no longer just startups trying to slow their burn rate by outsourcing development.

"The types of clients we're starting to get… are definitely expanding into the enterprise realm more, into significant brand names," said Frank Dudley, eRunway's chief marketing officer. Those same companies one year ago would not speak to a company with an offshore business model. Today they won't speak to companies without one, Canekeratne said.

As for travel fears and limitations, Canekeratne points out that people who live in Europe and Asia have been forced to live with the threat of terrorism for many years, and the security in airports has long been stricter because of it. Further, the fear of travel right now is greater in the United States than in the rest of the world.

"In the long term, it may still make sense to add low-cost labor as part of your portfolio of outsourcing sources," Keane's Vale said. Companies considering such arrangements need to reassess the risks, though.

"The worst case scenario now might be (that) it becomes impossible to do business out of India," he said, raising the possibility some future international crisis might force a company to shut down such operations. "A year ago, that would have been so improbable it would not be considered a worst-case scenario."

From *Boston Business Journal,* November 20, 2001, pp. 3, 8. © 2001 by Boston Business Journal.

UNIT 2
The Nature of International Business

Unit Selections

Key Points to Consider

- The world is growing smaller. How have improvements in transportation and communication affected international trade? As a manager, how would you take advantage of them?

- Economies are growing all over the world, but the most rapid growth is in the emerging countries of the Pacific Rim. How is this important to business people in the strategic planning of their businesses? Are there other areas of the world that might offer similar possibilities for growth?

- How has the mobility of production factors changed their importance when considering theories of international trade? As a manager, how would you deal with and take advantage of these changes in the international economy?

- How does the multinational corporation fit into the national economy and a theory of international trade?

 **Links: www.dushkin.com/online/**
These sites are annotated in the World Wide Web pages.

Center for International Business Education and Research
http://www.cob.ohio-state.edu/ciberweb/
Institute of International Bankers (IBB)
http://www.iib.org
International Labour Organization (ILO)
http://www.ilo.org
Lex Mercatoria: International Trade Law Monitor
http://lexmercatoria.net
Resources for Economists on the Internet
http://rfe.org
WashLaw
http://www.washlaw.edu

The world is growing smaller each day. Communication and transportation have made planet Earth more closely knit for the people who live on it.

Global growth is accelerating, especially in the developing countries of the Pacific Rim (who, while they have had a temporary setback, will continue to grow), and it is starting to increase in Latin America. In the second unit article, "International Trade: Globalization vs. Protectionism," the chairman of the Federal Reserve, Alan Greenspan, discusses the importance of international trade in raising the standard of living for all people. Industrialized countries, such as the United States, Japan, and Germany, will continue to grow. In addition to the new environment ushered in by September 11 there will be additional risks associated with doing business outside of one's own home market. People were aware of these risks in the past, but they have now been brought to everyone's attention, as seen in "Going Global: The Top 10 Risks." The consequences of this will certainly be felt in the political arena as well as in the economic sphere.

While international trade continues to grow, it continues to become more and more complex. "Integrating Multinational Firms Into International Economics" is no easy matter. It is, however, a simple equation. The more countries, the more trading blocs, and the more people involved, the more complicated trade becomes. Rules can be set, such as those associated with the General Agreement on Tariffs and Trade (GATT) and the World Trade Organization (WTO). But the more rules there are, the greater is the potential for gray areas between them. Not only is international trade becoming more complicated but it is also becoming more competitive. The developing countries of the world are challenging the established countries in a variety of areas. Software is being developed in India; electronics manufacturing is leaving Japan and going to other countries in Asia; and textiles, the traditional first step on the road to industrialization, has become major a industry in many emerging countries. Entrepreneurship, something that Americans may think is their private secret weapon in economic development, is being developed and successfully practiced in India, Korea, China, and Japan.

The United States, faced with such complexity and competition, must not revert to isolationism and abandon world trade. But, rather, it must embrace it. Education of the workforce is a key to success in the future, as well as an understanding of the sociocultural values of the societies in which companies plan to do business.

When most people think of powerhouse economies in Asia, they tend to think of Japan. However, that may be changing. As with many things, trying to measure something depends on how and what is counted. For now, Japan may be number one in Asia by most calculations. But is it really? (China is generally rated number two.) The United States is considered number one in the world. But why is that important? What will be the relationship between corporations and the governments and societies that spawned them? Lawrence E. Mitchell asks this question in "American Corporations: The New Sovereigns."

Theories of trade are also changing, and the resources necessary to engage in international trade are reflecting this change. In the past, utilitarians talked about the four factors of production—land, the entrepreneur, labor, and capital—and how each country had certain advantages over other countries in these areas. Today, that old analysis does not necessarily work. Transportation and communication have made the relative advantages in the four factors of production less important. The factor of land, or raw materials, has been made less imposing by the transportation system. Japan, for example, has virtually no natural resources, yet few would argue with the success of the Japanese economy. Education is likely to be the fifth factor of production.

The entrepreneurial factor can be seen everywhere. It is not just North Americans who start new ventures, but Chinese, South Americans, and Europeans. The former Soviet bloc more than demonstrates the ability of former communists to become entrepreneurs, as do developments in mainland China over the past 10 years. Even in Bangladesh, local financing is being used to help small entrepreneurs. True, these new beehives of entrepreneurial activity may have their problems learning to negotiate the world of business, just as infants have difficulty learning to walk. But eventually, just like small children, they will be on their feet and running everywhere.

Even labor, perhaps the most sedentary of all the factors of production, has shown signs of movement. Labor has always been willing to move, but historians have tended to view these movements as migrations of peoples, not as the movement of a mundane factor of production. Emigration from Europe to Australia, South Africa, and North and South America has been common for people seeking a better life for themselves and their families. This same kind of movement goes on today. Australia is still gaining population through immigration. Europe is experiencing waves of new workers from former colonies, whether they are Algerians in France or Indians and Pakistanis in Great Britain. Finally, the United States continues to receive immigrants, both legal and illegal, from all over the world, especially from Latin America and Asia. Whatever the reason for immigrating, these people certainly represent potential labor, at least, and they are all seeking better lives. Capital, or the means of production, has shown an ability to go global. Ever since the start of the industrial revolution, there have been countries that were "developed" (with the means of production) and countries that were "less" or "least" developed (generally without the means of production). But that is starting to change. Because of the global transportation and communications system, the location of production facilities is not as important as it once was. In addition, real and potential growth is now to be found in these developing countries. Any organization that is looking to grow will find it much easier to do so in an economy that is rapidly expanding than in one that is saturated and growing only as fast as the population. Capital and the division of production are global at last and will be even more so in the future. Successful companies will take advantage of this new aspect of the world economy and will need to direct their resources accordingly.

International Trade

GLOBALIZATION VS. PROTECTIONISM

Address by ALAN GREENSPAN, *Chairman of the Federal Reserve Board*
Delivered to the Committee on Finance, U.S. Senate, Washington, D.C., April 4, 2001

I am pleased to be invited to discuss some of the important issues concerning international trade and the attendant implications for the U.S. economy and the world economy more generally. In doing so, I want to emphasize that I speak for myself and not necessarily for the Federal Reserve.

One of the most impressive and persistent trends of the last several decades is the expansion of international trade. Trade across national borders has increased far faster than world GDP. As a consequence, imports of goods and services as a percentage of gross domestic products worldwide, on average, have risen from approximately 12 percent forty years ago to 24 percent today.

To most economists, the evidence is impressively persuasive that the dramatic increase in world competition—a consequence of broadening trade flows—has fostered markedly higher standards of living for almost all countries that have participated in cross-border trade. I include most especially the United States.

Globalization as generally understood involves the increasing interaction of national economic systems. Of necessity, these systems are reasonably compatible and, in at least some important respects, market oriented. Certainly, market-directed capitalism has become the paradigm for most of the world, as central-planning regimes have fallen into disfavor since their undisputed failures around the world in the four decades following World War II.

Globalization, in turn, has been driven importantly by advances in technology. By lowering the costs of gathering information and conducting transactions, new technologies have reduced market frictions and provided significant impetus to the process of broadening world markets. Expanding markets, in turn, have both increased competition and rendered many forms of government intervention either ineffective or perverse.

The recognition of this prosperity-enhancing sea-change in world markets and, in that context, of the counterproductive consequences of pervasive intervention has led many governments to reduce tariffs and trade barriers and, where necessary, to deregulate markets. These actions themselves have further promoted the very globalization that, interacting with advancing technology, spurred the deregulatory initiatives in the first place. The result of this process has been an advance and diffusion of technical change that has raised living standards in much of the world.

The international trading system that evolved has enhanced competition and nurtured what Joseph Schumpeter a number of decades ago called "creative destruction," the continuous scrapping of old technologies to make way for the new. Standards of living rise because the depreciation and other cash flows of industries employing older, increasingly obsolescent technologies are marshaled to finance the newly produced capital assets that almost always embody the cutting-edge technologies. This is the process by which wealth is created incremental step by incremental step. It presupposes a continuous churning of an economy in which the new displaces the old.

But there is also no doubt that this transition to the new high-tech economy, of which rising trade is a part, is proving difficult for a large segment of our workforce that interfaces with our rapidly changing capital stock day by day. This is most evident in the rising fear of job skill obsolescence that has induced a marked increase in experienced workers going back to school—often community colleges—to upgrade their skills for a rapidly changing work environment.

While major advances in standards of living are evident among virtually all nations that have opened their borders to increased competition, the adjustment trauma resulting from technological advances as well as globalization has also distressed those who once thrived in industries that were once at the cutting edge of technology but that have become increasingly noncompetitive. Economists will say that workers should move from the steel districts of western Pennsylvania to Silicon Valley or its equivalent. And eventually they, or more likely their children, will move. But the adjustment process is wrenching to an existing workforce made redundant largely through no fault of their own. It may be argued that all workers should have the foresight to recognize long-term job opportunity shifts and move in advance of obsolescence. Such forecasting abilities are not in great abundance among workers. But neither are they evident among business managers or the economists who counsel them.

Yet the protectionist propensity to thwart the process of the competitive flow of capital, from failing technologies to the more productive, is unwise and surely self-defeating. History tells us that, not only is it unwise to try to hold back innovation, it is also not possible over the longer run. Generation after generation has experienced episodes in which those rendered technologically obsolescent endeavored to undermine progress, often appealing to the very real short-term costs of adjusting to a changing economic environment. In the end, these attacks did not prevail, and long-term advances in standards of living resumed.

Nonetheless, the campaign to expand free trade is never won. It is a continuing battle. Though tariffs in industrial countries have come down sharply over the past half-century, other barriers have become more prevalent. Administrative protection in the form of antidumping suits and countervailing duties is a case in point. These forms of protection have often been imposed under the label of promoting "fair trade," but oftentimes they are just simple guises for inhibiting competition. Typically, antidumping duties are levied when foreign average prices are below the average cost of production. But that also describes a practice that often emerges as a wholly appropriate response to a softening in demand. It is the rare case that prices fall below marginal cost, which would be a more relevant standard. In the view of many economists, antidumping initiatives should be reserved for those cases in which anticompetitive behavior is involved. Contrary to popular notions about antidumping suits, under U.S. law, it is not required to show evidence of predatory behavior, or of intention to monopolize, or of any other intentional efforts to drive competitors out of business. In the end, economic progress clearly rests on competition. It would be a great tragedy were we to stop the wheels of progress because of an incapacity to assist the victims of progress.

Our efforts should be directed at job skills enhancement and retraining—a process in which the private market is already engaged—and, if necessary, selected income maintenance programs for those over a certain age, where retraining is problematic. Thwarting competition, by placing barriers to imports, will prevent markets

in the United States and other nations from deploying capital to their most productive uses, that is, the most cost-effective production of those goods and services most highly valued by consumers.

Protectionism will also slow the inevitable transition of the workforce to more productive endeavors. To be sure, an added few years may enable some workers to reach retirement with dignity, but it will also keep frozen in place younger workers whose opportunities to secure jobs with better long-run prospects diminish with time.

I regret that trade policy has been inextricably linked with job creation. We often try to promote free trade on the mistaken ground, in my judgment, that it will create jobs. The reason should be that it enhances standards of living through the effects of competition on productivity. It is difficult to find credible evidence that trade has affected the level of total employment in this country over the long run. Indeed, in recent months we have experienced the widest trade deficit in history with unemployment still close to record lows.

Certainly, the distribution of jobs by industry is influenced by international trade, but it is also affected by domestic trade. The relative balance of supply and demand in a competitive market economy determines the mix of employment. When exports fall or imports rise, domestic demand and relative prices have invariably adjusted in the long run to leave total employment generally unaffected.

I also regret that, despite the remarkable success over a near half-century of GATT, the General Agreement on Trade and Tariffs, and its successor, the World Trade Organization, in reducing trade barriers, our trade laws and negotiating practices are essentially adversarial. They presume that a trade concession extracted from us by our trading partners is to their advantage at our expense and must be countered. Few economists see the world that way; trade is not a zero sum game.

If trade barriers are lowered by both parties, each clearly benefits. In almost every credible scenario, if one lowers barriers and the other does not, the country that lowered barriers unilaterally would still be better off having done so. Raising barriers to achieve protectionist equality with reluctant trading partners would be neither to our benefit nor to theirs. The best of all possible worlds for competition is for both parties to lower trade barriers. The worst is for both to keep them up.

For these reasons, we should welcome the opportunity to contribute to the effort of working toward further trade liberalization. If we freeze competitive progress in place, we will almost certainly slow economic growth overall and impart substantial harm to those workers who would otherwise seek more-effective longer-term job opportunities. Protecting markets from new technologies has never succeeded. Adjustments to new technologies have been delayed, but only at significant cost.

Moreover, even should our trading partners not retaliate in the face of increased American trade barriers—an unlikely event—we would do ourselves great harm by lessening the vigor of American competitiveness. The United States has been in the forefront of the postwar opening up of international markets, much to our and the rest of the world's benefit. It would be a great tragedy were that process stopped or reversed.

The arguments against the global trading system that emerged first in Seattle and then spread over the past year and a half arguably touched a chord in many people partly, in the judgment of many analysts, by raising the fear that they would lose local political control of their destinies. Clearly, the risk is that support for restrictions on trade is not dead, only quiescent.

Those who protest against "globalization" appear too often to be self-designated representatives of developing country interests. For all the reasons that I have cited earlier, these protests, however well intentioned, are wrongheaded. In particular, it is essential to note that probably the best single action that the industrial countries could actually take to alleviate the terrible problem of poverty in many developing countries would be to open, unilaterally, markets to imports from these countries. Such countries need more globalization, not less.

In many important respects, the past half-century has represented an uneven struggle to repair the close linkages among national economies that existed before the first World War. The hostilities bred of war, the substantial disruptions to established trading patterns associated with that conflict, and the subsequent poor economic performance over the next few decades engendered the erection of trade barriers around the world that have taken even longer to dismantle. To repeat that error would increase poverty among a significant segment of the world's population.

The United States has been a world leader in terms of free trade and open markets for capital as well as goods and services. We have benefited enormously from the resulting international competition: We have a wide range of goods and services available for consumption; our industries produce and employ cutting-edge technologies; and the opportunities created by these technologies have attracted capital inflows from abroad. These capital inflows have reduced the costs of building our country's capital stock and added to the productivity of our workers. Most economists would argue that we must reaffirm the United States' leadership role in the area of international trade policy in order to improve standards of living in the United States and among all of our trading partners.

From *Vital Speeches of the Day*, April 15, 2001, pp. 386-388. © 2001 by Vital Speeches of the Day. Reprinted by permission.

American Corporations: the New Sovereigns

By Lawrence E. Mitchell

ONE of the most striking yet overlooked aspects of the current globalization debate is the quiet retreat of sovereign power—including that of the United States—in the face of imperial conquests by modern American corporations. At least until the recent downturns in the stock market—both the general one in 2000 and the sharper one following the attacks of September 11—a number of these companies, including Wal-Mart, Microsoft, Intel, General Electric, and Hewlett-Packard, have had market capitalizations larger than the gross national products of a number of developed and developing countries, including Spain, Kuwait, Argentina, Greece, Poland, and Thailand. The statistics overwhelmingly demonstrate that such corporations and American capital are increasingly dominant throughout the world. At last count, American institutional assets constituted an aggregate 66.8 percent of the total in five major foreign economies, including those of France and Germany.

Modern democracies are built to ensure the restraint of power and the pursuit of public will by forgoing efficiency for patience and consensus. In contrast, the modern American corporation, with its centralized control and absolute power in the board, is brilliantly and devastatingly built for economic efficiency—the ability to amass huge resources and deploy them instantly. No socialist economy has ever had the command-and-control capacities of the American corporation.

The scary thing is that we have come to see these corporations as built for a single purpose, to maximize stockholder wealth, and we have created them in a manner that exempts them from any of the normal moral constraints we expect from governments or individuals.

It has not always been so. Several factors led to the development of this new ethic over the last couple of decades. Among them were deregulation beginning during the Reagan era, together with an increased emphasis on wealth maximization as a social goal; the expectations created in stockholders by the quick money made in hostile takeovers, especially during the 1980s; and the charging bull market of the 1990s. Those phenomena have instilled stockholder expectations of large and immediate returns.

AMERICAN CORPORATIONS and their managers are thus increasingly driven by the faceless, soulless capital markets—markets composed of individuals with consciences but creating a collective that lacks one. Moreover, pressure on corporations to show higher stock prices fast has been increased by the enormous growth in institutional investors, which now own about half of the equity market in the United States.

They also dominate institutional investing in foreign markets like those of Western Europe. Institutional investors compensate their managers on the basis of their ability to raise the values of their portfolios immediately, so those managers have every incentive to push for short-term stock-price maximization over long-term gain and corporate stability.

In addition to the pressure of institutional investors, American investment banks, and consulting companies, markets are driven by nongovernmental organizations like the World Bank and the International Monetary Fund. Those players have implicitly, and sometimes explicitly, conditioned the supply of American capital (and in the case of the nongovernmental organizations, largely Western capital) to overseas markets on those markets' adoption of American-style, stockholder-centered, corporate capitalism.

To be sure, American corporations have brought the world great benefits: increased travel, communication, health, nutrition, and production capabilities. They have also brought Americans a higher material standard of living. But it is, in large part, the stockholder-centered nature of the corporation that leads it to behave in ways that no thoughtful person really wants, ways that most of us would consider to be irresponsible.

Although no legal doctrine requires it, American capitalist culture has adopted the view that maximizing stock price is the purpose of the corporation, its reason for being. Capital markets demand that maximization, and punish those corporations that fail to meet short-term expectations—just look at the stock price of any corporation that reports disappointing quarterly earnings. Corporate structure implies stock-price maximization: Only stockholders vote for directors, only stockholders have the right to sue, and only stockholders have the ability to sell the company out from under the directors.

Coupled with the maximization goal is the limited liability that shields the corporation. While corporations can be sued for causing harm, and sometimes even criminally prosecuted, the extent of their risk is finite. When a chemical plant in Bhopal, India, explodes because corners were cut, or Love Canal is poisoned because it is cheaper to pollute, or asbestos sickens thousands because the product is unsafe, the injured can recover only from the assets of the corporation. Directors and stockholders generally are not liable for its debts, and so many of the costs of maximizing stock price can be externalized onto all of those people and things, other than the stockholders, whom the corporation's behavior affects—workers, consumers, entire communities, the environment.

Layoffs are a fast way to cut costs and raise stock price. Saving a few dollars by placing a gas tank in not necessarily the safest spot, or by paying insufficient attention to tire safety, increases profit margins. Polluting entails limited risk of being caught and penalized, and the benefits, in terms of savings, sometimes exceed that risk. It's cheaper to shut down plants in areas of high labor cost and move them to other regions, no matter how dependent the community may be on the corporation.

Freed from the responsibilities of ownership, with surrogates directed to manage their corporations to maximize their wealth, American stockholders can, and for the most part do, wash their hands of responsibility for their corporations' behavior. Add to this the fact that most Americans tend to invest in corporations through intermediary institutions—mutual funds, pension funds, and the like—and yet another layer is placed between the stockholder and any feeling of responsibility.

WITH THESE CONDITIONS in place, American corporations have exported the dislocations they often cause at home through devices such as the leveraged, hostile takeover, and norms like stock-price maximization. *BusinessWeek* predicted (again, before the current recession) at least a $1-trillion mergers-and-acquisitions business in Europe, a region that has long celebrated its corporate stability. The profits drawn from such disruptions abroad go directly into the pockets of American stockholders, who demonstrate no concern with the effect of corporate behavior on anyone else. Arguments that transnational business helps the world's disadvantaged by raising their standard of living are disproved by the numbers. A recent United Nations report showed that American-style economic dominance has accelerated the widening gap between rich and poor throughout the world.

According to the UN's *Human Development Report 1999*, "the top fifth of the world's people in the richest countries enjoy 82 percent of the expanding export trade and 68 percent of foreign direct investment—the bottom fifth, barely more than 1 percent." That same wealthy population has 86 percent of the world's gross domestic product, and the income of that group was 74 times that of the bottom fifth in 1997, up from 60 times in 1990. And such data reflect only material wealth—not quality of life, leisure, education, or happiness.

> Because the goal of the corporation is to maximize stock price, managers use corporations narrowly and amorally as tools to achieve that end.

At least as dangerous as increasing inequality is the standard of behavior American corporate practices create for companies' managers. Because the goal of the corporation is to maximize stock price, managers use corporations narrowly and amorally as tools to achieve that end. When an ordinary human being with ordinary moral constraints walks into a board room or executive suite, he assumes those tunnel-visioned behaviors. That is, after all, his job. His own sensibilities can be left at the door—and even if they need not be, even if there is latitude (as there surely is) for good corporate behavior, he knows that the market will punish him unless his morality is reflected on the bottom line.

Like many social roles (that of a lawyer comes to mind), this one comes with a socially sanctioned set of expectations. But unlike most other roles, which exist and must interact in a wider social system, we so narrowly define the role of corporate actors as to give them a moral anonymity and a moral out. The corporate managerial role not only leads us to exculpate corporations for simply doing what we've created them to do, but it allows managers themselves to avoid feeling responsible, and being accountable, for their behavior. They have no personal contact with the people their decisions affect—those people are only numbers. The managers don't carry out the decisions themselves and witness the consequences, so they avoid the experiences that might help ensure empathy and restraint.

THE PROGRESS of the American corporation has been toward ever greater world dominance, not only in the products it sells and the services it provides, which export American culture throughout the world, but also in its exportation of American-style, stockholder-take-all capitalist practices. Given corporations' efficiency and speed in contrast to those of governments, corporations can establish strongholds and affect entire cultures long before those cultures have time to react. And once in place, corporate wealth and economic dominance allows them to remain firmly entrenched.

The problem is not only one of America against the developing world. American corporations, aided by the investment community, have also largely colonized the various forms of capitalism that used to distinguish Western European business from ours. Corporate behavior in Germany, France, Scandinavia, and Italy, for instance, was designed to provide for full employment, social stability, and social welfare. American companies, and American practices, have eroded those core values.

The European anger directed against President George W. Bush on his first visit there in June (somewhat abated since September 11 by a different anger, sympathy, and fear) is symptomatic of even the developed world's feelings of helplessness in the face of the continued onslaught by American-style corporate capitalism.

The recent terrorist attacks have been directed against sovereign governments. But to the extent that much of the unsettled state of the world derives from the increasing divide between haves and have-nots, to the extent that culture wars in America and abroad are driven at least in part by rearguard actions against disappearing ways of life, the cause lies less in the behavior of sovereign governments such as our own than it does in the collective behavior of corporate America and the American investment community.

Only government has the power, the resources, and the right to restrain corporate conduct and to demand corporate accountability. For far too long we've taken the attitude that business is business, as if that very mantra exempted corporations from the normal moral and responsible conduct that we expect from individual citizens. At the same time, we have granted our corporations almost all of the rights and freedoms of individual citizens. But unless we control our corporate goals and practices, unless our government regulates markets in a way that restrains our voracious drive for wealth, international strife and discord will only worsen.

Lawrence E. Mitchell, a law professor at George Washington University, is the author of Corporate Irresponsibility: America's Newest Export, *published recently by Yale University Press.*

From *The Chronicle of Higher Education,* January 18, 2002, pp. 18-19. © 2002 by The Chronicle of Higher Education. Reprinted by permission.

2001's Most Influencial People in World Trade

Some are Well-Known While Others Play Low-Key Roles

By Lara L. Sowinski

This has been quite a year for the industries collectively driving global commerce. From myriad new developments on the software and regulatory fronts to the paradigm-shifting events of "Nine-Eleven," 2001 will forever have its place in history.

Of course a year is an artificial measure of the passage of time—it can be memorable only because of the events—and people—that played a role in shaping its perceived character. WORLD TRADE MAGAZINE editors have compiled a short list of trade leaders for this year's final issue, though this grouping isn't meant to be a "Top Tier" by any stretch of the imagination. Rather, it's intended to provide a retrospective of the key figures who made a difference.

It may be somewhat difficult to quantify the achievements of U.S. Trade Representative **Robert B. Zoellick**, considering it hasn't even been one year since he was appointed. Yet, as President Bush's principal trade adviser and negotiator responsible for developing and coordinating U.S. international trade, commodity, and direct investment policy, this position undeniably wields significant power and influence. One of the highlights of Zoellick's first year in office was the resolution in April of a long-standing dispute between the U.S. and EU over trade in bananas. Other notable events include the World Trade Organization's endorsement of terms for China's entry into the global trade body, which will likely become effective as soon as this month or, possibly, early next year, after 14 years of negotiations. Zoellick also helped usher along the bilateral trade agreement with Vietnam, which will extend Normal Trade Relations (subject to an annual Jackson-Vanik waiver by the president) to that country and lower tariffs on hundreds of American goods and farm products. Meanwhile, the U.S.-Jordan free trade agreement, signed in October, will eliminate duties and commercial barriers to bilateral trade in goods and services originating in the U.S. and Jordan. In the position of U.S. Trade Representative, Zoellick also serves as vice chairman of the Overseas Private Investment Corporation, is a non-voting member of the Export-Import Bank, and is a member of the National Advisory Committee on International Monetary and Financial Policies.

European Trade Commissioner **Pascal Lamy** has also had a busy year, and the U.S. has figured prominently in his dealings. Not only are the U.S. and EU each other's largest single trade partners, but together they account for roughly 20 percent of the entire world's trade activity. While the EU generally sides with the U.S. on many trade issues, Lamy is working to overturn a number of U.S. trade barriers ranging from antidumping and countervailing measures to restrictions on the satellite communications market. One of the biggest sticking points between the two partners has been the U.S.' legislation governing Foreign Sales Corporations. The EU celebrated a ruling by a WTO panel earlier this year that deemed FSCs an illegal subsidy, and struck down its replacement as well. The U.S. is fighting the ruling, however. Lamy is also targeting the U.S. Helms-Burton Act, and the Iran and Libya Sanctions Act. On a more positive note, it seems the U.S. and EU are close to settling their differences over genetically modified organisms (GMOs), and the EU may allow imports from the U.S. to resume early next year. On another front, Lamy is helping to accelerate preparatory work on Russia's accession to the WTO.

The director-general of the World Trade Organization is so influential that it takes two people to hold this position. Well, not quite, but because of some irreconcilable differences, and in order to maintain a consensus, it was decided that New Zealand prime minister **Mike Moore** and Thailand's deputy prime minister **Dr. Supachai Panitchpakdi** would split the position. Moore began his three-year term on September 1, 1999, and Panitchpakdi will take over on September 1, 2002. At its best, the WTO can set global rules for free and fair trade, settle disputes between trade partners, lower trade barriers, and assure market access to its 142 member nations. Critics, though, have blamed the organization for advancing trade at the expense of the developing world, amongst other violations. Moore appears to at least acknowledge the WTO's shortcomings, and has tried to balance his duties and the organization's to appease as many as possible.

During the opening address to the 1999 ministerial meeting in Seattle, which was the scene of considerable protests, Moore said, "I have some empathy with some of these protesters outside. Not all are bad or mad. They are right when they say they want a safer, cleaner more healthy planet. They are correct when they call for an end to poverty, more social justice, and better living standards. They are wrong to blame the WTO for all the world's problems. They are especially wrong when they say this is not a democratic house. Ministers are here because their people decided so. Our agreements must be agreed by Parliaments. This is a Ministerial Conference."

Later in the speech, he added, "The concerns of the least-developed must not be left behind. What is the real cost to the wealthiest nations of dropping barriers to their exports—when these exports represent just half a percent of world trade? If we cannot make this small concession to the poorest amongst us, what hope is there for our grand commitment to poverty eradication in the 21st century? The least-developed countries are not threatened by globalization. They are threatened by 'de-globalization,' falling outside of the world economy and slipping ever further behind. This is not the fault of the trading system. Governments themselves have responsibilities. Some governments are paying up to nine times more on debt repayment then on health."

It's likely that Dr. Panitchpakdi will follow in Moore's footsteps when it comes to attending to the concerns of the developing world relative to increased globalization.

John Simpson, president of the American Association of Exporters and Importers in New York City, leads a diverse and respected group of traders, including exporters and importers, manufacturers, retailers, carriers, customs brokers, banks, attorneys, and insurance firms. AAEI is the only national association dedicated exclusively to representing the interests of both U.S. exporters and importers before U.S. government agencies, Congress, international organizations, and foreign governments. Congressional committees routinely consult with AAEI owing to its technical expertise on policy and regulatory matters involving global commerce. Among the issues on which AAEI has provided testimony are trade between the U.S. and China, fast track negotiating authority, extension of the Generalized System of Preferences, and changes to the administration of dumping regulations. AAEI also monitors export-related issues such as U.S. economic sanctions, export controls, intellectual property rights protection, and elimination of foreign barriers to U.S. exports.

Although it's only been in existence for just one year, the West Coast Waterfront Coalition, headed by president **Robin Lanier**, has an aggressive agenda to tackle. The national coalition, based in Washington, D.C., is made up of importers, exporters, retailers, carriers, and customs brokers who ship through West Coast ports— the location for five of the top ten U.S. container ports. There's already substantial business through these gateways, and cargo volumes are projected to triple by 2020. Congestion, a problem that West Coast ports have faced for a while, is one of the top issues the group is address-

ing, and it's making measurable headway. Part of the coalition's success is its ability to bring together a variety of voices from the industry with a common goal of finding a solution. This "all for one, one for all" attitude has helped the group maintain momentum and sustain dialogue among sometimes competing interests. The idea of extending terminal gate hours at the ports is one solution towards reducing congestion and improving productivity that the group is exploring, as is an appointment system for harbor truckers.

Ronald Schoof, chairman of the Joint Industry Group, is preparing to wrap up his two-year term. But, that doesn't mean the 150 or so Fortune 500 companies, trade associations, and businesses that make up the Washington, D.C. group's members are slowing down their efforts to facilitate growth in imports and exports. The JIG's members account for more than $350 billion in annual trade, and when they talk with officials from U.S. Customs, the Commerce Department, the Office of the U.S. Trade Representative, Congress, and other government agencies, their concerns are heard loud and clear. Committees within the JIG cover such topics as U.S. Customs' Automated Export System and importer requirements related to "informed compliance" and "reasonable care."

When it comes to representing a particular industry, one of the most vocal has been **Laura E. Jones**, executive director of the United States Association of Importers of Textiles and Apparel. Indeed, the New York-based USA-ITA's motto, "The Voice of Textile and Apparel Importers" sums it up in a nice little package. There are lots more complexities involved with textile imports than many other products—quota restrictions, classification, and country of origin issues to name a few, and Jones has helped keep the industry's concerns at the forefront.

While textile importers can count on the USA-ITA for support, advocacy groups covering other high-profile industries such as agriculture, footwear, and electronics abound, and their leadership and members have considerable clout when promoting their specific interests. And naturally, Washington, D.C. is the place to go to access policy makers, whether you're a lobbyist, consultant, industry spokesperson, union representative, or ordinary citizen.

In the meantime, there are a host of issues confronting the trade community, both domestically and abroad, and certainly more influential faces in the crowd than we can profile in a single year-end feature. Their efforts and achievements hardly go unrecognized, however, and WORLD TRADE MAGAZINE will continue to monitor their progress in the months ahead.

Lara is a features editor for WORLD TRADE *magazine.*

From *World Trade*, December 13, 2001. © 2001 by Business News Publishing Company.

Europeans covet U.S.

Foreign carmakers such as Maserati plan their return as others hunt ways to target Americans

By Nick Lico

JAPANESE CARMAKERS hit U.S. shores in force during the fuel-conscious 1970s, and South Korean marques have followed in the last 10 to 15 years. New foreign competition in the U.S. car market also could come from Asia.

And the most likely candidate may be a country that already is manufacturing much of what Americans buy—China.

"When you look at their economy and their wages, it certainly makes sense that they would begin building their own vehicles," says Stephen Roulac, CEO of the Roulac Group, a consulting company with headquarters in San Francisco and offices in Hong Kong and India.

Elsewhere in Asia, "It wouldn't be surprising to see Vietnam coming to the U.S.," Mr. Roulac says. "It's a country with a great deal of capacity, a strong sense of style and tremendous work ethic."

Mr. Roulac cautions Americans shouldn't expect to be able to purchase a vehicle from China or Vietnam in the near future. It may take a decade before it will be feasible to even consider such an option.

LOOKS FOR TRANSFORMATION

China would have to transform itself much like Japan did a quarter-century ago, moving from a producer of low-cost, inferior products to premium, high-quality offerings, Mr. Roulac says.

In Vietnam, the "government has to open up to become more conducive to an enterprise coming into their country and establishing a presence," he says.

In the nearer term, new incursions into the U.S. will come from the same continent that gave us our first car imports—Europe. And they're going to come from carmakers that earlier competed in, and abandoned, the U.S. market. Fiat's Alfa Romeo, Ferrari's Maserati and MG Rover Group are revving up to re-enter the U.S. market.

General Motors Corp. and Italian carmaker Fiat in 2000 linked in a venture under which GM got a 20% stake in the Fiat Auto arm. Fiat said at the time it would look for marketing synergies in the U.S. to bring back its Alfa Romeo cars, which had pulled out of the market in 1995. Current plans are to debut the Alfa Spider in the U.S. in 2005, following a European launch in 2004.

Paolo Vannini, VP-corporate communications at Fiat USA, confirms that the Alfa Spider will be "sold under the GM umbrella, but a decision as to whether it would be sold at Saab, Cadillac or other GM dealerships has not been announced." No agency currently handles Alfa Romeo in the U.S., and no review is under way.

"General Motors could arrange Alfa within premium brands. These vehicles could then be offered through an existing pipeline," says David E. Cole, director of the Center of Automotive Research at the Environmental Research Institute of Michigan.

Maserati next year returns to the U.S. after more than a decade's absence. The vehicles will be distributed through the dealer network of Fiat-owned Ferrari. Ferrari took control of Maserati from Fiat in 1997. No agency has been assigned ad duties.

Another likely competitor is the U.K.'s MG Rover Group, which displayed an MGF roadster at the 2001 Society of Automotive Engineers Congress in Detroit last month. MG Rover is "very interested in returning to the U.S., but with more than one product," says Kevin Jones, product communications manager. Any vehicle introduction in the U.S. wouldn't occur before 2005.

The Euro carmakers know that success in the U.S. is hardly guaranteed. Alfa, Maserati and MG tried before and ended up departing for home. Unlike the South Koreans, and the Japanese before them, the Europeans are not eyeing the entry-level market. Rather, they would be entering the near-luxury segment that, Mr. Cole notes, is already "over-represented with brands."

From *Advertising Age*, April 9, 2001, S4. © 2001 by Crain Communications Inc. Reprinted by permission.

Free Trade Bush's Way

On the eve of George W. Bush's recent tour of Latin America, Mexican writer Carlos Fuentes equated the advantages of a global free market with the peaks of the Himalayas, characterizing them as summits so inaccessible that the poor cannot even see them, let alone scale them. Fifteen years of US-prescribed free markets and trade liberalization in Latin America have generated an average annual growth rate of only 1.5 percent, far short of the 4 percent needed to make a serious dent in poverty levels. Add to that the Mexican peso meltdown of 1994, economic stagnation in Central America, the Brazilian currency crisis of three years ago, the political and economic collapse of Peru, endless war in Colombia, coup jitters in Venezuela and the staggering crash in Argentina, and one can understand Fuentes's pessimism.

"Trade means jobs," Bush said as he met with regional leaders and promised a harvest of benefits from his proposed Free Trade Area of the Americas (FTAA)—a thirty-two-nation pact Washington hopes to implement by 2005. But for all Bush's talk of a prosperous hemispheric future, his policy initiatives are mired in a cold war past. The Administration has just anointed a former Oliver North networker and interventionist hawk, Otto Reich, to head the State Department's Latin America section. And much as in the days of the Reagan wars in Central America that Reich helped promote, the Bushies seem to believe that the region's ills are better solved by guns than butter. No sooner had Washington signed off on the sale of a new fleet of F-16s to Chile (ending a two-decade ban on sophisticated-weapons sales to Latin America) than the Administration began asking Congress to increase military aid to Colombia and to lift all restrictions on its use. Those critics who argued that the $1.3 billion antidrug "Plan Colombia" would suffer mission creep and inevitably morph into a prolonged counterinsurgency war are now seeing their darkest fears confirmed.

On the economic front, Bush offered little more than warmed-over trickle-down Reaganomics to a continent in desperate need of a lift from the bottom up (the three countries he visited—Mexico, Peru and El Salvador—all suffer poverty rates of 50 percent or more). Certainly not lost on his Latin American audiences was the one-sided nature of the free trade offered by Bush. For nearly two decades now, Latin Americans have been told that by adhering to the "Washington Consensus" of market liberalization they will be able to partake of the rich American pie. But the cold fact is that the US market has remained closed to a cornucopia of Latin American goods.

Some remedy was found in the past decade's Andean Trade Preference Act, designed to lure impoverished Latin Americans away from local drug economies by allowing them to freely export a list of 4,000 goods into the United States. But since ATPA expired last year, the Senate and the White House have balked at its reauthorization because of protectionist pressure from conservative, primarily Southern, textile and agriculture interests. Its reinstatement could shift 100,000 farmers in Peru alone from coca to cotton cultivation.

Washington's refusal to depart from such unequal and inflexible models has—unwittingly—provoked some positive alternative stirrings. The use of armored cars and tear gas barrages in downtown Lima during the US-Peruvian presidential meeting was an official acknowledgment of the growing restlessness with the status quo. Newly elected President Alejandro Toledo has seen his popularity plummet to 25 percent as he has failed to offer economic alternatives. In Brazil center-left candidate Luiz Ignacio "Lula" Da Silva leads in this fall's presidential polls and vows to block the FTAA if elected. Even the incumbent, more conservative, President Enrique Cardoso has begun to steer Brazil toward more independence from Washington. It's still too early to predict how the developing debacle in Argentina will play out.

Finally, El Salvador, where Bush ended his Latin American tour, couldn't have provided a more fitting showcase for the current disjuncture between Washington and its southern neighbors. During the 1980s the United States was willing to spend billions to fight a war against leftist insurgents and promised a bright, democratic future. That conflict was settled ten years ago with a pact that opened up the political system but did nothing to address the social ills that provoked the war in the first place. And once the guerrillas were disarmed, Washington lost interest; in the past decade US aid has been reduced to a paltry $25 million a year. Today El Salvador languishes with vast unemployment, radical economic disparities and a murder rate forty times higher than that of the United States.

Democrats like California Assembly Speaker Antonio Villaraigosa are probably right when they claim that Bush's trip was aimed more at luring the domestic Latino vote than at building bridges to the South. During his 2000 campaign, Bush excoriated Bill Clinton for squandering a chance to improve relations with Latin America. But now Bush seems to be following in that same sorry tradition.

MARC COOPER

Marc Cooper, a Nation *contributing editor, is the author of* Pinochet and Me: A Chilean Anti-Memoir (*Verso*).

From *The Nation,* April 15, 2002, p. 4. © 2002 by The Nation. Reprinted by permission.

AMERICA'S FUTURE

SMART GLOBALIZATION

Being first and biggest in an emerging market isn't always the best way to conquer it.
A better tactic: Learn local cultures—and build a presence carefully

By **Pete Engardio**

A television ad running these days in India shows a mother lapsing into a daydream: Her young daughter is in a beauty contest dressed as Snow White, dancing on a stage. Her flowing gown is an immaculate white. The garments of other contestants, who dance in the background, are a tad gray. Snow White, no surprise, wins the blue ribbon. The mother awakes to the laughter of her adoring family—and glances proudly at her Whirlpool White Magic washing machine.

The TV spot is the product of 14 months of research by Whirlpool Corp. into the psyche of the Indian consumer. Among other things, the Benton Harbor (Mich.) company learned Indian homemakers prize hygiene and purity, which they associate with white. The trouble is, white garments often get discolored after frequent machine washing in local water. Besides appealing to this love of purity in its ads, Whirlpool custom-designed machines that are especially good with white fabrics.

Whirlpool hasn't stopped there. It uses generous incentives to get thousands of Indian retailers to stock its goods. To reach every cranny of the vast nation, it uses local contractors conversant in India's 18 languages to collect payments in cash and deliver appliances by truck, bicycles, even oxcart. Since 1996, Whirlpool's sales in India have leapt 80%—and should hit $200 million this year. Whirlpool now is the leading brand in India's fast-growing market for fully automatic washing machines.

Whirlpool's success story stands out in a time when Corporate America doesn't talk much about emerging markets. Things were different a decade ago. That's when Western economies had stalled, so expanding operations into the fast-growing, heavily populated lands of Asia, Latin America, and the old Soviet bloc was a top priority. The approach to globalization then was brutally simple: get in fast, strike megadeals with top officials, and watch the profits roll in. Multinationals figured local consumers would snap up their products at a premium. Thus AT&T promised some 20 ventures in China, from state-of-the-art telecom factories to research labs. Enron Corp. negotiated giant power plants and pipeline projects in India, Indonesia, and Bolivia. General Motors Corp. envisioned an Asia-wide network of car plants, led by its $1.2 billion facility in Shanghai.

SENSE AND SENSIBILITY. Many of these bets fizzled or disappointed. Enron's $4 billion Indian power plant is a debacle. Other multinationals saw that local competitors can catch up fast—and beat them in price and marketing. Tumbling trade barriers are making local production less essential. Meanwhile, a globalization backlash has forced companies to view their activities in poor nations in a different light. Exxon Mobil, Cargill, Freeport-McMoRan, and Royal Dutch/Shell became targets of local uprisings over oil, mining, and other projects in Indonesia, India, and Nigeria. McDonald's, KFC, and Philip Morris have endured withering criticism at home and abroad for aggressively pushing inappropriate products and ignoring local sensibilities.

The financial crises that ravaged nations like Mexico, Thailand, Russia, Brazil, and Turkey didn't help. Suddenly, "emerging markets" connoted excessive risk. Indeed, compared to the booming U.S. of the late '90s and a unifying Western Europe, emerging markets looked irrelevant to many execs. After

Succeeding Overseas
How Companies are Boosting Foreign Sales—and Cutting Risk

PRUDENT INVESTMENTS Rein in capital spending on new factories and acquisitions. Look for smaller, more focused projects.

BROADENING THE MARKET Look beyond upscale consumers to the 4 billion people earning the equivalent of $1,500 or less a year.

LOCAL LEVERAGE Where possible, use existing distribution networks and underutilized factories, rather than build from scratch.

CO-OPT THE LOCALS Don't wait for a backlash, involve local nonprofits, entrepreneurs, and officials in your project.

DON'T RUSH IN Most emerging markets are liberalizing investment rules: So wait until the terms are right.

explosive growth in the early 1990s, foreign direct investment by U.S. companies in East Asia, excluding Japan, plunged by 74% to $1.33 billion from 1997 to 2000, estimates the U.S. Commerce Dept. The drops have been nearly as dramatic in Latin America and Eastern Europe.

But as Whirlpool and other savvy U.S. companies such as Kodak, Citigroup, and Hewlett-Packard are proving, investing time and energy to understand societies in developing nations can pay rich returns. Rather than swinging for the fences with megaprojects or costly takeovers, the smarter approach is to methodically build a presence from the ground up. Some of the best investments are the most economical—small corner kiosks instead of full-blown stores or bank branches, say, or a tie-up with a savvy local player who owns a factory. Says Bain & Co. global strategist Chris Zook: "Companies are trying to figure out how to build on their strengths as opposed to throwing a bunch of Hail Mary passes in the hope they connect."

Above all, smart globalization requires extensive homework. Companies are starting to work closely with bureaucrats, entrepreneurs, and social groups at the grass roots. Not only is it easier to head off a local political backlash by cooperating with local players early; multinationals are also finding they can save enormous resources—and develop products local consumers really need.

Whirlpool has learned many of these lessons. Eight years after launching its global blitz in 1989, it took a $294 million writedown to shed two of the four appliance plants it built in China. "What we absolutely missed was how fast three markets would become saturated," concedes CEO David R. Whitwam. "We could build plants around the world, but where you fail is in the marketplace."

Now, Whitwam believes Whirlpool is on track. Besides its sophisticated marketing and inroads with local distributors, the company reorganized its global factory network. For all appli-

ances, it devises basic models that use about 70% of the same parts. Then it modifies its machines for local tastes. Whirlpool has an incentive to get it right: Through 2009, it expects demand for big appliances in the U.S. to remain flat, while it projects demand overseas will grow 17%, to 293 million units.

Similar dynamics are pushing other companies to renew their global focus. Developing nations are still likely to grow much faster than the industrial West for at least a decade (see chart). What's more, most multinationals today target mainly the richest 10% of the global population. They've yet to reach the 4 billion who earn the equivalent of $1,500 or less annually. Few can afford a PC, car, or mortgage now. But many experts argue they will be the greatest source of future global growth. That's why Hewlett-Packard Co. has launched a drive to help stimulate computer use in villages from Central America to Africa. The HP program also is politically shrewd: It promotes the beneficial aspect of globalization to the neediest.

Citibank's new campaign to broaden its traditional base of rich clients exemplifies the new approach to emerging markets. In Bangalore, India, it launched a program called Suvidha— Hindi for "ease." It persuaded midsized companies to set up retail bank accounts for their entire staffs, from janitors to top managers. To open accounts, customers need just $22. They get a card they can use to get cash, take out loans, pay bills at local ATMs, and buy groceries. In three years, Citi has gained 200,000 retail clients, doubling its base in India, for about $10 million.

Where the growth is Since 1997, Citibank clients in emerging markets who operate small businesses have risen sixfold, to 8.7 million

In corporate banking, Citi is targeting companies with revenues of $50 million or less. India's trucking business has been one priority. By opening offices in 23 cities offering credit, savings, and checking accounts, Citi now finances 10,000 truckers—most with fewer than 30 vehicles. It also is gearing up in Poland, Brazil, and the Philippines. Since 1997, small-business clients in emerging markets have risen sixfold, to 8.7 million. "The lower segments of these markets is where the growth is," says Citibank CEO Victor J. Menezes. Such markets earned Citigroup $2.7 billion in net profits last year.

Other U.S. companies are finding they can get ahead working with small entrepreneurs eager for new ways to make money. That's one reason emerging markets are a bright spot for Eastman Kodak Co. While Kodak has struggled in the U.S., in Asia, sales were up 9% last year. Much of this is because of Kodak Express photo supply and development shops, often owned by entrepreneurs such as Qiu Xing, 28. The Shanghai native, who says he had "always been a photography buff," invested $48,000 to open his shop in January. In a deal with a Chinese bank, Kodak lets Qiu use his developing equipment as loan collateral even though he hasn't fully paid for it. Kodak

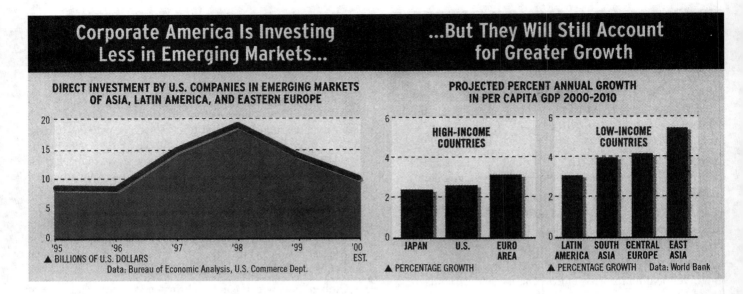

Corporate America Is Investing Less in Emerging Markets...

DIRECT INVESTMENT BY U.S. COMPANIES IN EMERGING MARKETS OF ASIA, LATIN AMERICA, AND EASTERN EUROPE

▲ BILLIONS OF U.S. DOLLARS

Data: Bureau of Economic Analysis, U.S. Commerce Dept.

...But They Will Still Account for Greater Growth

PROJECTED PERCENT ANNUAL GROWTH IN PER CAPITA GDP 2000-2010

HIGH-INCOME COUNTRIES

JAPAN U.S. EURO AREA

▲ PERCENTAGE GROWTH

LOW-INCOME COUNTRIES

LATIN AMERICA SOUTH ASIA CENTRAL EUROPE EAST ASIA

▲ PERCENTAGE GROWTH   Data: World Bank

also supplies monthly staff training. Qiu takes in $5,000 a month and makes a 25% profit.

Kodak has 6,000 Expresses across China and expects 10,000 by yearend. Its market share in China has doubled since 1995, to 60%. "We moved so fast, our competitors didn't have time to act," boasts John Tseng, a Kodak general manager for Asia.

In these turbulent times, when political and currency crises rock governments from Jakarta to Buenos Aires, it's hard to tell when emerging markets will be the predictable lands of oppor-tunity CEOs once foresaw. But that was always an illusion—and it's time Corporate America figures out what really works. "The next round of global expansion is as much about imagination as about resources," says University of Michigan management guru C. K. Prahalad: "Putting a billion dollars down does not in-volve imagination." With the mistakes of the '90s behind them, the winners will approach the world in a smarter way.

With Manjeet Kripalani in Bombay and Alysha Webb in Shanghai

Reprinted from the August 27, 2001 issue of *Business Week,* pp. 132-134, 136 by special permission. © 2001 by the McGraw-Hill Companies, Inc.

Integrating Multinational Firms into International Economics

James R. Markusen

As recently as the mid-1980s, research on multinational firms was almost entirely separate from research on international trade. The latter was dominated by general-equilibrium models using the twin assumptions of perfect competition and constant returns to scale. In this theory, there was little role for individual firms; indeed, theorists spoke only of industries, not firms. Multinational firms generally were approached from a case-study perspective, or at best in a partial-equilibrium setting.

To the extent that multinationals and foreign direct investment were treated at all in trade theory and open-economy macroeconomics, they were viewed as part of the theory of portfolio capital flows. The view was that capital, if unrestricted, flows from where it is abundant to where it is scarce. The treatment of direct investment as a capital flow was evidenced in data sources as well. There were lots of data on direct investment stocks and flows, but little on what multinationals actually produced, where they produced it, and where they sold it.

It took little staring at available statistics to realize that viewing direct investment as a capital flow was largely a mistake. The overwhelming bulk of direct investment flows both from and to the high-income developed countries and there is a high degree of cross penetration by firms from these countries into each other's markets. It also appeared that the decision about whether and where to build a foreign plant is quite separate from how and where to raise the financing for that plant.

Lastly, casual observation suggested that the crucial factor of production involved in multinational location decisions was skilled labor, not physical capital. By the late 1970s, I began to believe that location and production decisions should be the focus of a new microeconomic approach to direct investment while financial decisions should remain part of the traditional theory of capital flows.

Much of my work over the last two decades[1] has thus been to develop a microeconomic, general-equilibrium theory of the multinational firm. This theory should satisfy several conditions. First, it should be easily incorporated into general-equilibrium trade theory. Second, it should be consistent with important stylized facts, such as the large volume of cross investment among the high-income countries. Third, it should generate testable predictions and survive more formal econometric testing.

One useful starting point for theory is a conceptual framework proposed by British economist John Dunning, who suggested that there are three conditions needed for a firm to become a multinational. First, the firm must have a product or a production process such that the firm enjoys some market power or cost advantage abroad (ownership advantage). Second, the firm must have a reason to want to locate production abroad rather than concentrate it in the home country (location advantage). Third, the firms must have a reason to want to own a foreign subsidiary rather than simply license to or sub-contract with a foreign firm (internalization advantage).

I have used these ideas as conceptual guides in building a formal theory. In my models with Horstmann and Venables[2], the ownership advantage is modeled by the existence of firm-level as opposed to plant-level scale economies. The general idea is that there are knowledge-based activities such as R and D, management, marketing, and finance that are at least partially joint inputs across separate production facilities in that they can yield services in additional locations without reducing services in existing locations. We assume that activities can be fragmented geographically, so that a plant and headquarters can be located in different countries, for example. Finally, we assume that different activities have different factor intensities, such as a skilled-labor-intensive headquarters or components production and an unskilled-labor-intensive production plant. I have termed these properties jointness, fragmentation, and skilled-labor intensity respectively.

Jointness is the key feature which gives rise to horizontal multinationals, firms that produce roughly the same goods and services in multiple locations. For these firms, broadly defined trade costs constitute a location advantage, encouraging branch-plant production abroad. Fragmentation and skilled-labor-intensity are key features which give rise to vertical multinationals, in turn geographically fragmenting the production process by stages. For vertical firms, low trade costs may be a location advantage. Differences in factor endowments and prices across countries encourage geographic fragmentation, resulting in the location of stages of production where the factors of production they use intensively are cheap.

These elements are not difficult to incorporate into industrial-organization models of trade. The latter models are then enriched by allowing firms to choose their "type" in a first-stage, selecting the location of their headquarters and the number and location of their plants. The second stage decision may be a Cournot output game or a standard monopolistic-competition model. Multinationals arise endogenously, depending on country characteristics including country sizes, factor endowments, and trade costs.

Internalization advantages are not easily added to the same models. The issues here are the stuff of the theory of the firm and the boundaries of the firm in particular. The reasons for firms to wish to own foreign subsidiaries rather than to license technology, for example, include factors such as moral hazard, asymmetric information, incomplete and non-enforceable contracts, and so forth. It becomes technically awkward to incorporate these factors into general-equilibrium models, so they often are embedded in more specialized, partial-equilibrium models.

Nevertheless, my view is that the same properties of knowledge-based assets that give rise to jointness also give rise to the risk of asset dissipation, moral hazard, and asymmetric information. A blueprint that can be used easily in a foreign plant as well as a domestic one may also be copied easily or stolen. Licensees or possibly the firm's own employees may quickly absorb the technology and defect to start rival firms if contracts are not enforceable. Thus the theory is relatively unified, but internalization or choice of mode issues (for example, owned subsidiary, licensing, exporting) often are addressed in specialized models.

These new models yield clear and testable predictions as to how we should expect multinational activity to relate to country characteristics, industry characteristics, and trade and investment costs. Consider two countries, and an industry in which firms can decompose production into a headquarters activity and a production activity. Horizontal firms, which roughly duplicate the activities of home-country plants in foreign branch plants will tend to arise when countries are similar in size and in relative endowments, and when trade costs are moderate to high relative to investment costs (or technology transfer costs). In particular, it is the host-country's trade and investment costs that matter, not the home country's costs. The results on country size and relative-endowment similarity can best be understood by noting what happens in countries that are not similar in one of these respects. First, if there are plant-level scale economies, then a large difference in country size will favor single-plant national firms that are headquartered and producing in the large country, and exporting to the small country instead of incurring the high fixed costs of a foreign plant. Second, if countries are of similar size but differ significantly in relative endowments, then single-plant firms headquartered in the skilled-labor abundant country will have an advantage unless trade costs are very high. Third, when countries are similar in size and in relative endowments, there should be two-way direct investment in which horizontal firms penetrate each other's market via branch plants rather than through exports.

Vertical firms separating a single plant and headquarters, on the other hand, are encouraged by factor-endowment dissimilarities. Under the skilled-labor-intensity assumption just discussed, large differences subject to moderate or small trade costs should favor locating the headquarters in the skilled-labor-abundant country and having a single plant in the unskilled-labor-abundant coun-

try. Factor-endowment differences between countries will be reinforced if the skilled-labor-abundant country is also the small country. In the latter situation, the headquarters should be located in the skilled-labor-abundant country, while the single plant should be located in the other country both for factor-price motives and for market-size motives (minimizing total trade costs). Vertical activity generally should be one way, from skilled-labor-abundant (especially smaller) countries to unskilled-labor-abundant (especially larger) countries.

As indicated above, these are clearly testable predictions and suggest regression equations to explain world multinational activity. There are now a number of such studies published, including Brainard[3] and Carr, Markusen, and Maskus[4] with others forthcoming or in working paper form. The dependent variable is generally production in country j by affiliates of firms headquartered in country i. The right-hand-side variables (including interaction terms among these variables) are the country sizes, country factor endowments, trade costs in both directions, investment barriers, and industry-specific variables such as firm and plant scale measures, R and D indexes, and so forth. The general approach outlined above gets good support in the empirical analysis. Key variables have the correct signs and generally high statistical significance. Outward multinational activity from country i to country j (production by affiliates of country i firms in j) is increasing in the joint market size, decreasing in size differences, increasing in the relative skilled labor abundance of country i, increasing in country j's inward trade cost, and decreasing in country j's investment barriers. Across industries, affiliate activity is increasing in measures of firm-level scale economies such as R and D, headquarters activities, and advertising intensity, and is decreasing in plant-level scale economies.

There seems to be some consensus that, if one were to look for a single model that is effective in explaining a large proportion of multinational activity, we would clearly choose a pure horizontal model over a pure vertical model. The casual evidence discussed earlier is confirmed by formal econometric testing: multinational activity is highly concentrated among the high-income developed countries with significant two-way penetration of each other's markets in similar products. Such investments quantitatively dominate activity from developed to developing countries. Thus a theory based on knowledge-based assets and firm-level scale economies seems to be a much better approach than a more obvious and traditional theory based on factors flows.

To say that the horizontal approach is a better overall model than a vertical theory is not, of course, to say that vertical activity is unimportant. It is clearly important in many sectors and for many developing host countries and no one is suggesting otherwise. Recent empirical papers by Hanson and Slaughter[5] and Yeaple[6] are quantifying the range of strategies taken by multinational firms across industries and host countries. It is also worth emphasizing that some vertical activity, including assembly, footwear, and clothing production is carried out by independent contractors in developing countries and thus does not appear in the affiliate production statistics.

Future work will likely proceed on several fronts. In the theory area, more work on internalization or micro-theory-of-the-firm models would be welcome, creating a better understanding of the choice of mode by firms. It is particularly desirable if new models can be fitted together with the general-equilibrium models emphasizing ownership and location. Further work with the general-equilibrium models connecting production decisions with factor markets is important. There seems to be some two-way causality at work, where multinationals are only attracted to countries with minimum levels of labor skills and social infrastructure, yet the entry of multinationals in turn contributes to skill upgrading and skill accumulation.

In the empirical area, work on the choice of mode is also desirable. Why do we see owned-subsidiaries in electronics assembly, but rarely see them in clothing and footwear production which use independent contractors? When and why do we see licensing instead of owned subsidiaries? More clarification on the importance of vertical firms is also desirable, and on the use of certain countries as export platforms.

Research on policy issues also is needed. The two-way causality just noted is important for public policy and suggests the possibility of multiple equilibriums and low-level development traps. While much work has been done on taxes, there is virtually none on the importance and composition of government expenditure. Yet casual evidence suggests that social infrastructure, including physical, educational, and legal infrastructure, is very important in attracting inward investment.

Notes

1. *Most of my work on multinationals has now been rewritten, synthesized, and extended in: J. R. Markusen,* Multinational Firms and the Theory of International Trade, *Cambridge: MIT Press, forthcoming in 2002.*

2. *I. J. Horstmann and J. R. Markusen, "Endogenous Market Structures in International Trade," NBER Working Paper No. 3283, March 1990, and in the* Journal of International Economics *32 (1992), pp. 109–129; J.*

R. Markusen and A. J. Venables, "Multinational Firms and the New Trade Theory," NBER Working Paper No. 5036, February 1995, and in Journal of International Economics, 46 (1998), pp. 183–204; J. R. Markusen and A. J. Venables, "The Theory of Endowment, Intra-Industry and Multinational Trade," NBER Working Paper No. 5529, April 1996, and in Journal of International Economics, 52 (2000), pp. 209–35.

3. *S. L. Brainard, "An Empirical Assessment of the Proximity-Concentration Tradeoff between Multinational Sales and Trade," NBER Working Paper No. 4580, December 1993, and in* American Economic Review, *87, (4) (September 1997), pp. 520–44; S. L. Brainard, "An Empirical Assessment of the Factor Proportions Explanation of Multi-Nationals Sales," NBER Working Paper No. 4583, December 1993.*

4. *D. L. Carr, J. R. Markusen, and K. E. Maskus, "Estimating the Knowledge-Capital Model of the Multinational Enterprise," NBER Working Paper No. 6773, October 1998, and in* American Economic Review, *91 (2001), pp. 693–708. J. R. Markusen and K. E. Maskus, "Multinational Firms: Reconciling Theory and Evidence," NBER Working Paper No. 7163, June 1999, and in* Topics in Empirical International Economics: A Festschrift in Honor of Robert E. Lipsey, *M. Blomstrom and L. Goldberg, eds., Chicago: University of Chicago Press, 2001; J. R. Markusen and K. E. Maskus, "Discriminating Among Alternative Theories of the Multinational Enterprise," NBER Working Paper No.7164, June 1999.*

5. *G. H. Hanson, R. J. Mataloni, Jr., and M. J. Slaughter, "Expansion Strategies of U.S. Multinational Firms," NBER Working Paper No. 8433, August 2001.*

6. *S. R. Yeaple, "The Role of Skill Endowments in the Patterns of U.S. Outward Foreign Direct Investment," University of Pennsylvania Working Paper, 2001.*

Markusen is a Research Associate in the NBER's Program on International Trade and Investment. He is the Stanford Calderwood Professor of Economics at the University of Colorado, Boulder.

From *NBER Reporter*, Winter 2001/2002, pp. 5-7.

UNIT 3

The International Environment: Organizations and Monetary Systems

Unit Selections

Key Points to Consider

- Outline the role of international trade organizations. Do you think they are important? Why do you think they are developing and expanding?

- What are some things that are being done to stabilize world monetary markets?

- Do you think the balance of payments problem is serious? Why or why not?

- Do you think companies should attempt to minimize the taxes they pay? How far should they be willing to go?

 **Links: www.dushkin.com/online/**
These sites are annotated in the World Wide Web pages.

Chambers of Commerce World Network
http://www.worldchambers.com/
CIBERWeb
http://ciber.centers.purdue.edu
India Finance and Investment Guide
http://finance.indiamart.com/
Foreign Direct Investment Is on the Rise Around the World
http://www.neweconomyindex.org/section1_page04.html
International Economic Law Web Site
http://www.law.georgetown.edu/iiel/
United States Trade Representative (USTR)
http://www.ustr.gov
WWW Virtual Library Demography & Population Studies
http://demography.anu.edu.au/VirtualLibrary

One of the most obvious features of international trade has been the development international trade organizations. Some of these organizations have existed for several decades while others are very new. They all have several things in common. The first is that while there have been some global agreements such as the General Agreement on Tariffs and Trade (GATT) and the World Trade Organization (WTO), most of the trade organizations tend to be regional. The European Union (EU), the North American Free Trade Agreement (NAFTA), and the Asia Pacific Economic Cooperation Forum (APEC) are three of the more obvious examples.

The second common bond is that trade organizations involve nations in a sort of customs union that tends to lower and/or remove trade barriers among its members while maintaining, at a somewhat higher level, trade restrictions for products and services from outside the association. A few trade organizations, such as the EU, also have political ambitions of uniting the member countries into a political union. The headquarters of the EU is located in Brussels, Belgium. One of the problems that the EU has had over the years has been the struggle over sovereignty between the countries making up the union and its centralized government in Brussels.

One recently developed trade organization is the North American Free Trade Agreement (NAFTA), a trade agreement among the United States, Canada, and Mexico that took effect in January 1994. NAFTA was built on an agreement that was in force for several years between the United States and Canada. That agreement essentially removed the vast majority of trade barriers between these two countries. NAFTA included Mexico in the deal. This was not accomplished without great struggle in the U.S. Congress or without second thoughts, especially when the Mexican economy crashed shortly after U.S. ratification of the agreement in late 1993.

NAFTA does broaden opportunities for all businesses involved. One major problem, however, is going to be the integrating of Mexico, a country that for decades has seemed to be on the verge of joining the developed world, into a union with Canada and the United States. Integrating the Canadian and U.S. economies is a relatively simple task. The legal systems are based on the same philosophy of law, and the most-used language is the same. The political systems are very similar, and many United States and Canadian firms are already doing substantial business in each other's countries. Also, the standard of living, while not exactly the same, is certainly comparable. Mexico, however, is a very different story: the legal system is based on a whole different philosophy of law, the language is different, and, in Mexico, much of the business activity is aimed at export to the United States. Still, economically, geographically, or politically, it does not make sense to exclude Mexico from economic integration with the rest of North America. The difficulty arises in how to do it. As NAFTA has developed, other countries have become interested in exploring closer trading ties with North America. This is explored in "Free Trade Area of the Americas: NAFTA Marches South."

Another recent development in world trade has been the creation of the World Trade Organization (WTO). The WTO was created as a result of the Uruguay Round (1986–1993) of the GATT (General Agreement on Tariff and Trade) talks and in many ways supersedes GATT. Many challenges face the WTO. One of the first challenges is the trading conflict between the United States and Japan over a variety of products, This conflict has been going on for over 25 years, and it is part of a larger balance-of-trade problem between the two countries. Much of the conflict is not to be found in official government policy, but in the way individual firms do business, something that has always been difficult to control and will surely prove a thorny problem for the WTO.

Unfortunately, these organizations are not without their critics. Many people are less than enthusiastic about the development of these organizations. They often seem less than democratic and even somewhat dictatorial in their attempts to manage the world economy. Not everyone is happy about the actions of the IMF, as seen in "The Sacking of Argentina: The IMF Deserves to Be Blamed, but So Does the Country's Willing Political Class."

Financial markets have always been a major cause of concern for organizations engaged in world trade. Financial markets, along with the International Monetary Fund (IMF) and the World Bank, were the major focus of the Bretton Woods Agreement at the end of World War II. But the financial markets aspect of the agreement failed, and while the IMF and the World Bank have continued in their missions, the value of currencies has been unhitched and allowed to float. This has led banks and other international financial institutions to seek greater cooperation and stability in recognition that world trade conditions are fluid and subject to change, and that a mechanism is needed to help deal with the inherent risks associated with that change. Such a mechanism was found in the international market for currencies and the associated markets, such as derivatives, that have developed over the years. It is difficult to say what will happen in the future concerning the international monetary systems. But there is concern with how the IMF and the World Bank operate as may be seen in "Failure of the Fund: Rethinking the IMF Response."

Finally, the issue of taxes and accounting procedures has become one of concern to corporations. As more and more companies are doing business outside of their home markets, the question of what taxes are paid to which government becomes more important. Governments are looking for ways to pay for their various programs, and profits made by companies from outside the country provide an inviting target for taxation. The problem for many firms is that their profits are often taxed numerous times before they are able to get them, making doing business outside the country less attractive. Companies realize that they are going to have to pay taxes, but they only want to pay them once, not three or four times, and then as little as possible, as noted in "Accounting Challenges Overseas."

Where the elite preens itself

The World Economic Forum or Davos (actually it's held in New York this year) brings together the world's wealthiest and most powerful people. But don't expect any insights.

By **Jenni Russell**

"Y ou're off to the World Economic Forum?" asked the Oxford economist, enviously. "How very impressive. They've never invited me."

Three days later, I queued in the snow outside the conference centre in Davos, standing behind mink coats and cashmere overcoats, watched over by Swiss policemen with machine-guns. "Reporting press? You can't come in here. Side entrance, please." I stood in line again, this time behind Puffa jackets and *Newsweek* journalists, waiting to collect my orange badge. Once inside, I found that the seminar I wanted to go to was being held in a half-empty room. "You can't sit here. All seats are reserved for white badges. Coloured badges have to stand."

An acquaintance invited me to a dinner he was hosting: "There are people I'd like you to meet." The green-badged Forum employee stopped me at the door. "This is a participants' dinner. Orange badges are not allowed." Then, later, reluctantly: "If you're coming in, please can you turn your badge around? Diners may be upset if they see you're a colour."

"Why does anyone put up with being treated like an epsilon?" I asked a *Financial Times* correspondent. "Because we all live in hope of becoming white badges," he said. "Then we'll know what's really going on."

A leading British businessman was wearing a white badge, but it bore a small logo on the top left-hand corner: GLT. "What's a GLT?" I asked.

"Ah," he said, "well, it's a Davos club. I'm a Global Leader for Tomorrow."

"That sounds very important," I said. "Yes," he said, "I thought so myself, until I bumped into the man who'd sponsored me, on the way to my first meeting. I asked him if he was coming, and he said, 'Oh no, dear boy, I don't bother with that any longer. I'm not a GLT any more, I'm an IGWEL.' 'What's an IGWEL?' I asked him. 'A member of the Informal Group of World Economic Leaders of Today.'"

The World Economic Forum has employed a simple psychological truth—that nothing is more desirable than that which excludes us—to brilliant effect. Year after year, its participants apply to return, in the hope that this time they'll be a little closer to the real elite. Next year, they, too, might be invited to the private receptions for Bill Clinton, Kofi Annan or Bill Gates, instead of having to stand on the conference centre's steps like teenage rock fans.

It's the sheer concentration of individuals in possession of power, wealth or knowledge that makes the privately run Forum so desirable to its participants. The thousand chief executives who attend its annual meeting control, between them, more than 70 percent of international trade. Every year, they are joined by a couple of dozen presidents and prime ministers, by senior journalists, a changing selection of leading thinkers, academics and diplomats, and by rising stars of the business world. Access to the meeting is by invitation only, costs several thousand pounds a time for business participants, and is ruthlessly controlled.

If Kampala is full of Japanese cars, why can't Uganda sell beef to Japan?

The Forum prides itself on being not just high-powered, but high-minded—dedicated to finding solutions to global problems, identifying trends, encouraging corporate responsibility and extending the benefits of capitalism worldwide. Its critics would describe it in more brutal terms—as a group dedicated to keeping the world safe for big business, no matter what the cost.

For 30 years, the Forum has met in the Swiss mountain resort of Davos, where it began. This year, it will be different. The annual meeting is to take place at the Waldorf Astoria Hotel in New York at the start of February. Klaus Schwab, its founder, says that moving this year's meeting is a gesture of support for a city traumatised by terrorism. Cynics suspect other motives, largely to do with the Americans' current reluctance to leave their shores. Security is another issue. Last year, the meeting was under siege by anti-globalisation protesters; snowball-throwers in woolly hats were met by Swiss police firing water cannons. This year, the potential threats are thought to be altogether more serious.

Within the conference itself, the issue of how to respond to the newly dangerous world will dominate the official programme. Schwab has said that the meeting must be more than a talking shop: he wants it to come up with solutions. There's no doubting his earnestness. The programme is studded with sessions on how to deal with fundamentalism, bridge religious divisions, respect differences and reduce poverty. Yet, considering its record over the past few years, it will be a surprise if the Forum comes up with any original conclusions, or any inspired forward thinking. Despite its impressive invitation list, its intoxicating range of subjects for discussion and its enormous self-importance, the organisation has proved surprisingly poor at foreseeing both problems and opportunities.

In 1998, Davos staged a handful of sober sessions on the catastrophic collapse of the Asian economies. No one predicted that, over the next year, the financial turbulence would deepen and spread, causing Russia to implode, and driving stock markets down worldwide. The following year's meeting failed to spot the impending dotcom boom, and, to compensate, 2000's programme was stuffed with internet entrepreneurs in open-necked shirts, holding oversubscribed seminars on how you, too, could make millions in months. Nothing said by the Forum indicated that this was a bubble, which was to burst within three months.

At one of the first dinners I attended in Davos, the charming businessman next to me had risen the minute coffee was served. "Excuse me—I must just catch the president of Ghana," he said. Twenty-five minutes later, he was back. "Did you speak to Rawlings?" I asked. "Too much of a crowd," he said. "But I caught the president of Kazakhstan. He invited me to open one of my businesses there. I think I will. There are, oh, two hundred thousand individuals there with a net worth in excess of a hundred grand."

"Is this why you come?" I asked. "Yes. The contacts you make here are invaluable. When I want to see him, I'll call his private secretary, say we met at Davos, and I'll go straight through… I do a deal a year at Davos. It's worth half a million a time to me."

Other participants don't even bother with the formal schedule. Skiing alone through the woods on the cross-country trail one lunchtime, I was overtaken by an American banker, in charge of lending millions to the rest of the world. He'd been chauffeur-driven from Geneva directly to the ski shop. He worked for Goldman Sachs. Was he going to the afternoon sessions? "Naw." Why not? "I look at it this way. Subject I know about, I guess I know more about it than anyone else in the room. Subject I don't know about—say, the brain—I think, well, do I need this? And the answer's no. So I don't waste my time."

The gulf between the values the Forum professes and what it actually does depresses and bewilders one contingent at the annual meeting: the representatives of the poorest countries in the world. They are excluded from the deal-making by sheer lack of resources, and they find the Forum hypocritical and ineffective, even when it comes to upholding its own most fundamental belief—that of free trade.

Four years ago, President Museveni of Uganda came to Davos to lobby for a change in the terms of trade. Most heads of state were staying in five-star hotels; Museveni and his entourage could afford only a small, bare flat on the edge of town. He made an impassioned speech asking why, when Kampala was filled with imported Japanese cars, he couldn't reciprocate by selling Uganda's beef to Japan. We don't want aid, he said. We keep being told we must accept free trade, but it's all one way: we aren't allowed to export food and textiles into protected western markets. We don't want dependence. We want opportunities.

I asked him whether he thought his lobbying would be successful. "I don't know," he said, sounding troubled. These were, he said, the most powerful people in the world. He had hoped they would support his case once they had heard it.

Campaigners have been puzzled at the lack of any effective response to their pleas. Every year, the Forum restates its commitment to the ideals of free trade, and yet the companies supporting the declaration include some of the most protectionist in the world. What they fail to recognise is that Davos can make no concessions, offer no compromises. It is not a negotiating body, like the World Trade Organisation. It cannot make promises on behalf of nation states. It has no leverage over the companies that attend. There is no necessary connection between its flowery resolutions and any activity, because no mechanism for that exists.

The irony is that, for a body so dedicated to identifying and associating with power, the Forum has none of its own. It simply offers a platform on which the elite can parade, talk and listen, thrilled by their proximity to one another. Even its futurology is unreliable. When the sonorous conclusions are issued in New York early next month, it will be worth remembering how little it all means.

From *New Statesman*, January 28, 2002, pp. 28-29. © 2002 by New Statesman Ltd.

REPORT ON POST COLD WAR LATIN AMERICA

Free Trade Area of the Americas:
NAFTA MARCHES SOUTH

BY CLAUDIO KATZ

The U.S. plan to create the Free Trade Area of the Americas (FTAA) as a hemisphere-wide successor to, and expansion of, the North America Free Trade Agreement (NAFTA) is a strategic project aimed at consolidating U.S. supremacy in the region by means of increased U.S. exports, more investment controls and sophisticated financial-flow monitoring methods.

Planning for the FTAA began seven years ago, but the project remained at a standstill until 1998. At their meeting last year in Quebec, the region's presidents agreed to speed up the planning process and finish FTAA negotiations by 2005. The initiative has received new impetus from the Bush administration, which, as we write, is trying to convince Congress to approve so-called "fast-track" legislation that would give the U.S. executive branch the authority to negotiate trade agreements while reducing Congress' oversight role. The immediate objective of the United States is to find external trade outlets to compensate for the U.S. economic slowdown. Unlike Asia and Europe, Latin America represents a possible new export niche for North American companies[1] The FTAA would slow down competing European moves into Latin America by obstructing negotiations over alternative free trade agreements, like those promoted by Spain. U.S. officials also hope the agreement would help shore up regional military alliances threatened by the recent deterioration of many Latin American political regimes.

The 500 U.S. companies with the closest links to Latin America are pushing for fast implementation of the FTAA. They want the new pact to be modeled on NAFTA and on World Trade Organization (WTO) provisions on commerce, and to incorporate the types of financial discipline imposed by the International Monetary Fund (IMF).

The FTAA negotiations were initially secret and although they are now public, the pact still faces strong opposition from U.S. industries with few international ties. They believe they would be worse off under the agreement. Representatives of this sector successfully prevented Congress from giving former President Clinton fast track authority.

The importance of the political-military interests behind the FTAA is less obvious, but more decisive. For several years, highly organized popular movements with clear social demands have been growing stronger in both rural and urban areas of many Latin American countries. These movements highlight the erosion of political systems that have become delegitimized because of their inability to meet popular claims. Lack of confidence in existing regimes accelerated the end of a presidential term in Peru and led to government dissolution in Ecuador, the effective collapse of the state in Colombia and the disintegration of traditional political parties in Venezuela and Mexico. Preserving stability in the face of this upheaval is a priority of a U.S. government that identifies these crises with a weakening of its own regional security role. The FTAA would be a means for the United States to strengthen its covert military intervention in Colombia, continue with the regional re-armament associated with the U.S. "war on drugs," conduct more Vieques-style military exercises and use diplomatic pressure to get more Latin American support for sanctions against states the State Department considers pariahs: Cuba, Iraq, Libya, and North Korea. The United States successfully opposed the establishment of independent nuclear programs in Argentina and Brazil and now intends to expand this "discipline" to the rest of the world even as it moves forward its own anti-missile defense system.

Nobody disputes that, at present, the FTAA is a U.S. project aimed at increasing its own hegemony in the region. However, after a decade in which neoliberal ideology has been in the ascendency, some now idealize U.S. supremacy. In the past, great power domination was crit-

Brazil: Neoliberal decades bring down "emerging power"

By Emir Sader

The historical period that began with the fall of the Soviet Union and the advent of the United States as the world's only superpower changed Brazil's international position. Up until then, Brazil had been one of the so-called "emerging intermediate powers." Among these it occupied a special place because of its dynamic economy, one so well-endowed with natural resources and technological capacity that when the 1980s began, Brazil was active in all the important economic sectors, including information technology. But the following two decades were marked by a traumatic turnaround, in which Brazil's international profile was sharply reduced, along with its possibilities for economic expansion and for playing a leading international role.

Brazil had the fastest growing economy in the world between 1930 and 1980, but the "debt crisis" of the 1980s interrupted this five decade-long expansion. Then, beginning in 1990, the productive and competitive capacity that had been built up over previous decades was substantially weakened as a succession of Brazilian governments adopted U.S.-promoted neoliberal policies. Deregulation and the brusque opening of Brazilian economy to the international market promoted the replacement of industrial capital by finance capital as the economy's driving force. This made the economy more fragile and in seven years increased the public debt eleven-fold. Brazil began to be strongly dependent on foreign capital in order to keep its accounts current, and it lost is sovereignty to international financial organizations in which the United States plays a preponderant role.

Mercosur, the regional customs union that might have played a key role in affirming the international power of Brazil and other nations of the region, also ended up as a victim of neoliberal policies. [See "Free Trade Area of the Americas: NAFTA Marches South"] The priority given to fiscal adjustment and monetary stability forced the region's governments to impose artificial exchange policies. When differences between member nations' exchange policies produced a marked economic disequilibrium between member countries instead of their integration, Mercosur's final crisis began. In light of this, the proposal for the Free Trade Area of the Americas (FTAA) may represent a consolidation of Brazil's loss of sovereignty. Brazil could be the principal victim of a form of supposed integration that in reality signifies total subordination to the United States. Brazil's natural resources, labor power and massive potential internal market are the booty to be snatched by the United States and its huge corporations.

Brazil now finds itself at a turning point. The possibilities for fiscal adjustment have been exhausted, and so have the political possibilities of the governments that were on the scene during the 1990s. The 2002 presidential elections will occur in a setting that will either permit an opposition victory or give new life to the current model. This means either a rupture with the neoliberal "Washington Consensus" economic plan which is now in effect in Brazil or a continuation of it. There would be continuity even with the victory of a "third way" candidate in the style of Argentina's de la Rua and Mexico's Fox. Such a government would maintain the current economic program despite promises to re-emphasize economic development, combat unemployment, and implement more social problems.

The main left opposition candidate, Luiz Inacio da Silva, known as Lula, hasn't yet clearly defined an external or foreign policy, but if he wins, the nature of his government will certainly depend on how he chooses to act internationally. Brazil must be reintegrated into the international system, and this would mean renegotiation of the debt, because the current payment schedule would make it impossible for any popular government to implement its program, as de la Rua's current situation in Argentina shows. It would also mean redefining international alliances in order to obtain sufficient power to carry out the renegotiation; this would imply not merely the rejection of FTAA, but also an active international policy aimed at creating diversified alliances, with priority given to closer ties with the big nations of the South China, India and South Africa among others.

Without redefining its own relations with the United States and affirming its sovereignty, Brazil won't be able to build a just society or again take up the task of economic and social development. It needs to do these things at home if it is to take on an international leadership role which would allow it to bring together the great majorities of the world who are today excluded from power and from access to most of the world's goods.

icized and the dominant states were accused of imperialism and colonialism; now there are those who argue that such domination is useful. Some maintain that the FTAA will help counteract a supposed lack of entrepreneurship among Latin Americans; they use anthropological, geographical and racial justifications to back up their claims. Others predict that if the region does not take this opportunity to accept U.S. leadership, it will not escape future poverty and decadence[2] It is, however, very difficult to show that Latin America was ever in the past free from U.S. patronage, especially during the last decade, when previous social and economic progress was being undone in many places. During this period, the region's economies were unbalanced by four factors—growing external debt, export specialization, unequal exchange rates and lower purchasing power. These were not the result of Latin America's moving away from the United States. Rather, they reflect the effects of the consolidation of Latin America's subordinate relation to the United States. The region's economic crises are not a consequence of the built-in defects of Latin Americans, but of Latin America's increasingly dependent role in the world market.[3]

Other analysts argue that "domestic markets are not sufficient to overcome underdevelopment" and claim that the FTAA will help us streamline our export capabilities and will facilitate access to the largest market in the world, that of the United States.[4] Do Latin American consumers already have such vast purchasing power and high levels of consumption that markets at home have been exhausted? How can Latin American exports successfully penetrate what is not just the largest, but also the world's most competitive and demanding market? What will be the effect of the enormous gaps in productivity that have so far thwarted access to this market? Answers to any of these queries bring into question a naive belief in a regional "take-off" based on the FTAA. Opinion makers, however, do not weigh their illusions against actual developments, but reiterate their faith in increased exports and investment inflows.

Many of those promoting the FTAA also support dollarization, that is, the adoption of the U.S. dollar as a legal currency. Nevertheless, dollarization supporters have not provided any proof of its advantages for the Central American economies that have already adopted this policy, Guatemala and El Salvador. They also ignore the fact that in Ecuador dollarization was implemented as an emergency measure in the face of financial collapse. Panama is the only country that has had a dollarized economy for an extended period of time, and it certainly does not represent a model of poverty eradication and adequate employment. Over the last decades, Panama, like any other debtor country in the region, had to abide by 17 IMF stabilization programs.[5]

Dollarization is associated with the FTAA project, but it is not integral to the initiative since there is still heated debate within the United States government about its advantages. Consequently, those Latin American countries that give up control of their national currencies by dollarizing do not get in return any commitment from the U.S. Federal Reserve that the Fed will act as a lender-of-last-resort in case of a banking crisis, as it would do in the United States. And while small economies that are commercially integrated with the United States can tolerate the fact that, under dollarization, U.S. officials have more power over individual Latin American economies than

national officials do, such inequality would have disastrous consequences for larger, more independent economies like those of Argentina or Mexico.

For now, however, U.S. interests in FTAA are basically commercial. As with any business initiative, FTAA's introduction has been accompanied by a major marketing campaign that seeks to recreate the fantasies that surrounded privatization plans in the 1990s. But, as with everything neoliberal, the predicted prosperity is a promise for the future, while sacrifices are immediately required for implementation.

As negotiations progress, there is less talk about "brotherhood" and "integration" among Americans, North and South, and more demands by particular groups of U.S. corporations. U.S. corporations that operate in service industries intend to step into the areas of insurance, education and health care in Latin America. These areas are particularly profitable because, given the dire state of Latin America's public services, the upper middle classes tend to use private services. In the area of investments, FTAA negotiators are considering provisions that would grant foreign companies the right to resort to an international court that would have more authority than any national legal system. Such legal entities are already part of NAFTA, and have ruled in favor of companies that filed complaints against several states in Canada and Mexico when the states tried to enforce environmental and other local laws.[6]

In the area of public sector procurement, the elimination of rules that give preference to local suppliers is being discussed. North American consortia will be able to push aside any local competitor that does not have as much access to international credit as they do.[7]

In terms of customs barriers, U.S. negotiators want more open Latin American economies but will not allow for increased imports in return. U.S. non-tariff trade barriers—mainly discriminatory anti-dumping measures—affect 34% of the products on the export list of the regional customs union, Mercosur. Under this mechanism, Argentine honey exports were recently penalized with a 60% tariff.

Agriculture is a key area in the agreement. As "agribusiness" corporations make progress in destroying regulations that protect Latin American small farmers, they also block any traces of free competition at home. U.S. Secretary of Commerce Donald Evans has already declared that the $97 billion in U.S. farm subsidies "will not be discussed in the FTAA negotiations."[8] What's more, the resolution of this issue does not depend on negotiations with Latin America, but on talks with the European Community for the reduction of European agricultural subsidies. If this dispute is not solved, all expectations that Argentine exporters, for instance, might have for the FTAA will be frustrated. Some estimate that the agreement will ultimately result in a 30-35% increase in Argentine imports and a 4% reduction in exports.[9]

The FTAA will once and for all consecrate intellectual property rights which brought a windfall to U.S. high-tech companies after the demise of the Argentine and Brazilian information industries. The most important current patent dispute concerns the pharmaceutical industry's objections to a Brazilian government project that produces cheap, generic versions of patented AIDS drugs without the permission of the patent holders. Though this program saves lives and heals patients, it does not meet the profit requirements of the international laboratories.

Last, but not least, the FTAA will authorize the United States to continue violating environmental protection agreements. As a result of NAFTA, several border regions in Mexico became toxic sewers and it is estimated that 40% of the forests in the Mexican state of Guerrero have been destroyed as a result of pollution.[10] The FTAA will also promote more wage flexibility based on the Mexican maquila model. The overall effect of the agreement will undoubtedly be a regional economic cycle more dependent on the U.S. GNP. This will deepen the vulnerability of the Latin American productive sector to downswings.

As it stands, the FTAA will also signify the demise of Mercosur. This customs union, currently made up of Argentina, Brazil, Paraguay and Uruguay, cannot survive in a general free trade zone.[11] For U.S. corporations competing with European rivals, Mercosur represents an obsolete method of protecting the Europeans via tariffs and national or regional subsidies. The United States has clearly expressed its intention of dissolving the South American association in proposals for bilateral agreements with Chile, recently extended to Argentina. But conditions are very different in these two countries: Chile has a small industrial base and has developed a complementary trade with the United States in mineral, fruit and timber products. Argentina, by contrast, still possesses the sort of industrial sector that would see its final days under the FTAA.[12]

There is no doubt, however, that U.S. efforts are directed mainly against Brazil, which boasts the most coveted market and an industrial sector that is still mostly independent of U.S. corporations. Unlike other countries, Brazil cannot acquiesce to the FTAA without sacrificing the international market shares it has already gained. For this reason, the Brazilian government opposes moving up the agreement's start date and wants to make Venezuela a strategic ally. These pressures are increasing Mercosur's tendency toward internal disintegration. Ten years after its creation, Mercosur promoters acknowledge its deterioration. It failed to make progress in the establishment of a common currency, and in the foundation of regional political and judicial institutions. Neither were customs pacts consolidated because common tariffs were never implemented. No arbitration court for conflict settlement was ever established and disagreements regarding subsi-

dies and government procurement systems were not solved.[13]

These disagreements were deepened by the way each country reacted during the debt crisis. While Brazil decided to devalue its currency and lift tariffs, Argentina opted for convertibility and trade opening. All those economists and politicians that propose "to enter the FTAA from Mercosur" cannot explain how joint talks could succeed if more basic agreements were never reached in ten years.[14]

Unlike the European Community (EC), the FTAA does not seek to create a zone of homogenous economic development—the agreement will encourage no backward member country to move closer to the level of the powerful economy which stands behind the pact. No North-to-South budget transfers are planned and gaps in living standards between Latin American countries and the United States will remain. The differences between the EC and the FTAA are obvious: The EC is constituted as a power bloc seeking to challenge the United States, while the FTAA is a pawn of U.S. supremacy used to confront such a challenge. It is therefore appropriate to define this initiative as an imperialist, neocolonialist project for Latin America. If the agreement is put into effect, it will change the nature of the regional bourgeoisie, ending the debate about whether it is dependent or transnational.[15] What is clear is that the Latin American dominant classes are unable to take on the task of creating an integration project of their own. The Andean and Central American pacts experienced the same defeat that Mercosur is suffering now. While during the twentieth century the regional bourgeoisies were unable to develop their Bolivarian dream of integration, they have now lost any interest in such an objective because their level of association with metropolitan—U.S.—capital is substantially higher than it used to be.

Genuine integration between countries cannot be achieved with the obstacles to sustainable development created by the external debt. Payment defaults obliterate all efforts toward regional development.

Mercosur's ten years of existence were also characterized by unprecedented attacks on worker living conditions. Instead of common labor laws and protection of salaried workers, unemployment rates and labor insecurity soared in member states. This experience demonstrates that any genuine integration project among peoples should be based on different principles. First, it should start from the satisfaction of basic demands, such as increased minimum wages, unemployment insurance, free education and health care. The prerequisites for policy coordination towards these goals are solidarity, promotion of labor stability and improvement of living standards rather than competitiveness, capital mobility, and business efficiency.

Second, genuine integration cannot be achieved under the obstacles to sustainable development imposed by the external debt, as illustrated by the 1995 Mexican, the 1998 Brazilian, and the 2000-2001 Argentine crises. Payment defaults obliterate any regionwide effort towards development, and continuing IMF adjustment programs prevent reconstruction of devastated Latin American economies. Finally, an integration project should be conceived as part of a socialist transformation process given that capitalism poses an impossible barrier for Latin American countries to overcome their periphery status. There is a direct link between the old dreams for Latin American unity and the establishment of new forms of ownership and collective economic management.

The debate on these proposals is now framed within the new international political climate created by recent protests against globalization. FTAA negotiators encountered hostile street demonstrations in Buenos Aires and Quebec. The novelty is that many demonstrators not only proclaim that "an alternative world is possible" but also define such a world and the ways to reach it.

Notes

1. Luis Bilbao, "Democracia amurallada," *Le Monde Diplomatique, Buenos Aires,* May, 2001.
2. Andrés Oppenheimer: "Geografía y cultura: ¿factores de progreso?" August 1, 2000; "La posible partición de las Américas," August 6, 2000; and "Qué se espera para América Latina," January 2, 2001, all in *La Nación,* (Buenos Aires).
3. For more on this topic, see Claudio Katz: "Las nuevas turbulencias de la economía latinoamericana," *Periferias,* No. 8-2, 2000, Buenos Aires.
4. Mariano Grondona: "América Latina: ¿se salvará con el ALCA?" April 12, 2001, *La Nación,* (Buenos Aires).
5. Sebastián Edwards: "El dólar no es la cura mágica,"May 13, 2001, *Clarín* (Buenos Aires).
6. Maude Barlow, "Area de libre comercio y la amenaza para los programas sociales," The Council of Canadians, 2001, www.canadians.org.
7. IDEP, "Los capitales únicos ciudadanos del ALCA," *Nosotros*-ATE, 3/2001, *Buenos Aires.*
8. Donald Evans quoted in *Página/12,* April 10, 2001, Buenos Aires.
9. Eduardo Locita, "ALCA un proyecto hegemónico,"*Realidad Económica,* No. 178, 2-3/2001.
10. Document of the Argentine Committee against the FTAA, March 2001, Buenos Aires.
11. Mercosur "emerged as a free trade zone in 1991, and became a customs union in 1995, when common import duties—which currently average 13.5%—went into effect for a list of products entering from outside the bloc." Marcela Valente, "Fissures Appear in Mercosur Trade Bloc," Inter-Press Service, September 28, 2001.
12. The Argentine final position is a mystery because, at this writing, the country is on the verge of a suspension of payments and a potential deflationary collapse. While this chaos subsists, the government will have an undefined position vis-a-vis Mercosur and the FTAA. Under the present crisis, some measures taken point to either option but these are actually improvised measures with no clear objectives.
13. Roberto Bouzas, "El bloque puede desaparecer,"April 12, 2001, *Página/12.*
14. Marcela Bordenave, "Mercosur o ALCA," April 10, 2001, Página/12; Alieto Guadagni, "El ALCA desde el Mercosur,"March 29, 2001, *La Nación.*
15. James Petras suggests that this change has already occurred. See *Rebelión,* March 17, 2001; *Página/12,* May 13, 2001.

Claudio Katz is an economic researcher and professor at the University of Buenos Aires and Conicet. This article originally appeared in Nueva Sociedad, *July-August, 2001. Translated from the Spanish by Carolina Escalona.*

From *NACLA Report on the Americas,* February 2002, pp. 27-31, 44-45. © 2002 by NACLA Report on the Americas.

The Deficit That Just About Everyone Overlooks

Clive Crook

One of the most startling aspects of America's economic performance in recent years has been one of the least noticed. It affects the outlook for inflation, and hence for interest rates, yet it attracts next to no attention on Wall Street. It is bound up with how or whether to spend the budget surplus, yet the topic is scarcely mentioned on Capitol Hill. If the economy's current slowdown should turn really bad, experts may call it the fatal flaw in the miracle of the late 1990s. Yet the financial press, which was obsessed with this very matter for much of the 1980s, now ignores it altogether.

THE UNITED STATES IS A NET DEBTOR TO THE TUNE OF MORE THAN $1.5 TRILLION. IT'S THE WORLD'S BIGGEST DEBTOR, BY FAR.

The subject in question is the deficit in the international balance of payments. In 1991, America's trade deficit stood at less than $30 billion. It has been rising ever since. Last year, it grew to some $360 billion, more than twice as big as it was at any point in the 1980s. Back then, such a sum would have been regarded as impossible, and the prospect would have caused consternation. This run of deficits has added, year by year, to America's foreign debts, because the country must attract capital to cover the gap between imports and exports. The United States was a net creditor to the world throughout much of the 20th century. Now foreigners' claims on the country stand at roughly $9 trillion; subtracting American claims on foreigners, the United States is a net debtor to the tune of more than $1.5 trillion—the world's biggest, by far.

Everybody has noticed what a colossal budget surplus America is running at the moment: Its size is driving the entire domestic-policy debate. Yet the budget surplus, in all its awesome, politically transforming immensity, represents less than 2.5 percent of the gross domestic product. The deficit in the external accounts is pushing 4 percent of GDP.

When people do decide to worry about the external deficit, admittedly, they tend to get carried away. The dangers are easy to exaggerate. They were, without question, greatly exaggerated during the 1980s. These moods of alarm and neglect are familiar: Usually, economic pundits are either celebrating deliriously or rendering their garments. At the moment, thanks to the new economy and the slowdown, some of both is going on. If things turn out very badly, and the mood swings all the way to misery, the dread meaning of the external deficit will come too much to the fore again. At the moment, though, it is too much ignored. How about a middle position—one that makes sense whether the economy soars or stalls?

To begin with, consider the case for seeing the deficit as no cause at all for concern. It goes like this: In a financially integrated world, it is the flow of capital that drives the external balance, not the flow of goods and services. The external deficit is an excess of imports over exports; it is also a net inflow of capital. In the past, external deficits were regarded as a sign of weakness partly because economists concentrated on the trade side: If a country imported more than it exported, its industries must be internationally uncompetitive. This was the fear in America in the mid-1980s—and it seemed plausible whenever growth slowed. Already, however, thanks to financial integration, this way of thinking is out of date. Modern finance means that trade flows change to accommodate capital flows, not the other way round.

In the late 1990s, this became obvious. As the economy roared ahead, nobody gave much thought to America's lack of competitiveness. Surging growth showed once and for all that trade deficits were not a sign of weakness. Success made it easier to view the external deficit from the capital-flows side—which, in a financially integrated world, is the right perspective.

Over the past five years, America's stunning growth has sucked in capital from all over the world. Far from signifying weakness, it was a resounding vote of international confidence in the U.S. economy. The trade imbalance was just a harmless byproduct of this influx of capital, as foreigners rushed to buy a share in America's success. Best of all, this financial inflow sustained a higher rate of domestic industrial investment than would otherwise have been possible. It fed, and continues to feed, the very growth that attracted it in the first place.

All this good news is true, as far as it goes. It was also true in Britain in the late 1980s, where conditions were similar in some ways to those in America today: strong growth, budget surplus, capital inflow, booming investment, big external deficit. Britain's finance minister in those days was Nigel Lawson. He was so keen on the good-news argument that it was known for a while in international policy circles as the "Lawson doctrine"—the idea that a big external deficit was a good thing, not a bad thing, so long as the capital was drawn in by private investment and not by public borrowing.

I remember endorsing this view at the time. I also remember, soon after, having to explain why Britain's new economy had fallen headlong into recession—a reversal that, among other things, wrenched the government's budget from surplus to deficit (thus transforming a good external deficit all at once into a bad one).

Oddly enough, this calamity did not discredit the Lawson doctrine. Economists were still citing it in the mid-1990s, when they sought to explain why the big external deficits of countries such as Thailand and South Korea were really a sign of strength, not weakness. Again, the fiscal position was all right. Again, the trade gaps reflected inflows of capital, the vote-of-confidence effect, surging private investment—certainly not any lack of competitiveness. Again, ev-

erything was fine—until it all went horribly wrong. You hear less about the Lawson doctrine nowadays.

All of this raises questions that matter very much for the U.S. economy. Where was the error in that plausible but discredited theory? Should the United States expect to suffer a fate similar to that of Britain in the 1980s and East Asia in the 1990s—or will the good-news theory that proved wrong in those cases be vindicated, in the end, in America?

The mistake, thanks to the benefit of hindsight, looks pretty obvious now. When governments are running fiscal surpluses, big external deficits are the counterpart of rapidly rising private debt, incurred by businesses and households. Everything depends on the soundness of those liabilities. You cannot take it for granted, as the Lawson theory assumed, that everything will be all right if the investments financed by the increase in debt are carried out by the private sector. In Britain's case, too much of the capital washed into the housing market. A real estate bubble followed. When the bubble burst, the debt turned bad. Businesses and consumers had to cut their spending sharply to restore their finances. The result was recession. Something similar happened in Scandinavia soon after. In broad terms, this is also the story of the East Asian shambles of the 1990s: too much borrowing, inflated asset prices, financial overstretching, and collapse—leading in the end to severe recession.

Most likely, this will not be America's fate. Still, it is useful to understand just why America has less reason to worry. It is not because a privately driven external deficit is necessarily a

sign of strength, or because booming debt-financed investment is always a good thing. Neither is true, as those other cases have shown. Debts can get too big, especially when banking systems prone to error (as banking systems are) serve as the intermediaries. At times of irrational exuberance, investment can be wasted, causing financial liabilities to grow faster than productive assets.

No, the reason to be sanguine is simply that in America, the signs of financial overstretching are less pronounced. In particular, real estate bubbles—a uniquely hazardous variety of asset-price inflation—played a big role in most of those other cases. The rise in real estate prices has been far more muted in the United States. Other signs of reckless or grossly wasteful investment are harder to find as well. The surge in output of the late 1990s, whatever the outlook from now on, was real enough while it lasted. The crashlanders of the 1980s and 1990s could not point to any comparable surge in the underlying productivity of their assets.

There may be less cause to be alarmed, but there is surely good reason to stay alert. America's financial overstretching may be milder, but it cannot be denied altogether. Look at the disappearing rate of saving. Look at Wall Street, despite the recent correction, still buoyed by personal and corporate borrowing. Look at the rate of bankruptcies, rising ominously. Look at the Federal Reserve's anxiety over "financial fragility." These are all counterparts of the influx of foreign capital—which has indeed, in this sense, been too much of a good thing. Give a thought now and then to the deficit that got away.

From *National Journal*, February 17, 2001, Vol. 33, Issue 7, p. 468. © 2001 by Natural Journal Group Inc. All rights reserved. Reprinted by permission.

The Sacking of Argentina

THE IMF DESERVES TO BE BLAMED, BUT SO DOES THE COUNTRY'S WILLING POLITICAL CLASS.

TIM FRASCA

Buenos Aires

It is sobering to witness one of the greatest cities in the world slip, despite its deceptively placid surface, into a state of premodernity. Traffic lights in this metropolis of 12 million people still turn from red to green, newspapers in the kiosks report the latest bad news and Argentines occupy cafe tables, smoke a lot and shake their heads in disgust as they have for centuries. But money has ceased to exist. Oh, there are coins and bills, and cash still manages to facilitate exchange—except when the peso's value oscillates by 40 percent in three days, as it did in March. But money as the basis of a modern, capitalist economy, money that can be lent and borrowed, created or liquidated by central banks, money as the lubricating oil of investment and production—that has disappeared.

In normal times, María Esperanza Alvarez, 63, could be fairly considered a bit eccentric, if not a nut case. Standing outside the Spanish consulate where her niece is trying to get papers in order to abandon the country, she confides that for the past thirty years she has kept her savings in a box—thousands of dollars (which were always available) accumulated from her clothing business, which once employed twenty-three seamstresses. Having defied all common and expert sense for three decades, María Esperanza now deserves an Einstein award: She never for a moment believed the banks' basic pledge that they would give her back her money when they promised to do so. And she was right.

Lisandro Orlov, by contrast, was more trusting, perhaps in keeping with his professional outlook as a Lutheran pastor. Engaged for years in projects aimed at reintegrating social outcasts—street dwellers, drug users, people facing AIDS-related discrimination—the 59-year-old Orlov lost his pension fund in the December bank freeze-up. Like many Argentines, Orlov assumed that the austere entities in cavernous downtown palaces like HSBC, Citibank and BankBoston would honor their commitments. Now he's fighting in court to regain access to his dollars, already forcibly converted to 1.4 pesos each, or less than half the 3-to-1 rate the greenback now commands on the street.

In December of last year, Argentina's decade-long and highly celebrated experiment as the poster child of monetarist orthodoxy came to a crashing halt. While the International Monetary Fund is not the only responsible party, its spokespeople have now conveniently forgotten their laudatory worship of the main architect of the project, former President Carlos Saúl Menem, and the fund's gleeful funding of it throughout the 1990s. The IMF is now forcing Argentines to pay the price of its decadelong collusion with what it now says was a flawed performance all along.

So a once-wealthy country is suddenly seeing its sophisticated middle class driven into the streets, both to protest and to put food on the table. However, this extraordinary descent cannot simply be blamed on the opportunism of the free-trade globalizers. The sacking of Argentina could not have occurred had not a willing political class put out the FOR SALE signs long ago. Peronism, Argentina's peculiar form of nationalist populism from the 1940s and '50s, capitalized on the country's postwar largesse and lulled the populace into accepting political rot in exchange for fairly broad access to a share of the loot. After Menem came to power in 1989, he took a major detour from the Peronist vision. While preserving the rhetoric, the party structures and the patronage, he engineered huge privatizations, dismantled trade barriers and freed financial flows into and especially out of the country. The cornerstone of his monetarist policy, adopted at a time of hyperinflation, was the guarantee that a peso was a dollar was a peso, now and forever.

As a result of Menem's policies, what was once just old-fashioned corruption gave way to bargain-basement sales of the family silver. Now, with nothing left, citizens have awakened to the calamity. Although they may not be staging an active revolt for the moment, their unprecedented rejection of a whole generation of leaders has profoundly changed the political landscape.

Argentina's current plight is a lesson for those countries and their citizens that have toed the free-trade line and assume they will be rewarded accordingly. Now that things have fallen apart, the foreign beneficiaries of the fat years quickly wash their hands of responsibility and blame local elites, while turning their sights elsewhere for the next opportunities.

The Implosion

Last December the IMF, realizing that Argentina was a bottomless pit, turned off the cash spigots. Facing bankruptcy, President Fernando de la Rúa of the Radical Civic Union and his financial Rasputin, Economy Minister Domingo Cavallo, declared a *corralito* on bank deposits. This apt metaphor, suggesting cows liable to wander off and teams of neoliberal horsemen reining them in, meant, in practice, seizure. Confiscation. Argentines suddenly could withdraw only 1,000 pesos a month of their own money; otherwise, old-fashioned bank runs would have collapsed the system.

Implicit in the *corralito* was acknowledgment not only of the country's bankruptcy but also of the huge falsehood that had underpinned the entire economy for a decade: that the Argentine peso was worth one US dollar. Like the military dictatorship's assurances to the public in 1982 that the Falklands/Malvinas war would conclude with a glorious triumph, the political leadership simply couldn't give up its steady fix of convenient mendacity until it was far too late. The Argentine military still hasn't recovered from that debacle and the subsequent airing of its horrendous crimes during the local version of the war on terrorism, and in fact no one suggests the generals are in any way itching to get back into the political game, much less stage a coup.

But neither does the country's discredited political leadership, mostly Peronists and Radicals, seem to have much of a clue how to navigate the ship of state. "While the businessmen bankrupted the country," says Santiago Kovadloff, a former de la Rúa official, "the political leadership was directly complicit." Although not everyone would have subscribed to that radical indictment until recently, today Kovadloff's views are probably on the moderate side. The implications of this repudiation for Argentina's future are enormous. There is even a name for spontaneous outbursts of popular rage: the *escrache*, which in the local slang means, "in your face."

When the impact of the nationwide grand larceny first set in, the dispossessed victims surged into the streets. In December, police killed twenty-seven demonstrators before the teetering Radical government realized it had lost all legitimacy. De la Rúa had to be hauled from the presidential palace in a helicopter. His first replacement, a delusional provincial governor who immediately promised to create a million new jobs, lasted a week. Finally, on January 1, Eduardo Duhalde, a Peronist warhorse from Buenos Aires's suburban rust belt, took over. Duhalde, the loser in the 1999 presidential election, made immediate noises about breaking the deadly grip of the financiers and boosting the "productive" sector.

Virtually all progressive voices in Argentina today say a new strategy of this sort is urgently needed: pump-priming to generate internal demand, help for pulverized local industry and a break from the monetarist straitjacket. But even some of Duhalde's direct collaborators, who have since resigned, say it's all talk. Economist Héctor Valle, who worked for Duhalde for thirty-five days in the ministry of production, says his team's emergency recovery plan assumed that no foreign investors would touch Argentina with a ten-foot Brady bond and that the regime would have to cast its lot with local industry to reactivate the economy. "This meant confronting powerful interests and generating political support for more sacrifices," says Valle. "But Duhalde has no stomach for bold moves; he's a ribbon-cutter, and he's wasting crucial time."

Patacones and *Quebrachos*

What do governments do when they have no money? Under the theory on which convertibility of the dollar and peso was based, the governors of Argentina's twenty-three provinces should have slashed their payrolls and cut costs. But in some areas, over half the work force is state-employed, and salaries were often held up due to cash shortages even before the current disaster. With no jobs anywhere and no safety net, provincial bosses have been in no mood to commit political suicide for the IMF.

Instead, to avoid violent upheavals, the states have taken to issuing their own "bonds" or IOUs to pay their bills, including salaries. All over Buenos Aires, shop windows advise potential clients that they will accept one or more of the dozen quasi currencies that have sprung up to replace old-fashioned money: Chaco in the north issues *quebrachos*; Buenos Aires Province offers its employees *patacones*. At last count, there were fourteen of these funny moneys circulating. Desperate shopkeepers accept them, after knocking a percentage off their face value. The IMF wants them eliminated, as one of its many conditions for restarting the flow of emergency cash.

The retailers' desperation arises from the other predictable result of the anti-inflationary miracle: a devastating recession, now in its fourth year. It doesn't take an economics degree to see that the artificially expensive peso drove Argentine products off world markets and wrecked local industry through a flood of cheap imports. Argentina's economy has shrunk some 20 percent since 1998, and the free fall is just beginning.

Unemployment, now officially 22 percent, can only go higher. Just in the first two weeks of March, 20,000 businesses failed, each employing an average of ten people. Retail shops all over the capital are liquidating merchandise at a loss before closing their shutters for good. The only buyers in town are foreigners, including hordes of Chileans crossing the Andes to scoop up bargains. Poverty now affects 16 million Argentines, 43 percent of the population. Twenty percent are officially destitute. When a livestock truck overturned near the city of Rosario just before Easter, residents rushed to the highway and slaughtered the stunned cattle on the spot.

Another dramatic example of Argentina's accelerating creep toward prehistory are the barter clubs that have sprung up everywhere as a way around the fact that nobody can buy anything, while plenty of useful and needed products are in ample supply. While Spain sends charity food shipments—equivalent to sending donations of corn to Iowa—all over the capital long lines of people form with packages and shopping carts waiting patiently for one of the prized stalls in a church basement where the weekly session of frenzied commodity exchange is about to begin. In one club in upscale Palermo Viejo, at least 1,000 people clamored for a chance to crowd in and use their paper "credits"—another money substitute—to pick up food or used clothing or offer their skills as hairdressers, fumigators or aromatherapists. There are now upward of 4,000 of these clubs, with their deceptive air of a 1960s food co-op, generating the annual equivalent of $300 million in "commerce."

A recurrent slogan in the popular assemblies, pot-bangings and other demonstrations is "¡Que se vayan todos!"—the local equivalent of "Throw the bums out!" Some organizations actually promote dispensing with all leadership, a sign of the depth of revulsion for what has led them to this sorry pass. Others worry that the blanket rejection of "politicians" is a dangerously reactionary sentiment—readying Argentina for a Fujimori-type solution, a "nonpolitical" Bonaparte on a white horse.

There is certainly no shortage of motives for these sentiments. That the political class is corrupt to the bone, the civil service featherbedded beyond recognition and the union leadership complicit with every imaginable scam is no longer in question. Congressional deputies are so shameless that even during the current mass repugnance at their felonious antics, one Elsa Lofrano from Chubut Province could be appointed to a vacant Peronist seat, despite having received a pension for "physical and mental disability" for the past fifteen years. (The vote to seat her was 100 to 94.) But when a longtime Cassandra, congressional deputy Elisa Carrió from the center-left Movement for a Republic of Equals (ARI), and Otto Reich, George W. Bush's deputy for Latin America at the State Department, both put the blame for Argentina's problems on "corruption," they're not describing the same phenomenon.

'When the torturers go free, then anyone who steals or makes crooked deals can go free as well.' —Congressional deputy Elisa Carrió

Carrió, 43, was part of the alliance that brought de la Rúa into power in 1999. She broke with the ill-fated regime early on and is now one of the half-dozen recognizable politicians who can walk the streets without fear of an escrache. Carrió warned early on that corruption and incompetence were tearing the model apart. Wearing her signature mega-crucifix, Carrió says the ostentatious hand-washing by the IMF and Bush officials is just cynical amnesia. "Corruption in Argentina operates in complicity with foreigners. I had to go to Washington to denounce money-laundering because the US Embassy here was covering up for Citibank," she says. "All the biggest corruption scandals here involved American companies," she adds, noting that the laundering was enthusiastically carried out by top foreign banks. If so, today's finger-pointers were happy to cash in while the corruption they denounce redounded to their allies' benefit.

Political Response

More than the current government, the Argentine state faces a vast crisis of legitimacy. Any plan with a chance of success will require even more pain and therefore patience from a severely battered populace—patience that can only be won by leaders they can believe in and trust. Those are so scarce that one economist suggested in dead seriousness importing a team of Finns to run the central bank.

The escrache is the most graphic symbol of this prostrate leadership. There are several varieties: Crowds may suddenly recognize a hated figure from the political or business elite at an airport and confront him with curses and even physical threats. An escrache can also be an old-fashioned demonstration, focusing on personal shaming rather than political demands. One took place on March 23, organized by HIJOS, or Children for Identity and Justice and Against Silence and Forgetting, composed of surprisingly youthful relatives of those disappeared and assassinated in the 1970s. One of their two targets was the former archbishop of Buenos Aires, known for his sympathies with the dictatorship.

Impunity is indeed the problem, says Carrio, but she worries that the escrache hints of private revenge. "We have to know what happened in the genocide of the 1970s, plus who robbed us blind and all the deals that were made." She blames the recent brigandage on the continuing impunity for human rights crimes. "Those who tortured were liberated! Those who disappeared people! That's where the system of truth and justice broke down. When the torturers go free, then anyone who steals or makes crooked deals can go free as well." Neither does it escape Argentines that the liberator of the generals and admirals convicted of some of the most vicious crimes in modern history was none other than Carlos Menem himself, who granted them an amnesty in 1990. The spin then was that Argentina needed "stability," because, as a Swiss banker elegantly told me at the time, "You can only stir the shit so far."

Given the total discredit of most political parties, people eager for action and participation have flocked to ad hoc neighborhood assemblies, now slowly institutionalizing themselves. These expressions of popular wrath have mushroomed, and their representatives appear with their increasingly worn banners at rallies and demonstrations of all sorts. It's not clear what sort of long-term impact the assemblies can have on broader policy decisions, and the weekly pot-banging sessions have already turned slightly routine. But their appearance is clearly breaking down the hegemony of the traditional party structures, as the experience of Gladys Quinteros illustrates.

Quinteros, a 40-year-old housewife in what was once the heavily Peronist suburb of Merlo, decided to join the demonstrations in December but found her own community "asleep."

After a few lonely vigils in the local plaza, she and some allies managed to drum up 300 people for a protest march against the situation. As they made their way through the streets, they were suddenly set upon by a well-organized band of thugs armed with homemade weapons. Twenty people were injured, and others were further abused in the local hospital where employees are beholden to the local bosses, clearly in no mood to tolerate spontaneous dissidence. "The idea was to intimidate us, and they succeeded," says Quinteros. "People sympathize, but now they are afraid to join in." Later, Quinteros's home was set afire and one room badly damaged.

Meanwhile, Peronism, if not its current representatives, still exercises a mystical lock on many Argentines. Portraits of Evita pop up unexpectedly: in union halls of the left-wing Argentine Workers Federation (CTA) or on the mantels of disgusted dissidents and lapsed Peronist Youth. Gabriel Guga, 31, was a Peronist captain in the La Matanza suburb until he became disaffected with Menem's neoliberal deviation. He recognizes that Peronism uses public coffers to buy political support and enrich the party elites, as well as its pronounced authoritarian streak, its vote-rigging, its links to the drug trade and organized crime. But Guga remains in his heart loyal to Peronist principles, "what our fathers and grandfathers stood for."

What Next

IMF teams were in Buenos Aires in March and April to dictate the terms for new loans. These include measures that worked so well for Herbert Hoover in the early 1930s, like more spending cuts, which will further reduce internal demand. In addition to seeking abolition of the provincial quasi currencies, the IMF wants civil service ranks reduced and bankers let off the hook. While the tiny US downturn last year was promptly treated with oceans of cash, the Argentines are supposed to swallow more neolib medicine. This is likely to occur, given the dearth of creative alternatives from Argentina's current leadership. With no popular support, they will probably turn to Washington to help prop themselves up, for now. The clear political quid pro quos involved in the next IMF loan, such as voting against Cuba at the UN or helping with Plan Colombia, are already done deals.

Some observers are convinced the United States wants to make an example of Argentina and undermine its MERCOSUR regional trade pact with Brazil, to clear the path for a US-dominated free-trade zone in the Americas. "We're the economic Guernica," says psychoanalyst Silvia Bleichman. "They have decided to punish us, to crush all resistance." But some of the IMF demands are in themselves reasonable. Any new government will have to deal with corruption, padded civil service rosters, the unsustainable provincial deficits. The question is who will take charge of the major surgery and to what ends.

The sheer scale of the rapine committed by Argentina's leaders over the past decades, sometimes in uniform, sometimes not, has left the nation ripe for a sharp break with the past. People who feel systematically tricked by their banks, their armies, their presidents and even their bishops will either despair or figure out how to put their trust in one another and construct something new. Carrió, one of the few who dare to predict anything, says radical change is now as unstoppable as a hurricane. "A whole class is disappearing, and after a brief period of anarchy, there will be new leaders, and not just political ones," she assured me.

Although not everyone shares her optimism and fighting spirit, Argentines are now alert to bullshit like never before. People show up at street-corner assemblies to patiently consider the activists' speeches or the comments of their neighbors, clearly inexperienced in such matters but of necessity eager to understand what's taking place. But for the most part, says Bleichman, Argentines simply refuse to look ahead—what has already happened is so unlikely, so implausible, that predictions or indeed logical faculties seem useless. Only one, usually unspoken, sentiment garners universal agreement in Buenos Aires today: The worst is yet to come.

Tim Frasca is a US journalist who has lived and worked in South America for twenty years.

From *The Nation*, May 6, 2002, p. 26. © 2002 by The Nation. Reprinted by permission.

Failure of the Fund

Rethinking the IMF Response

JOSEPH E. STIGLITZ

*T*he world is just emerging from the Asian financial crisis, perhaps the most cataclysmic event to affect global capitalism since the Great Depression. While the United States emerged from this event unscathed—some might argue that it even benefited from the crisis as plummeting commodity prices reduced domestic inflationary pressures—many developing nations were not so lucky. Whereas the Great Depression induced a great deal of soul searching about capitalism's basic principles, the seemingly quick global recovery from the financial crisis and its limited effect on industrial countries have brought a more mixed response—self-congratulation on the part of some, renewed criticism of the impacts of globalization by others. In both instances, however, the global economic arrangements were clearly inadequate. The international financial institutions and arrangements established at the end of World War II to guard against another global economic depression are widely viewed as incapable of managing the modern global economy. The International Monetary Fund (IMF), in particular, has failed to perform the tasks for which it was designed. Today, the institution requires serious reform to ensure a more stable global economic environment.

Beggar Thy Self

The IMF's philosophy has moved far away from its roots. In this past financial crisis, the IMF provided funds under the explicit condition that countries engage in more contractionary fiscal and monetary policies than they might desire. The money went not to finance more expansionary fiscal policies but, instead, to bail out creditors from the more industrialized countries. The beggar-thy-neighbor policies that were so widely condemned gave way to even worse "beggar-thy-self" policies, with disastrous effects both for the home country and for its neighbors. The downward spiral in the region accelerated as declines in domestic GDP led to cutbacks in imports, thereby reducing regional exports. The beggar-thy-neighbor policy at least had the intention of making the nation's own citizens better off. No such benefits resulted from the IMF's beggar-thy-self policies. A country was told to build up its foreign-currency reserves and improve its current-account balance; this meant that it either had to increase exports or decrease imports. But exports could not rise overnight—in fact, as the country's neighbors' incomes plummeted, the prospects for increasing exports were even bleaker. Thus imports had to be reduced without imposing tariffs and without further devaluation. There was only one way that imports could be reduced in these circumstances: by reducing the consumption and investments that relied on imports. The immiseration of those at home was thus inevitable.

There is a further irony in the policies that the IMF pursued: while the IMF was created to promote global economic stability, some of its policies actually contributed to instability. There is now overwhelming support for the hypothesis that premature capital and financial market liberalization throughout the developing world, a central part of IMF reforms over the past two decades, was a central factor not only behind the most recent set of crises but also behind the instability that has characterized the global market over the past quarter century.

The Indictments

There is now widespread agreement that the IMF response to the Asian crisis was a failure. Although exchange rates stabilized, interest rates dropped, and the world eventually emerged intact from the crisis, none of this turnaround can be attributed to the IMF when we judge the success of its policies by whether the downturn was unnecessarily long or imposed unnecessarily high costs on workers. Of the four crisis countries in Asia, Indonesia remains in deep depression. The political turmoil there has proven a nearly insurmountable obstacle, but there is little doubt that the magnitude of the economic downturn contributed to the severity of the social and political unrest, that the turmoil was anticipated, and that IMF policies contributed to the magnitude of the economic downturn. Thailand has been the IMF's most faithful student, carefully following its dictates for several years; yet it has still to regain its pre-crisis output level. With almost 40 percent of bank loans non-performing, the country's future prospects are far from rosy. The two success cases are Malaysia, which avoided an IMF program, and South Korea, whose recovery can be attributed, at least in part, to its deviation from the IMF prescription in important ways. For instance, South Korea was told to restructure by dispensing excess capacity in industries such as computer chips. But the excess capacity was purely cyclical, and the passing of the downturn put billions of dollars into South Korean coffers, greatly aiding the country's recovery. Had it followed the advice of outsiders, Korea would be in a far worse position today. Similarly, South Korea was urged to shut down or sell off two of its major banks; instead, it effectively nationalized them.

While there is some disagreement about the appropriateness of the policies pursued in East Asia, there is general consensus that the IMF pursued excessively contractionary fiscal policies, and that the manner in which it handled financial-sector restructuring, at least in Indonesia, was a dismal failure. Beyond this specific crisis, widespread evidence exists of other failures, such as the inability of the rescue packages in East Asia, Brazil, and Russia to sustain the exchange-rate cost of billions of US dollars. This money will come not from taxpayers in the United States or Europe, but largely from the pockets of those in the developing world, especially unskilled labor.

Intellectual Incoherence

There was a certain coherence in John Maynard Keynes's post-World War II conception of the IMF and its role. Keynes believed that a market failure occurred when the actions of one country had spillover effects on others. Today, however, the dominant view inside the IMF is sometimes characterized as *market fundamentalism*, a strong belief that markets, by and large, work well, and governments, by and large, work poorly. One might suppose that an inherent tension exists here: the IMF, after all, is itself a governmental body, and many of the arguments concerning governmental inefficiency and incompetence hold with equal or stronger force at the international level than they do at the national level. From this perspective, the IMF's economists would expect an international governmental body such as itself to be marked by failures.

Developing a coherent policy for an international agency such as the IMF thus requires identifying important instances in which markets might not work and analyzing how particular policies might address

these failures. The IMF has, to date, failed to articulate a coherent theory of market failure that would justify its own existence and provide a rationale for its interventions in the market.

One of the IMF's arguments in defense of its intervention is that an ongoing crisis in one country will spill over to its neighbors. This concept of contagion is a devastating criticism to market fundamentalism because it implies an inherent market failure. If it is desirable to take international collective action to address the consequences of a crisis, it is equally desirable to take international collective actions to reduce the likelihood that crises will occur. If an increase in the ratio of foreign short-term indebtedness to reserves (in excess of some critical threshold level) substantially increases the likelihood of a crisis, then there should be international pressure to limit short-term indebtedness; yet the IMF has pushed for capital-market liberalization, the effect of which is precisely the opposite.

> **The IMF has, to date, failed to articulate a coherent theory of market failure that would justify its own existence and provide a rationale for its interventions in the market.**

Other examples of intellectual incoherence were displayed throughout the management of the Asian financial crisis. While the IMF recognized that weak financial institutions were a key factor in the crisis, it continued to use outdated macromodels that do a grossly inadequate job of incorporating the financial sector. This was remarkable, given the widespread discussion in the United States of how the failure of much more sophisticated models used by the US Federal Reserve had led to inadequate policy responses. While it should have been apparent that concern about bankruptcy was at the heart of the problem in Southeast Asia, the models used by the IMF (and worse still, the reasoning of senior IMF officials) gave no scope for bankruptcy and default and took no account of how their actions might af-

fect either bankruptcy itself or lenders' concerns.

There is a certain irony in this lack of intellectual coherence: the IMF is often accused of following an excessively rigid formula, a one-size-fits-all approach. I would agree with these accusations. The IMF has an ideology; a particular lens through which it looks at the world, but one should not confuse an ideological straitjacket with intellectual coherence.

The IMF Evolution

Since the creation of the IMF, there has been a subtle change in mandate, a change that, were it made explicit, perhaps would not have been widely accepted. The conflict between the effective mandate and the original mandate created a tension that manifested itself in numerous ways, including intellectual incoherence.

The IMF's original mandate was to provide liquidity in a world of imperfect capital markets, so as to enable countries to maintain output as close as possible to full employment. Assistance was conditioned on the recipient nations engaging in appropriate expansionary policies. Today, the mandate often appears to be that of a bill collector for lending nations: its objective is to make sure that the debtor country has as large a war chest as possible to repay outstanding loans and to ensure the maintenance of overvalued exchange rates in order to easily acquire foreign currency. These objectives require achieving a massive trade surplus as quickly as possible, regardless of the costs to the country or its neighbors. Capital-market liberalization also reflects the interests of the financial community in advanced industrialized nations. In part, the IMF is opening up lesser-developed markets to an industry in which the advanced nations have a comparative advantage.

The IMF focuses on the repayment of loans far more than on the maintenance of the affected country's GDP. Senior officials at the IMF repeatedly speak of defaults or standstills as an abrogation of the sanctity of contracts. They do not recognize that bankruptcy is a central institution of capitalism, that the high interest rates and high unemployment rates that their policies cause are an abrogation of the social contract under which these countries had so successfully operated for a third of a century, and that such an abrogation— and the public bailouts that follow—is the action that truly undermines capitalism and the long-term stability of society. The problem is that the IMF cannot openly announce its new mandate, and so it formulates an amalgam of policies that were both ineffective and lacking in intellectual coherence.

There is now a widespread consensus about one key aspect of this reform: the IMF should be restricted to crisis management in order to limit the damage that its mistaken policies might impose.

Other aspects of the IMF, such as its organizational structure and rules of conduct, also contribute to its policy blunders. The institution has a hierarchical structure, not uncommon among organizations that are designed to deal with crises; one cannot have intellectual debates on the best way to fight a fire in the midst of a fire. But whatever its merits in dealing with crises, such a structure often leads to organizations that do not adapt quickly. In addition, the IMF conducts much of its business behind closed doors, without transparency. The normal checks on institutional behavior, the pressures to alter its models, and the criticism of peers that is a normal part of intellectual and democratic processes simply do not exist. The IMF makes assertions and predictions concerning its policies that are consistently proven wrong, yet its leaders are seldom held accountable. With each failure, the IMF has looked to others to explain away its mistakes. Its effectiveness and credibility as an advisor are under mined by its refusal to lay out clearly the consequences of its actions and by the fact that it has lost touch with basic economics. Its success as a market psychologist is undermined by its recurring inability not only to predict but, increasingly, to affect market reactions. And its effectiveness as a political actor is weakened not only by the first two failures but also by the growing perception that its policies are dominated by the political interests of the US Treasury.

A Mandate for Reform

The simplest and most straightforward reform—one advocated by many economists on both the left and the right—is the abolition of the IMF. Some of the "public good" functions, such as data collection, could be transferred to other bodies, such as the UN Statistics Division. Monitoring could be performed by private agencies, and if considered insufficient, by existing or newly created peer-review groups like the Organization for Economic Cooperation and Development. Its development and transition programs could be assumed by the World Bank, but its core crisis-management functions would be abolished. With flexible exchange rates, the IMF simply interferes with the functioning of the exchange market, and its recent performance has reinforced the widespread view that even if markets do not work perfectly, bureaucrats are unlikely to improve matters. Without abolition, there cannot be a credible commitment not to engage in bailouts, and without such a credible commitment, lenders will have an incentive not to engage in sufficient due diligence. Excessive lending without due diligence contributes to economic instability.

Despite such arguments, governments consistently react in the same way to crises: they want someone to seem to be in charge. If the IMF were dissolved, it would almost surely be re-created when the next crisis occurs. Thus, given that the IMF exists and will certainly continue to do so, how should it be reformed?

There is now a widespread consensus about one key aspect of this reform: the IMF should be restricted to crisis management in order to limit the damage that its mistaken policies might impose. Its other functions should be given to other institutions. But limiting the IMF to crisis management clearly does not solve the problem. After all, problems in managing the recent global crisis were what precipitated the debate over reforming the international financial architecture. Thus reforms must focus on what the IMF does in response to a crisis. Three sets of reforms are crucial.

First, the IMF must become more transparent. This increased transparency would subject its policies to more critical scrutiny; it would hopefully make it more difficult for it to use outdated and inappropriate models. Part of this increased transparency would require the IMF to disclose the models it used and to predict the consequences of its policies. Outsiders could then independently ascertain the accuracy of these forecasts. In addition, if the IMF paid insufficient attention to the consequences of its programs on poverty, there would likely be a significant outcry before the damage was done.

Second, the IMF's interventions need to be limited. Huge bailouts should be a thing of the past. In effect, the advanced industrial countries provide the funds for the developing countries to repay the developed countries' banks, but the real burden is borne by taxpayers in the developing countries, since the IMF is almost always repaid. There should be a *prima facie* case that if a huge bailout is required, the exchange rate should not be at an equilibrium level.

Third, the conditions imposed by the IMF need to be reformed. Supporters of the IMF often point out that all lenders impose conditions to make sure that the funds are used as promised by borrowers. But the IMF's conditions are different. They are not necessarily designed to enhance the likelihood that the loan will be repaid; in some cases the conditions actually have the opposite effect. In other cases, the conditions have little or nothing to do with the crisis. For example, South Korea's crisis had nothing to do with loose monetary policy leading to excessive inflation, yet the IMF entered into the political sphere demanding reforms of Korea's central bank to make it focus exclusively on reducing inflation and becoming more independent. Forcing Korea to move up the timing of some trade liberalization measures to which it had previously agreed had absolutely nothing to do with the crisis; it was simply a crude political power play.

Even when there are particular structural weaknesses that can be linked to a crisis, reforms must be carefully timed and paced. What would have happened had the United States gone to the IMF in the midst of its 1989 financial crisis? The IMF would have insisted on abolishing the special tax treatment of real estate and agricultural subsidies, which serve to inflate the price of land. Had it done so in the midst of the Savings and Loan debacle, the United States would have had a full-blown crisis.

The rapid abolition of tax preferences would have had a devastating effect on real-estate prices, and thereby on the entire banking system. Eventually the United States should eliminate the real estate preferences as they interfere with the productivity of the US economy, but adverse effects from the rapid elimination of these preferences would have more than outweighed any gains from improved efficiency. IMF conditions thus need to be greatly circumscribed, limited only to actions that are absolutely essential to ensure the repayment of the loan and/or to mitigate externalities, such as those associated with excessively contractionary policies.

Some reformers have argued that the IMF should be de-politicized. They observe that some of its worst lending practices, such as the loan to Russia in 1998, are based not on economic analyses (which showed that Russia had unsustainable debt dynamics and an overvalued exchange rate), but on political motivations. Such an argument, however, runs contrary to the idea that one of the key problems is the IMF's lack of political accountability. It would be one thing if the IMF's bureaucrats were engaged in totally technical operations. But as we have repeatedly seen, they are engaged in actions that are inherently political, whether it involves a decision to bail out international creditors at the expense of the domestic economy, or designing bankruptcy laws that are more creditor friendly than debtor-friendly.

Beyond the Rhetoric

While markets are by and large the most effective way of increasing output and promoting growth, they often fail. Thus, within national economies, the government must often assume some role. But just at the time when the need for international economic institutions has increased, confidence in global institutions has eroded, and for good reason. Reforms must focus more on what the IMF does and how it does it. But we should also be aware that the IMF is a political organization that has survived and expanded over the past 50 years; while its adaptation may not have enabled it to better stabilize the world economy, it has enabled the IMF to survive—some say even to prosper. Thus, we should expect the rhetoric of the IMF to seriously consider such critiques. True reform needs to look beneath the surface, beneath the rhetorical veneer.

JOSEPH E. STIGLITZ was Chief Economist at the World Bank and is presently a Professor of Economics at Stanford University.

Reprinted with permission from *Harvard International Review,* Summer 2001, pp. 14-18. © 2001 by the President of Harvard College. All rights reserved.

Accounting Challenges Overseas

Accurate Reporting of Financial Results to U.S. Parent Companies Critical for Overseas Operations

By Mel Mandell

Finding and hiring competent accountants. It's one of the many nagging problems for corporations expanding abroad—especially public ones that have to report results in timely fashion. Here are just two of the challenges:

- Converting fluctuating foreign currencies into dollar values.
- Inducing openness on the part of overseas executives, businesspeople who aren't accustomed to publicizing detailed financial details and whose compliant accountants are accustomed to delivering statements that report what the clients want to hear and not necessarily reality.

Then there's the challenge of doing business in countries that don't have a long history of free enterprise, such as current or former communist nations like China, Romania or Russia. In these nations, the accounting problems could persist for years, according to Professor Gregory Miller of the Harvard Business School. Why? "Because there are few, if any, knowledgeable teachers to train the many needed accountants," Miller says. The professor has a deep understanding of the needs of U.S. multinationals because he was previously associated with one of the "Big Five" accounting firms—Andersen.

Fortunately, there is progress in achieving what's described as a "desirable convergence of global accounting standards." These are the words of Edmund L. Jenkins, chairman of the Financial Accounting Standards Board (wwwfasb.org) in Norwalk, Conn., a private, non-governmental association devoted to raising American accounting standards. The FASB not only participates in overseas conferences on accounting standards, but also works closely with the recently created international Accounting Standards Board (www.iasb.org.uk) in London. FASB often provides overseas accounting organizations with its informative publications.

There's still another factor promoting higher accounting standards overseas: More and more corporations abroad want to list their shares on American exchanges.

Finding Accountants

Obtaining competent outside accounting services abroad is much easier if a multinational deals with one of the Big Five. That's because these giant accounting firms have expanded overseas very aggressively, setting up branches or linking up with affiliates in scores of trading nations. And, if they don't have affiliates in a nation into which a client plans to expand, they will help find competent accountants, according to Miller. They will even detail members of the firm to travel abroad and help solve local accounting problems.

What if your outside accountants don't have an affiliate in a nation in which your company acquires an income-producing (or losing) subsidiary? One obvious answer is to contract with one of the Big Five that has a branch or affiliate in the nation of interest. Of course, your present outside accountants could see this as a threat to their tenure. Nevertheless, they would have no option but to cooperate with the overseas accountants. (Requiring two or even more outside accounting firms to cooperate is a common problem today as a result of all : the cross-border mergers and acquisitions.)

Other than dealing with one of the Big Five, how does a CFO locate and hire competent accountants abroad? There

Beware High "Opacity"

A portion of the latest Opacity Index developed by PriceWaterhouseCoopers for many national economies. Here, the index is arranged in decreasing opacity—the lower the rating the better. Obviously, the opacity of a national economy is a prime factor affecting the promptness and relevance of the financial statements of its public and private corporations. It's interesting to note that the formerly controlled Hungarian economy is more transparent than that of some nations with much longer histories as presumably free economies. To view the complete list and a detailed explanation of how it is compiled, see www.opacity.com.

Country	Rating	Country	Rating
China	87	Brazil	61
Russia	84	Taiwan	61
Indonesia	75	Japan	60
Turkey	74	South Africa	60
South Korea	73	Egypt	58
Romania	71	Greece	57
Czech Republic	71	Israel	53
Kenya	69	Hungary	50
Ecuador	68	Italy	48
Thailand	67	Mexico	48
Poland	64	Hong Kong	45
India	64	UK	38
Venezuela	63	USA	36
Pakistan	62	Chile	36
Argentina	61	Singapore	29

are several possibilities. One is to network with other American or foreign corporations with substantial subsidiaries in the nation of interest, especially those with whom you have current dealings, such as a major supplier. American commercial attaches abroad should also be consulted.

The Chinese Riddle

One of the most-difficult nations in which to engage rigorous accounting services is China. Besides enjoying the distinction of having the most opaque economy among trading nations (See sidebar), there's the high risk that any company with which an American multinational forms a joint venture is controlled by—if not owned outright—by the state. This means, of course, the priorities of the Beijing government would most likely outrank those of the business objectives of the venture.

To avoid such problems, Robert Quillinan, CFO of Coherent, Inc., a Santa Clara, Claif., manufacturer of laser equipment, offers this sharp advice: "I would not get into a joint venture with any state-owned company because there's a good chance of being bitten on the rear end."

Even if there's a need to consolidate financial results from a subsidiary or joint venture in a nation with accounting on par with that in the U.S. (such as in most of the English-speaking nations) issues can arise. For instance, Miller says, assets in Australia are treated as having their current value. In contrast, assets in the U.S. are accounted for based on their historical cost. In the UK, chartered accountants generally create financial reports that are "more conceptual and less specific" than those of American CPAs.

Euro Helps

Fortunately, the problem of converting foreign currencies into dollars will lessen with the introduction of the euro on January 1. Instead of having to convert a dozen currencies into dollar values, American CFOs will only have to worry about one, according to Quillinan. To prepare for this important introduction, many corporations outside the EEC are already reporting results in euros. For instance, many Swiss multinationals are already reporting in euros even though Switzerland is not in the EEC, although it might join.

Are currency devaluations a problem in accounting for overseas financial results? It depends, says Miller: "If you own a financial institution in a nation that devalues its currency, it's a big headache. However, if your subsidiary makes soft drinks, it shouldn't be a problem." Quillinan adds that devaluations are usually more of a problem for overseas suppliers.

How do overseas accountants charge? In general, they charge less than American CPAs, except in Japan, where charges are actually higher, Miller says.

Globalization is forcing all trading nations and their companies to raise their levels of accounting, no doubt reluctantly in some instances. Although only a minority come close to performing according to the "generally accepted accounting principles" of the American accounting community, the situation is improving, according to the experts. In any event, if an American corporation wants to acquire or start subsidiaries overseas or engage in joint ventures abroad, it has no choice but to contract for competent accounting services. It's just another of the many challenges of expanding globally.

Related Websites

- Opacity Index www.opacity.com

Mel Mandell is an international business writer and consultant based in New York.

From *World Trade,* December 1, 2001. © 2001 by Business News Publishing Company.

THE EURO

What the New Currency Means to the European Economy

By Bruce Barnard

The arrival of euro bills and coins in January will give Europe a second chance to create a single pan-continental economy to rival the United States. The euro has failed to live up to the hype that surrounded its launch in January 1999 when Europe's politicians and business leaders predicted it would soon challenge the dollar as a global currency, attract a flood of capital into the continent, hasten deregulation, and put the finishing touches to the fifteen-nation single market.

The euro's performance has been mixed and its impact muted over the past three years. It has lost a quarter of its value against the greenback, which still remains the world's superpower currency. Economic growth in the euro zone has lagged behind the US, and there has been a net capital outflow of around $240 billion across the Atlantic. Furthermore, the fledgling European Central Bank has yet to establish its credentials in the financial markets, and labor market rigidities persist.

The euro has also not yet equalized consumer prices across the European Union. Gasoline remains 15 percent cheaper in Luxembourg than in Germany, and new cars cost 10 percent more in Austria than in neighboring Italy.

On the plus side, the euro has definitely knitted European economies closer together, triggered a boom in cross-border mergers and acquisitions, cut the cost of capital, eliminated foreign exchange risks, and abolished the competitive devaluations—like the UK's and

Italy's in the early 1990s—that distort the European economy. Meanwhile, the strict limits on government deficits and borrowing in the Maastricht Treaty, which created the euro, have had a major impact on public finances with many euro-zone countries boasting budget surpluses.

The euro's impact was limited because it was a "virtual" currency, its use restricted to European Union budgets, corporate accounts, bond and stock markets, and other non-cash transactions. That will all change on January 1 when it goes "live" with the conversion of the currencies of the twelve euro-zone countries, worth roughly $320 billion, into "real" euros.

Despite military style preparations, the changeover will encounter teething problems that could undermine consumer confidence. That's to be expected in an operation involving the simultaneous introduction of 14.5 billion new notes and 50 billion coins and the withdrawal of twelve national currencies, which cease to be legal tender on February 28. Simply put, it is "the most important operation of changing a currency in world history," according to Pedro Solbes, the European commissioner for economic and monetary affairs.

But it won't take long for the euro to gain legitimacy as it becomes the sole currency from the frozen north of Finland to Greece's Aegean islands. It will boost cross-border trade and recruit the euro zone's 300 million consumers in the creation of a genuine single European

economy. "On January 1, 2002, 300 million people will for the first time be able to cross twelve national borders and discover that the currency which their neighbors are using is the same as the one they are using at home," said Wim Duisenberg, president of the European Central Bank. "Europeans will realize they are at home throughout Europe."

Big business will take the currency conversion in its stride because it has been preparing for years. IBM, for example, began offering euro-related services as long ago as 1996. Ahold, the Dutch supermarket giant, started to switch its suppliers over to the euro in 1999. Most large European retailers have been pricing goods in national currencies and the euro for well more than a year, and their cash registers and staff are ready for the changeover.

Small and medium-sized companies, however, are trailing in their preparation for the introduction of euro cash, according to the European Commission. One in five of 2,800 companies polled by the EU's executive say they will not be able to operate entirely in euros on January 1 though nearly half of the medium-sized businesses employing between 50 and 249 workers believe they will be ready.

The switchover to euro cash will initially increase costs for business. The Association of German Banks reckons the conversion cost will exceed $60,000 per branch in additional insurance, transportation, staff training, and customer information campaigns. Euro Commerce, a Brussels-based retailers' association, estimates conversion will present euro-zone retailers with a bill of more than $28 billion, or 2 percent of sales.

Economists warn that the costs of the changeover, delays in circulating the new cash, and consumers' initial reluctance to spend the new money until they are comfortable with it, could clip growth in the euro zone by at least 0.25 percent in 2002, a big hit when the economy already is slowing sharply.

Furthermore, some worry the switch to euro cash will stoke inflation as manufacturers and retailers take advantage of the confusion among consumers to increase prices by stealth or by simply rounding up prices in the new currency. UK prices rose 3 percent after decimalization in 1971, but this increase resulted more from excessive wage awards and a lax fiscal policy than gouging by retail-

ers. Economists play down the inflationary threat. "Given that rounding up [of euro prices] would go equally likely upwards or downwards, the impact on the aggregate prices should be negligible," according to Goldman Sachs analysts.

The "real" euro is being launched at a time when the euro zone is still reeling from the economic fallout from the September 11 terrorist attacks on the US and is not expected to recover until well into 2002. However, euro bills and coins are entering circulation amid signs that the twelve euro economies finally are starting to converge, making it easier for the European Central Bank to run its one-size-fits-all monetary policy in a region where conditions vary widely. When the euro was launched in 1999, annual growth ranged from a high of 10.8 per-

cent in Ireland to a low of 1.6 percent in Italy, a 9.2 percent gap that is expected to more than halve in 2002. Similarly, the 3.5 percent difference between the highest inflation rate (5.3 percent in Ireland) and the lowest (1.8 percent in France) in 2000 is set to narrow to just 1.8 percent next year.

Euro bills and coins are hitting the streets at a difficult time for the European economy, but a year from now consumers could be wondering what all the fuss was about. That, indeed, will be a mighty achievement for the architects of the pan-European economy.

Bruce Barnard, based in London, is a EUROPE *contributing editor.*

From *Europe,* December 2001/January 2002, pp. 10-12. © 2002 by European Commission.

UNIT 4
Foreign Environment

Unit Selections

Key Points to Consider

- Do you think the euro will become an important currency? Do you think it will rival the dollar?

- Why do you think people are concerned about globalization? Do you think they should be? How would you feel if you lost your job when the plant moved to some foreign country?

- Do you think corporations should be doing the types of services normally associated with governments? What if they are more efficient? What if they get better results? The same results? For less money?

- Do you think antitrust-type laws are appropriate for international corporations operating in a variety of countries? How would you apply them?

 **Links: www.dushkin.com/online/**
These sites are annotated in the World Wide Web pages.

International Marketing Review
http://www.mcb.co.uk/imr.htm
The Development Gateway
http://www.developmentgateway.org/
Research and Reference FAQs (Library of Congress)
http://lcweb.loc.gov/faq/research.html

For centuries most American businesses focused on the domestic markets. There were many reasons for this. The first was that during the 1800s the United States was probably the most rapidly developing country in the world, a huge continental market limited only by the Atlantic and Pacific Oceans. This was true until the end of World War I, when the United States, for the first time, became the world's leading industrial nation. But distances between countries seemed greater than they do today, and communication was not as swift or sure. In addition, most Americans tended to have at least a partially isolationist outlook on the world. There were exceptions, notably in mining, agricultural commodities, and oil. The time between World Wars I and II was also marked by the worldwide Great Depression of 1929–1939, which was almost immediately followed by World War II. After World War II, the United States stood alone as the great industrial power. It was not really until the 1970s that the United States received notice, in the form of the first gasoline crisis, that its position in the world economy had changed.

While many U.S. firms did extensive business outside the country, in the early 1970s these arrangements represented only about 6 percent of the total business in the United States. But, now, this figure is close to 33 percent. This means that non-domestic business activity matters greatly to U.S. companies. What goes on in Europe and the Pacific Rim has a direct impact on what happens on Wall Street as well as Main Street, U.S.A. Doing business outside the United States is different from doing business within the country. First of all, there is the monetary problem. Every country has a different currency, banking system, and regulations affecting the financial system, and the problems this can cause are illustrated in "Economic Focus: Big MacCurrencies." Currency fluctuations can play havoc with the assets and profits of a firm. But financial institutions are working to solve this problem and keep the markets stabilized, as seen in "What the New Currency Means to the European Economy."

Economic and socioeconomic forces also play a role. While the cold war is over and the United States and its allies have won, it does not mean that doing business in Singapore is just like doing business in Denver. True, with a few minor exceptions such as Cuba and North Korea, capitalism is rapidly becoming the preferred method of organizing an economy. That organization, however, will not necessarily be a clone of the system in the United States. There is Indonesian capitalism, Chilean capitalism, and Hungarian capitalism, just as there is American capitalism, British capitalism, and Japanese capitalism. Each system will be based on the same general principles, but each will be different, with its own unique twists. These variations in capitalism will cause people to question a growing trend to dictate the same rules to corporations and nations in how they involve themselves in world trade. People will want a say in the development of the coming global economic system and they will not want to be excluded from the discussion.

One factor that is going to have tremendous impact on international trade is the need to develop infrastructure in the developing world and to maintain appropriate infrastructure in the developed world. Asia alone is expected to have over $1 trillion in infrastructure needs in the foreseeable future. Add to this the maintenance and modernization needs of the developed world,

plus Latin America and Africa, and it is clear that there will surely be no shortage of work for contractors and engineers who are willing to go into these markets.

Among the fascinating aspects of the global environment are the differences in culture and ideas, as well as the many similarities. Human beings have a wide variety of answers to seemingly mundane, everyday questions. Customs and culture often play a role in how successful organizations will be when dealing in a foreign market. What may be rude and offensive in one society may be accepted or even expected behavior in another. Understanding these differences and why they are important can be a key to success in any market. For example, offshore Chinese firms are a unique group of organizations that play a significant role in Asia and other parts of the world, as discussed in "Empires Without Umpires."

The political environment also plays an important role in international trade. Some countries are more politically stable than others. Nationalization of foreign assets is not unheard of, and corporations have little or no recourse when their assets are suddenly appropriated by the government. History teaches that this is a real risk. "Analyzing and Managing Country Risks" is something that multinationals have to do and that countries are going to have to recognize. Since the end of the cold war, however, the climate has changed and generally for the better. Some, in fact, may argue that it has gone too far, as Tony Clarke does in "Serving Up the Commons: A Guest Essay." Some countries are also having problems coming out from under the cloud of dictatorship and are having trouble making their way with their new political freedom, as shown in "Chile's Democratic Challenge."

The laws of many nations when dealing with world trade are in the process of developing. Industries are now international in scope. The world is a market for small, as well as large, businesses. Illegal business practices are being identified because their cost is huge. Different laws in different countries concerning the same issues can contribute to confusion and misunderstanding. Different laws can lead to different rules being applied to the market and the company, as seen in "International Alliance Negotiations: Legal Issues for General Managers." Antitrust is now a more important issue for world trade than it was a few years ago, as corporations start to merge across international boundaries. Those mergers may or may not be approved, as in the case of Honeywell and GE, where the merger was turned down by the Europeans, as discussed in "The World According to Monti."

Economics focus
Big MacCurrencies

In the history of the Big Mac index, the dollar has never been more overvalued

CURRENCY forecasters have had it hard in recent years. Most expected the euro to rise after its launch in 1999, yet it fell. When America went into recession last year, the dollar was tipped to decline; it rose. So to help forecasters really get their teeth into exchange rates, *The Economist* has updated its Big Mac index.

Devised 16 years ago as a light-hearted guide to whether currencies are at their "correct" level, the index is based on the theory of purchasing-power parity (PPP). In the long run, countries' exchange rates should move towards rates that would equalise the prices of an identical basket of goods and services. Our basket is a McDonald's Big Mac, produced in 120 countries. The Big Mac PPP is the exchange rate that would leave hamburgers costing the same in America as elsewhere. Comparing these with actual rates signals if a currency is under- or overvalued.

The first column of the following table shows the local-currency prices of a Big Mac. The second converts these into dollars. The average American price has fallen slightly over the past year, to $2.49. The cheapest Big Mac is in Argentina (78 cents), after its massive devaluation; the most expensive ($3.81) is in Switzerland. By this measure, the Argentine peso is the most undervalued currency and the Swiss franc the most overvalued.

The third column calculates Big Mac PPPs. Dividing the Japanese price by the American price, for instance, gives a dollar PPP of ¥105, against an actual exchange rate of ¥130. This implies that the yen is 19% undervalued. The euro is only 5% undervalued relative to its Big Mac PPP, far less than many economists claim. The euro area may have a single currency, but the price of a Big Mac varies widely, from €2.15 in Greece to €2.95 in France. However, that range has narrowed from a year ago. And prices vary just as much within America, which is why we use the average price in four cities.

The Australian dollar is the most undervalued rich-world currency, 35% below McParity. No wonder the Australian economy was so strong last year. Sterling, by contrast, is one of the few currencies that is overvalued against the dollar, by 16%; it is 21% too strong against the euro.

Overall, the dollar now looks more overvalued against the average of the other big currencies than at any time in the life of the Big Mac index. Most emerging-market currencies also look cheap against the dollar. Over half the emerging-market currencies are more than 30% undervalued. That implies that any currency close to McParity (eg, the Argentine peso last year, or the Mexican peso today) will be overvalued against other emerging-market rivals.

Adjustment back towards PPP does not always come through a shift in exchange rates. It can also come about partly through price changes. In 1995 the yen was 100% overvalued. It has since fallen by 35%; but the price of a Japanese burger has also dropped by one-third.

Every time we update our Big Mac index, readers complain that burgernomics does not cut the mustard. The Big Mac is an imperfect basket. Hamburgers cannot be traded across borders; prices may be distorted by taxes, different profit margins or differences in the cost of non-tradable goods and services, such as rents. Yet it seems to pay to follow burgernomics.

In 1999, for instance, the Big Mac index suggested that the euro was already overvalued at its launch, when nearly every economist predicted it would rise. Several studies confirm that, over the long run, purchasing-power parity—including the Big Mac PPP—is a fairly good guide to exchange-rate movements.

Still, currencies can deviate from PPP for long periods. In the early 1990s the Big Mac index repeatedly signalled that the dollar was undervalued, yet it continued to slide for several years until it flipped around. Our latest figures suggest that, sooner or later, the mighty dollar will tumble: relish for fans of burgernomics.

The hamburger standard

	Big Mac prices		Implied PPP* of the dollar	Actual dollar exchange rate 23/04/02	Under(-)/over(+) valuation against the dollar, %
	in local currency	in dollars			
United States†	$2.49	2.49	-	-	-
Argentina	Peso 2.50	0.78	1.00	3.13	-68
Australia	A$3.00	1.62	1.20	1.86	-35
Brazil	*Real* 3.60	1.55	1.45	2.34	-38
Britain	£1.99	2.88	1.25‡	1.45‡	+16
Canada	C$3.33	2.12	1.34	1.57	-15
Chile	Peso 1,400	2.16	562	655	-14
China	Yuan 10.50	1.27	4.22	8.28	-49
Czech Rep	Koruna 56.28	1.66	22.6	34.0	-33
Denmark	DKr24.75	2.96	9.94	8.38	+19
Euro area	€2.67	2.37	0.93§	0.89§	-5
Hong Kong	HK$11.20	1.40	4.50	7.80	-42
Hungary	Forint 459	1.69	184	272	-32
Indonesia	Rupiah 16,000	1.71	6,426	9,430	-32
Israel	Shekel 12.00	2.51	4.82	4.79	+1
Japan	¥262	2.01	105	130	-19
Malaysia	M$5.04	1.33	2.02	3.8	-47
Mexico	Peso 21.90	2.37	8.80	9.28	-5
New Zealand	NZ$3.95	1.77	1.59	2.24	-29
Peru	New Sol 8.50	2.48	3.41	3.43	-1
Philippines	Peso 65.00	1.28	26.1	51.0	-49
Poland	Zloty 5.90	1.46	2.37	4.04	-41
Russia	Rouble 39.00	1.25	15.7	31.2	-50
Singapore	S$3.30	1.81	1.33	1.82	-27
South Africa	Rand 9.70	0.87	3.90	10.9	-64
South Korea	Won 3,100	2.36	1,245	1,304	-5
Sweden	SKr26.00	2.52	10.4	10.3	+1
Switzerland	SFr6.30	3.81	2.53	1.66	+53
Taiwan	NT$70.00	2.01	28.1	34.8	-19
Thailand	Baht 55.00	1.27	22.1	43.3	-49
Turkey	Lira 4,000,000	3.06	1,606,426	1,324,500	+21
Venezuela	Bolivar 2,500	2.92	1,004	857	+17

Sources: McDonald's; *The Economist*

*Purchasing-power parity: local price divided by price in United States
†Average of New York, Chicago, San Francisco and Atlanta   ‡Dollars per pound   §Dollars per euro

From *The Economist*, April 27, 2002, p. 76. © 2002 by The Economist, Ltd. Distributed by the New York Times Special Features. Reprinted by permission.

Nike's Voice Looms Large

by Jeff Ballinger

There has been a tremendous accomplishment in consciousness-raising on the issue of sweatshops since the mid-90's. News reports of worker abuse in shoe and apparel production got thousands of young people to join the recent protests against corporate-dominated globalization. In terms of victories, however, there's little to show.

One reason is the capitalist press. When Clinton officials and industry spokespeople started to tout "dialogue" and corporate codes of conduct as a solution, most editors and reporters began to address the issue as one of good-faith compliance. The stories began to carry less information about strikes, firings and protesting workers.

One substantial victory is the students' establishment of the Workers Rights Consortium to gather first-hand information in a systematic way and connect solidarity groups in the consuming countries with the workers producing specific apparel items. This is a rare example of code of conduct discussions leading to meaningful action (since most student groups started—in the period 1998–2000—by negotiating such codes with university administrators). Significant, too, are principled stands by a coach (Jim Keady—his story can be found at www.nikewages.org) and an Olympic athlete named Kevin McMahon, who recently protested the decision of U.S. track officials to sell advertising space for the Nike "swoosh" on all team apparel.

Former President Clinton's administration was determined to change Americans' perceptions of worker conditions in developing countries. Clinton had sold the free trade agenda as "win-win"—U.S. consumers would get cheap shoes and apparel, workers would get good jobs. As the Nike case showed, consumers were paying high prices while workers were cheated and suffered under inhumane factory conditions. Editorial cartoonists and a host of newspaper columnists used Nike and Kathie Lee Gifford to highlight the "lose-lose" part of the story, resulting in a crushing legislative reversal as Clinton's team failed to win fast-track negotiating authority.

The dramatic emergence of the sweatshop story was akin to a train wreck. The big-name brands and department stores began outsourcing all of their production to contractors (the industry was moving to the most corrupt and repressive places in the world.) At about the same time,

changes in information-sharing technologies made it possible for activists to link up with nascent unions and insurgent groups of workers. While business school case studies were heaping praise on corporations for shedding responsibility for manufacturing, the seeds were being sewn for a tremendous upheaval that would come to fruition once the contractors' brutal practices were exposed.

It didn't happen overnight. The Nike-Indonesia stories started in the Jakarta newspapers around 1988; they became well known regionally soon thereafter. Policy-makers, at least, took note: in the years between 1988 and 1996 Indonesia's minimum wage rose more than 300% (from 86 cents to $2.46 a day), largely because of the acutely embarrassing and well-documented Nike story. While the international press reports were few and far between, the all-important gathering of information was taking place.

As the Nike case showed, consumers were paying high prices while workers were cheated and suffered under inhumane factory conditions.

First, a USAID - funded survey documented widespread minimum wage violations. This was followed by a comprehensive study of the Indonesian shoe industry by the Hague-based Institute for Social Studies partnered with the Institute of Technology at Bandung, West Java. Other European groups became interested, and the United Kingdom-based Christian Aid undertook a regional (SE Asia) look at the shoe business. Later, the Italian Center for A New Model of Development, and the Swiss Berne Declaration sent researchers to Indonesia. Country-wide consumer-information campaigns were launched in Holland (IRENE, Komite Indonesie and the Clean Clothes Campaign), France (Agir Ici), Belgium (CMOS), Germany (Sudwind) and Canada (Development and Peace). Nike's greedy and intransigent contractors in Indonesia unwittingly helped to deliver a wage increase to millions of Indonesian workers and, due to favorable local press reports about shoe-worker uprisings, strike activity increased in other industries. In addition, the demand for independent trade unions rose sharply.

The *Harpers'* magazine story during the 1992 Barcelona Olympics and the CBS-TV story the following year lulled Nike executives into thinking that they could safely dismiss protesting workers as "troublemakers" and international solidarity groups as "flat-worlders." This changed when Charles Kernaghan and Barbara Briggs of the National Labor Committee made Kathie Lee cry, lighting the fuse for an unprecedented level of reporting on the issue. The archives that Indonesian, European and North American labor rights groups had constructed on Nike's operations in Indonesia—along with Phil Knight's flippant denials of worker abuse—assured Nike a top spot on the anti-sweat coalitions' hit-lists. Soon, Nike was hustling well-known board members off to Asia (to fight an "anti-sweat" resolution from religious shareholders), debating Roberta Baskin, an award-winning TV journalist, about its Vietnam operations, and grousing about unfair treatment from Garry Trudeau (Doonesbury) and the *NY Times'* columnist Bob Herbert. Little changed in the Asian factories, however, because Nike refused to force contractors to deal in dignity with workers. Instead, Company spokespeople became obsessed with defending wage rates, the number of factory fire exits, lighting conditions, etc.

. . .the demand for independant trade unions rose sharply.

Phil Knight kept performing like the "evil capitalist overlord" (*Time* magazine) from Central Casting—complete with photos showing him with a scowl and sunglasses. In the summer of 1998 came a rhetorical change, at least. Knight tried to pass off a "reformed" attitude under the tutelage of former Bush image advisor, Maria Eitel. (She was soon joined by Vada Manager, a Democratic publicity consultant.) Both must have viewed the Apparel Industry Partnership (AIP), which began as a Clinton-Administration initiative, as a partial solution to the image problem.

AIP morphed into the Fair Labor Association, a coalition of industry representatives, NGOs and universities. Trade unions and the Interfaith Center on Corporate Responsibility, which were part of the AIP, decided not to join the FLA due to profound disagreements about transparency and "No-Sweat" certification procedures. According to Patagonia's Kevin Sweeney, AIP's passage into the Fair Labor Association (FLA) could not have been accomplished without the determined effort of Nike's Washington lawyer, Brad Figel. Indeed, what other company in the FLA more needed the cover it promised? Still, Eitel and Manager (and a staff which had swelled to over ninety, according to *Business Week*) had to know that the continuing abuses by Nike's recalcitrant contractors could not be rectified by the transpar-

ency-challenged FLA. More serious image-making was in the works.

Got problems with NGOs? Start your own! That is exactly what Nike did with the Global Alliance for Workers and Communities. Rick Little, whose wobbly International Youth Foundation (IYF) was being weaned from the megagrantor Kellogg Foundation, spotted the opportunity. IYF's new specialty became corporate responsibility and, soon after Little convinced Nike to pledge seven million dollars to the Global Alliance, he talked Lucent and Nokia into outsourcing their "responsibility affairs" to IYF for another $15 million.

The nefarious nature of Nike's Global Alliance strategy was revealed in the February 2001 report about nine Nike contractors in Indonesia. The fifty-page Global Alliance report (accompanied by a 56-page "remediation plan" from Nike) failed to mention strikes, fired workers, wage cheating and, most importantly, the fact that no Nike shoe or apparel contractor in Indonesia was presently engaged in meaningful collective bargaining—even though independent unions have been legal in Indonesia for nearly three years. While admitting other serious wrongdoing, the aforementioned omissions do nothing to alter the perception that Nike has nothing but scorn for worker activists and truly representative, worker-controlled unions.

The anti-sweatshop movement's challenge is to find resources to get local NGOs and independent unions talking to workers in an organized fashion so the story can get out and independent unions can be built. Participatory Action Research (PAR) holds great promise as a union-building activity. Using survey work, Indonesian activists interviewed tens of thousands of rank-and-file workers in the early- to mid-Nineties. The surveys functioned as a story-sharing vehicle; the frequency of strikes quadrupled. Workers concluded that complaints had to be raised to draw attention to their grievances about low pay, abusive supervisors and punishing work-loads. PAR may be coupled with a brand-based and country-specific approach (i.e. Motorola in Malaysia) or, survey work may be designed to document lax labor code enforcement by corrupt inspectors.

China looms large. Serious talks with rights groups and unions in Hong Kong about how best to undertake campaigns aimed at companies which use law-breaking contractors on the mainland must take place. Chinese authorities must be convinced that consumers care about what goes on in these factories and that there will be a serious backlash if our friends in Hong Kong (or workers they talk to) are imperiled for bringing these stories to campaign groups in the consuming countries.

Other producing countries will likely continue to repress trade unions and fail to provide even minimal protections for workers. Vietnam provides some useful insight. In the early days of Nike contractors' operations there, unions and the press vigorously protested the abusive practices of shoe factory managers. This agitation ended as it became clear to Vietnam's autocratic rulers that foreign investors expected no constraints once the factory gates slammed shut.

Little help for workers, then, can be expected from governments desperate to build export-driven economies. The AFL-CIO's American Center for International Labor Solidarity (ACILS), supported by the U.S. government, has offices in many developing countries. It is a great help to workers, but far more can be done if we can get individual unions, religious organizations and the broader human rights community into direct relations with these courageous bands of labor activists in the developing world.

Chinese authorities must be convinced that consumers care about what goes on in these factories. . .

We need to build a database of labor practices—starting with the shoe, toy and apparel industries. As we network with interested groups and individuals in the producing countries, we may eventually gain the confidence of the socially responsible investment funds and, some years down the road, help them to offer investors reliable "sweat-screens" the way environmental groups have helped to create "green-screens."

The anti-sweatshop movement must do all it can to protect protesting workers and their advocates. There are certain to be cases of workers being dismissed for leading legitimate protests. Our first irreducible demand must be that lost wages are paid and wrongfully discharged workers are re-hired before agreeing to talk with any corporation about labor issues.

Jeff Ballinger is founder and director of Press for Change, which monitors workers' rights in Asia. (www.nikeworkers.org.) He is a research associate at Harvard's Kennedy School of Government; was the "Farah pants" boycott national student coordinator; worked for the Textile Workers' J.P. Stevens organizing campaign; founded an international support committee to relay information to New York-based media outlets from Poland's underground Solidarity trade union; as director of the Youth Institute for Peace in the Middle East, worked with young Palestinian and Israeli unionists (early 1980s); and worked for the AFL-CIO (1984–1995) directing A.I.D.- and union-funded programs in Indonesia, Turkey, Azerbaijan and Kazakhstan.

From *Social Policy*, Fall 2001, pp. 34-37. © 2001 by Organize Training Center.

GLOBAL SOURCING

Social Accountability in
Central America

NOT JUST ETHICAL, BUT *ECONOMICAL*

BY TIM VICKERY

Everyone loves a bargain. Yet, as globalization grows, scenes of child labor and other unconscionable human rights violations have made "sweatshop" a household word.

Mention "social accountability audit" to U.S. executives who source goods in Central America and they may be seized by visions of activists picketing their headquarters, a surprise visit from *60 Minutes* and stock price drops akin to a trap door opening underneath their desk chair.

These days though, veteran managers at some of the most venerated U.S. brands and WORLD TRADE 100 companies are finding that ethical sourcing can be economical.

"If you work with factories to make them better places of employment, quality improves, productivity goes up, there's less waste and you retain workers longer," says Amanda Tucker, director of business compliance at Nike, the athletic footwear and apparel manufacturer based in Beaverton, Ore.

Suppliers realize tangible gains too. "The competitive advantages trickle down to the factories," says Mary Howell, vice president of the 700-member American Apparel and Footwear Association based in Arlington, Va. "They attract more business by being a good employer."

Home to thousands of *maquilas* employing hundreds of thousands of workers and some of the best-respected rights monitoring groups, Central America is an incubator for socially responsible innovations in supply-chain management.

Preferential trade terms, free trade zones, geographic proximity, easy market entry and the low skill-levels required made apparel manufacturing a lifeline for Central American economies. "Apparel became the only sustainable income source after Hurricane Mitch," says Stephen Jordan, head of corporate citizenship for the Association of American Chambers of Commerce in Washington, D.C. A 1999 Department of Labor report named Mexico the No. 1 source of U.S. apparel imports (50 percent greater than second-place China). The Dominican Republic ranked No. 4 behind Hong Kong, Honduras, Guatemala, and El Salvador occupied top spots as well.

Apparel jobs can mean life and death to governments and workers alike. Activists say that dependency leads to exploitation. "It takes a worker in [the Dominican Republic] 6.6 minutes to make a sweatshirt that retails for $22.99 and they get only 8 cents," says Charles Kernaghan, Director of the National Labor Committee, an advocacy group in New York. World Bank figures for 2000 show Dominicans' per capita GDP equaled less than $6 per day and Hondurans earned less than half that amount.

Therein lies part of the problem. Many governments adopted international labor standards to get access to the U.S. market, but commonly neglect to enforce those laws for fear of driving away U.S. buyers and (often) Asian factory owners. Sheer lack of resources and corruption play roles as well.

Apparel and footwear brands aren't alone. Experts say conditions in factories producing other consumer goods

Standardization Groups

A veritable cottage industry of commercial and non-profit social compliance auditors have sprung up to help socially responsible companies verify conditions at supplier factories. The lack of an enforceable global standard, numerous company codes and differing local laws gave rise to four major standardization and accrediting groups:

- **The Fair Labor Association**, (*www.fairlabor. org*), was the first U.S. organization to standardize codes, accredit external monitors, systematically compare factory performance and hold companies accountable for shortcomings. Funded by member fees and governed by a council of brand executives, university representatives, consumer and religious groups, FLA has accredited 11 commercial and non-profit monitoring groups to certify brands.

- **SA8000** (Social Accountability International), (*www.cepaa.org*), is a supplier certification program drawing on ISO standards to measure social compliance. Unlike FLA, SA8000 includes non-apparel/footwear brands and requires factories to pay a "living wage"—often substantially higher than the legal minimum in Central America. SA8000's eight accredited certification organizations have approved 85 factories in 22 industries. None are in Central America.

- **The Workers Rights Consortium**, (*www. workersrights.org*), is a Washington, D.C.-based activist-monitor hybrid that does no certification. Focusing exclusively on university licensees, WRC conducts fact-finding investigations and training to raise workers' awareness of their rights. WRC distinguishes itself by publicly disclosing results of all investigations and refusing corporate funding.

- **Worldwide Responsible Apparel Production**, (*www.wrapapparel.org*), is the brainchild of the American Apparel and Footwear Association. A "pay to play" factory certification program, WRAP believes that suppliers who commit to accountability gain competitive and economic advantages. "You can't eliminate sweatshops unless you get factories to buy in," explains Lawrence Doherty, WRAP's Executive Director. WRAP monitors compete to win factory audits. Since last year, four WRAP-accredited commercial firms have approved 151 factories. Another 615 are in process. Funding comes from application fees and certification must be renewed annually. Audit reports go only to board members and the factory.

are sub-par, too. But as high profile, ubiquitous targets, apparel and footwear brands became Public Enemy No. 1 one in fair labor campaigns. "There's an intimacy that's not there with auto parts—even though workers making wiring harnesses are walking across the border to sell blood for food money," says NLC's Kernaghan.

To defuse the charge of activist campaigns, scathing exposés and mounting consumer demands for sweat-free goods, Levi Strauss, Nike, The Gap, Liz Claiborne, Reebok and others who rely on tens of thousands of workers in thousands of factories, adopted voluntary codes of conduct, established internal monitoring teams, and spent millions of dollars on blue-chip auditors for reputation assurance. Despite the safeguards, embarrassing labor abuses continue to surface.

"Let's be real," says Auret van Heerden, executive director of the Fair Labor Association, one Washington, D.C. group formed to accredit social accountability monitors. "Compliance is a process not an event. I'm skeptical of any factory that's got a badge on the door saying, 'We're perfect.' What's important is having the will and capacity to fix the problems."

Just Do… The Math

Even for the most dedicated brands, will and capacity are light years apart. Worldwide, some 80,000 factories employing millions of workers feed the U.S. appetite for consumer goods. Wal-Mart alone buys from more than 20,000 factories worldwide. No single organization is capable of monitoring such a massive number—especially companies whose core business is sneakers or T-shirts.

Social compliance auditing is poised for explosive growth. By certifying supplier factories, WRAP and SA8000 can ease the staggering backlog. However, leading brands say they won't stop auditing themselves. "We don't want to use (external) monitors as a crutch," says Daryl Brown, vice president of Human Rights for Liz Claiborne. Nike's Tucker agrees, "If we could only buy from certified factories and had to wait for them to sign up, we'd never be able to keep up with demand."

Whether done by companies, monitoring organizations, governments or an international body, vigilant enforcement alone won't bring sourcing economies. "The key is education, education, education… employees, factory managers, NGO's, and consumers," says AAFA's Howell.

To educate consumers and respond to critics who fault brands and monitor-the-monitor groups for a lack of transparency, Nike has begun posting results of external audits and interviews with factory workers on its Web site, *www.nikebiz.com*. "The report included some very disconcerting details and there was a lot of concern within Nike about releasing it," Tucker says. "It was a gamble, but a good one."

Rights advocates applauded Nike's candor. "Companies have to realize they can't stick their heads in the sand," says Nolan of the Lawyers Committee on Human Rights. "The more they're honest and the further they extend verification and remediation, the more credibility they get."

The value of such counterintuitive brand building can't be quantified. Nor have conclusive studies quantified the costs of *not* monitoring suppliers. But experts argue the damage to brand value, share price and sales caused by boycotts, campus protests, media exposés and consumer revulsion far outweigh the costs of social monitoring.

"The truest test of the value of monitoring is companies are facing shrinking margins and making layoffs yet the same companies are increasing investment in social compliance—they're voting with their budgets," says Aron Cramer, vice president of human rights at Business for Social Responsibility, a 1,400-member business organization based in San Francisco.

In the end, supply-chain efficiencies and corporate citizenship aside, ignorance can be deadly. "Companies have to ask themselves, 'How much can I possibly know if no one goes independently to check it out?" says FLA's van Heerden. "Enron is a good analogy."

Tim Vickery is a freelance writer who divides his time between Europe and the U. S. writing on international business and social issues.

From *World Trade,* April 2002, pp. 48, 50, 53. © 2002 by Business News Publishing Company.

ECONOMY FEATURE

Ascension Years

On 11 December 2001 China became the 143rd nation to join the WTO,
bringing to a conclusion negotiations that stretch back 15 years to 1986 when China
first applied to enter the General Agreement on Tariffs and Trade (GATT).
Tsugami Toshiya *discusses the transformation—through "reform and opening"—of the*
Chinese economy that has taken place during that time.

IN short, the essence of the WTO is the principle of market economics. The WTO is based on the idea that the overall welfare of the global economy will be maximized by introducing the market economy principle to every nook and cranny of the world's economy and by doing its utmost to eliminate trade barriers and discriminatory measures. The proselytizers of the market economy at the WTO displayed their character even more strongly when they lowered tariff barriers and made new rules during consecutive rounds of negotiations, in particular when they expanded the scope of regulations to include trade in service and the protection of intellectual property rights, when the shift was made from GATT to the WTO.

Even so, the WTO is a system that has always approached problems in a member country from the viewpoint of foreign trade and investment, and it lacks the clout to force the internal systems of all countries to harmonize in a market economy focus. That's why problems arose in the negotiations on entry for China—a country that was in a state of transition (and was thus known as a "transition economy") from a traditional socialist economy to a

market economy—involving how far a market economy could be developed in China by utilizing WTO rules.

INCONGRUITY OF THE TRANSITION ECONOMY

The reform and opening of China in the 1980s was generally limited to the conspicuous introduction of foreign investment in "special economic zones" in coastal areas such as Shenzhen. In the 1990s, a genuine movement to switch the domestic economy to a market economy began. Substantive negotiations on China's membership in the WTO, then known as GATT, began in 1994. But coming just five years after the Tiananmen Square incident in 1989, the "reform and opening" policy was still in a precarious position. As a result, people were repeatedly asking, "Will China really not backpedal on its reform policies to open up to the outside world?"

The negotiations on China's accession initially began with the seemingly interminable process of confirming whether or not

there was significance in having China join the WTO and indeed whether or not China was qualified to do so. For example, under its traditional planned economic system, prices of goods and services as well as supply and demand were controlled by the government, and almost all companies were state or public-owned enterprises under the influence and guidance of the government, on matters from production and sales to personnel and finance. The relationship in between was purely hierarchical. It was naturally thought then that even if the customs duties of such a country were reduced, the government might still continue to decide for the country how much to import, instead of leaving the decision up to the market.

Responding to these concerns, the delegation from China emphasized their plans to consecutively abolish price controls and import restrictions and to end direct government involvement in the management of state-owned enterprises in the future. They probably had the feeling that "the cup is already half full," but the WTO member countries not only felt that "the cup is still half empty," they also wondered whether they could even believe China's claims that the cup is really being filled. In 1994 and 1995, another serious problem was that virtually no preparations were being made for opening China's service market, a field whose importance rivaled that of trade in goods.

Facing these problems, however, not only did China declare unilateral market opening measures in 1994, 1996 and 1997, but as the negotiations dragged on, China also attempted to show its desire to join by implementing those measures one by one. But there was another factor underlying China's more-than-a-few unilateral market opening measures, even though no decision on China's WTO membership was in sight.

"REFORM AND OPENING": A DRIVING FORCE FOR MARKET OPENING

China promised unilateral market opening measures to the WTO because the promised measures were also necessary from the standpoint of the domestic "reform and opening" policy.

The nature of China's "reform and opening" can be roughly summarized in three points. First was state-owned enterprise reform, under which state-owned enterprises, long the main vehicle for economic activity, should become independent of the government, acquire the authority to manage themselves, and become more responsible actors. The second point is the switch in government functions. The government role should change from drafting economic plans, giving orders to companies, and managing them, to making and overseeing the rules of economic activity, building infrastructure and redistributing income through taxation and expenditure. These two points work in combination to achieve the aim of handing over the economy from the government to the market, where rule-based competition was expected to prevail. And the third point is market opening. China lacks both capital and technology. Open markets are a means by which China can obtain the products, capital and technology it needs from foreign countries. Simultaneously, market openness enables it to invite the products, companies and the market economy model that it should follow.

So this "reform and opening" represents a policy for obtaining the essential elements of production, including the capital and the technology necessary for eco-

nomic development, and for adopting market mechanisms that were supposed to make the economy operate more efficiently.

Needless to say, the purpose of all this was to bolster the Chinese economy, escape from poverty and underdevelopment, and restore China to the pantheon of great nations in the twenty-first century. China's willingness to institute many painful reforms during negotiations was superficially to gain entry to the WTO, but its real driving force came from the desire to become wealthy and advanced. It is only a slight exaggeration to say that the WTO membership negotiations were, in a sense, a way in which domestic Chinese reforms, which needed to be adopted sooner or later, were "sold" to members for a good price.

MEMBERSHIP NEGOTIATIONS AND REFORM/OPENING

But at the same time, the prerequisites for WTO membership were viewed by pro-reformers as "foreign pressure" that worked well for winning over anti-reformers, and so the desire for membership was valuable for accelerating "reform and opening" and not allowing them to slip back. This was particularly striking in the process that led up to the November 1999 U.S.-China bilateral accord. The market opening measures that China promised then were so bold in nature that they caused gasps from the WTO negotiators. Those measures could not possibly have been achieved without the strong motivation to achieve a settlement with the United States, the most important gateway on the path to WTO entry.

It is also necessary to note that the WTO provided various institutional frameworks for ways to reform and liberalize the domestic economy, and it also played a role as a pacesetter. China learned much from WTO member countries' demands for market opening and from the requirements of the rules of GATT and GATS (General Agreement on Trade in Services). It was particularly so when China was formulating timetables for opening markets for services such as finance and electronic communications as well as when it was formulating the policy for reforming the import-export control system.

It may be said that China's entry into the WTO and "reform and opening" have proceeded as if they were two sides of the

same coin. With the advance of domestic reform and opening in China and its track record of unilateral market opening measures in 1997 to 1998, a feeling grew among the WTO member countries that the time to reach an agreement might be coming close.

RAPID PROGRESS OF PRIVATIZATION

It may be said that until the early 1990s, China viewed the introduction of foreign capital and advanced technology as a major (if not the only) means of promoting economic growth. This was because China's domestic capital accumulation was extremely meager and it suffered a vast technological lag. This was a time when China's economic growth depended on foreign countries, and for that reason, accession to the WTO was a pressing issue.

This aim of China basically remains unchanged today. However, a new aspect to China's economic growth has developed recently because of the permeation of the market economy, the improvement of China's economic level, and in particular, domestic capital accumulation. Part of this new aspect is the rapid progress of the "privatization" of China's economy.

Even in China, a socialist country with a system of state ownership, privately owned companies appeared in the 1980s. For ideological reasons, however, they were neglected and discriminated against for a long time. But with the spread of the market economy and the weeding out of weak companies, the private companies that survived suddenly came to the forefront and began to be bathed in attention. Recently, a clutch of venture companies modeled after those in Silicon Valley and launched by highly educated businesspeople has emerged. In fact, the share of China's GDP accounted for by the "state-owned economy" has already declined to roughly 25 percent. The reason why privatization occurred so rapidly in China can be easily understood if one considers the situation from the aspect of "capital."

An adequate supply of capital is necessary for the sound growth of a market economy, and the national government must invest capital in companies as long as it means to protect the ideology of a state-owned system of companies. However, China does not have the financial wherewithal to supply capital commensurate with the size of the country's economy and to keep up with the speed of its economic growth. As a result, starting in the mid-1990s, China was forced to choose between protecting its ideology and maintaining its growth. There was no other way for the Chinese Communist Party but to say farewell to the ideology that had served as its base in convincing the people of the legitimacy of its rule and take the path that would lead to greater wealth.

Today China is a country that already has personal deposits close to the equivalent of ¥100 trillion. What needed to be done was to allow those who have money to supply capital. This led in 1999 to a revision of China's Constitution wherein private companies and non-government companies, hitherto only seen as "supplement" constituents of the socialist economy, were promoted to "important organizational constituents of the socialist market economy." Thus began the abolition of systemic discrimination against private enterprises. The private economy had been given full recognition.

During this process, to differentiate from opening to foreign interests, a new phrase was coined, namely "inward liberalization." To gain entry to the WTO, China allowed entry on a large scale by foreign companies into sectors that had traditionally been monopolized by state-run enterprises, including finance and telecommunications. The new phrase coined in response to this carried the meaning of, "If you are going to allow the entry of foreign companies, then you should also allow the entry of domestic private companies and thus come even closer to a level playing field." This way of thinking is intriguing as a case study to show how the concept of competition is taking root among the Chinese people.

In just this last one or two years, yet another new trend has emerged. This is the change in the forms of corporate ownership, which is made utilizing the capital market. To be specific, large state-owned companies are being listed on the overseas stock exchange, and managers and employees are buying out the smaller but sound state-owned companies and the public-owned companies in agricultural regions (so-called xiangzhen giye). Trading on the Chinese stock market opened at the beginning of the 1990s, but it was then nothing more than a place to raise "public money." But the spread of the market economy endowed the stock market with two new meanings. The stock market is going to replace the government as the supervisor of compa-

nies and represent an exit for capital that the government had previously invested. A policy was started for state-owned companies that carried heavy social burdens (like pensions and welfare) wherein the good part of the company that could survive is split off from the rest that needs to be liquidated, and the liquidation expenses for the latter are met with the proceeds gained from listing the former on the stock exchange. Recently, China's leading state-owned companies, such as oil and steel manufacturing, were listed on the New York Stock Exchange.

One cannot deny that the stock market in China still faces numerous problems, but the concept of "capital" is steadily changing the nature of the Chinese economy. Such rapid privatization was not anticipated by anyone among the WTO member countries during negotiations. The changes may be seen as another step toward the market economy, although no agreement in the WTO obliges China to proceed with such privatization. Once things have come this far, it does not really matter whether or not you call China a socialist country, at least with regard to its economy.

THE FATE OF THE CHINESE ECONOMY

Of course, not every outcome of WTO membership or the spread of the market economy has been positive for China. One negative is the fact that regional wealth disparities have probably widened, and another is the uncertainty that surrounds the future of farming and farm villages, following market-opening measures. The regions that have emerged winners are the coastal areas, and the southern coastal area in particular. Even there, massive numbers of people have become unemployed because of the restructuring of state-owned enterprises, but the well-developed private economy is absorbing them. Consequently, reforms there are proceeding smoothly. But the impact of market-opening measures is reaching the interior regions, where the outcome is reversed.

It is possible that the problems of agriculture will be the greatest challenge China faces in the coming 10 years. As the result of obsessional policies for increasing food production in the past, Chinese agriculture today is surprisingly inefficient, and there is a big negative spread between the prices of major grains in China and the international market price. Henceforth, the prices

of agricultural products will inevitably fall with bold market opening measures, and when that happens, economically borderline farm families will no longer be able to earn a living. Chinese farm villages, which have traditionally served as overflow basins for the surplus labor supply and which together are home to some 800 million people, will soon be unable to support so many people. Most likely the only choice will be to move the excess population to the cities, particularly those in the coastal areas, where they will be able to eat. But this will entail moving a population in excess of 100 million, and the social impact will be incalculable.

The key to alleviating these kinds of inconsistencies is government finance. However, there are actually massive hidden liabilities that will become evident in the future, including future pension liabilities and the disposal of non-performing loans that accumulated in the past. To alleviate the inconsistencies while avoiding financial ruin, the only solution is for high growth to continue for as long as possible. The prospects for the future of the Chinese economy certainly are not clear, and so it remains to be seen whether China can safely navigate its way through this narrow pass.

However, the reform and opening of China have clearly progressed since 1998 when Chinese President Jiang Zemin and Prime Minister Zhu Rongji joined forces. What is admirable is how they are allowing the people to enjoy success in promoting reforms that will open the door to the future, even if times are tough now. In reality the Chinese economy has a multitude of serious problems. If there is a bright side to the Chinese economy now, it should be viewed that the efforts of the Chinese people, who have accepted a number of hardships to promote reforms, are beginning to produce dividends. Although the situation is still far from perfect, given that they have come so far in such a short period of time, one can only take a fair attitude as a rival and say, "Well done!"

THE IMPLICATIONS OF CHINA'S WTO MEMBERSHIP FOR JAPAN

In Japan, concerns have recently been raised over the negative repercussions of China's WTO membership. However, membership negotiations are basically a process for unilaterally opening the market of the candidate country, and undoubtedly the net effect on Japan will be positive. This year, Japanese exports to China are likely to see a fairly large increase. As the World Bank has pointed out, Japan is likely to be the biggest beneficiary of China's WTO membership.

The reason why some are nonetheless voicing concern over the negative fallout is not because of the WTO membership itself but rather because at least some elements of the Chinese economy have rapidly posted real gains in power and efficiency because of the "reform and opening" that proceeded in tandem with the membership negotiations. Last year saw trade friction between Japan and China in agricultural products, but trade friction between the two countries is likely to occur routinely now. "What's wrong with selling high-quality products at low prices?" was a line the Japanese fre-

quently repeated to the Americans during past bouts of trade friction between the United States and Japan. Recently, however, in an increasing number of situations Japan is likely to be in the same position as the United States was in then.

With the Chinese economy rising before our eyes, the "Chinese economic threat" is a hot topic of debate in Japan. However, if the growth of the Chinese economy is interpreted as reward for China that has taken very difficult "reform and opening" measures, then it becomes clear that the correct response to the challenges presented by China is for Japan to work on its own reforms, so as not to be outdone by the Chinese. Japan must recognize the rise of China and work to reform itself, a process that must include changes to its industrial structure. In that process, a search for a win-win relationship with China will

likely yield the maximum benefits to both parties.

TSUGAMI Toshiya is a senior guest fellow at the Research Institute of Economy, Trade and Industry, and director of the Northeast Asia Division of the Ministry of Economy, Trade and Industry (METI). For two years starting in 1994, he was in charge of WTO membership negotiations as the head of the Office of Trade Policy Review in the Ministry of International Trade and Industry (now METI). For four years starting in 1996, he was councilor to the Economic Division of the Japanese Embassy in China. He was involved in the negotiations for China's accession to the WTO for a total of seven years, until China received membership.

From *Look Japan,* May 2002, pp. 12-14. © 2002 by Look Japan.

Special report **Japan**

The non-performing country

If Japan does not write off its bad loans, will the world write off Japan?

TOKYO

WHEN George Bush and Junichiro Koizumi met in Washington last June, it was the American president who seemed the more politically insecure and the Japanese prime minister who was riding high. Now, as they prepare to meet in Tokyo next week, their positions seem to be reversed. Mr Bush looks more sure-footed than he did last summer, and he has the kind of sky-high public approval once enjoyed by his Japanese counterpart. Mr Koizumi's fall from grace, meanwhile, has been swift and stunning. Since he sacked his popular foreign minister last month, his poll numbers have plunged. Worse, Mr Koizumi's plight may make him more helpless than ever against Japan's triple menace of debt, deflation and political deadlock.

That is why Mr Bush's anti-terrorism campaign will not seem the most pressing issue when he arrives on February 17th, starting a week-long tour of Japan, South Korea and China. Of course, Mr Bush will want to discuss the regime in North Korea, which he has recently fingered as a member of his "axis of evil". He will also praise Japan for sending support ships to the Indian Ocean to help America in the Afghanistan campaign. But all eyes next week will be on Japan's economic slide, and on Mr Koizumi's newest set of promises—to be unveiled for Mr Bush's benefit—that he will do something about it.

Those glancing in from a distance may find it hard to tell Japan's current mess from the general doom and gloom of the past decade. But people watching more closely see three especially strong reasons to tremble now. The first is that deflation and depressed spending continue unabated, bringing fears of an accelerating downward spiral. Consumer prices have fallen every month for more than two years. Retail sales have fallen for more than three years, and were down by nearly 6% in the year to December. GDP is once again falling in real terms; nominal GDP is falling even faster (see chart 1).

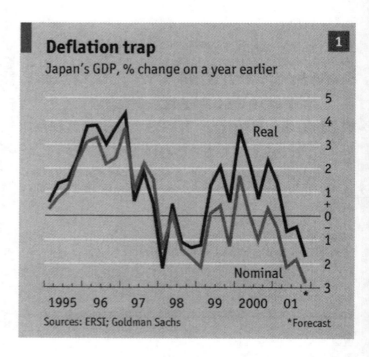

Only a few months ago many Japanese economists were still saying that Japan's deflation might be healthy, since lower prices make life better for consumers. Those optimists have gone silent, however, as falling prices have continued to be matched by dwindling jobs. Japan's unemployment rate rose to 5.6% in December, the highest since the second world war and nearly a percentage point above the rate a year ago (see chart 2). More than a million heads of Japanese households are now out of work.

The job losses follow collapsing balance sheets at weak Japanese companies, as falling prices squeeze profits and make it

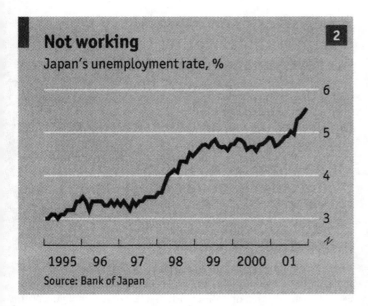

Not working
Japan's unemployment rate, %

Source: Bank of Japan

harder for them to service their debts. More than 19,000 companies went bankrupt last year, many of them small and mid-sized suppliers feeding Japan's bigger conglomerates.

Worse, the job cuts keep accumulating. Successive waves of lay-offs eat further into national income and confidence, hampering household spending and sending slightly healthier firms to the wall. Last year, such well-known corporate giants as Fujitsu, Hitachi and Toshiba announced massive cuts in employment as their profits collapsed. These were matched by countless smaller lay-offs at less well-known Japanese firms.

Banking blues

This deflationary trend is one reason why informed observers now feel so jittery. A second reason stems from Japan's rickety banking system (a natural consequence of all those indebted companies), and from the common knowledge that the government must one day accept that it will have to do more to deal with the burden of banks' bad loans. Although this has been obvious for years, a confluence of coming events has persuaded many investors that the day of reckoning is near.

On April 1st, Japan will start a new financial year, which this time round will set off a pair of decisive changes. Banks, which own lots of Japanese equities, will be made to value these shares at market prices. Because equity prices have fallen sharply since the shares were bought, the banks will have to show losses of more than one-and-a-quarter times their operating profits. Although those losses have already occurred, admitting to them could cause fresh problems if it prompts more depositors or investors to flee.

Depositors are anyway nervous, because of another change due on April 1st. After putting it off last year, the government will finally begin rolling back the blanket deposit insurance that it introduced in 1998. The first stage will affect only time deposits, and will limit insurance to ¥10m ($75,200) per depositor at each bank in which the person or institution holds an account.

Many depositors have already moved their money, spreading it around in ¥10m instalments and transferring much of the rest into other types of deposits, which will remain insured for another year. The risk remains that the partial repeal will cause bank runs. Some Japanese have been buying gold for safety.

These looming changes, by raising the odds that Japan's long-awaited crisis will at last arrive, leading to some kind of economic meltdown that could be cathartic but might be disastrous, have helped to send asset prices tumbling. Share prices have fallen yet again, to their lowest levels since the mid-1980s. The Nikkei 225 stockmarket average, which in its proudest moment in 1989 approached 40,000, now languishes at around 10,000 (see chart 3).

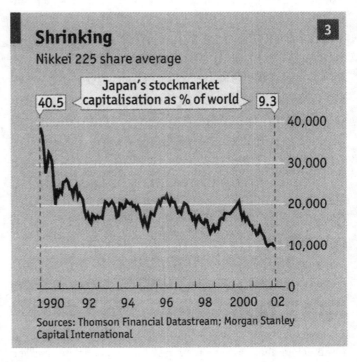

Shrinking
Nikkei 225 share average

Japan's stockmarket capitalisation as % of world
40.5   9.3

Sources: Thomson Financial Datastream; Morgan Stanley Capital International

Worse will follow if bond investors come to share the alarm. So far they have been subdued, keeping the government's debt-service payments in check. But, after running up fiscal deficits throughout the past decade's slump, Japan's official public debt has risen to 130% of GDP. Even the fuzziest maths cannot disguise that the real problem is much worse. For a start, Japan's deflation is causing nominal GDP to shrink, driving up the debt-to-GDP ratio even without any new spending. Add to that a continuing annual deficit, to avoid adding fiscal contraction to the economy's other woes, and the debt ratio will go on rising. The budget that Mr Koizumi wants to pass, which is modest by his ruling party's standards, will easily drive the ratio above 140% within a year.

None of this includes the cost of the government's other liabilities, stemming from publicly-backed corporations, social-security promises, and, if it is forced to nationalise the banks, the cost of cleaning up their balance sheets. Japan's fiscal position is, in short, pretty dreadful. This has already prompted downgrades by the rating agencies: this week, Moody's said it might lower Japan's credit rating to the same levels as Poland and South Africa. The only blessing is that foreigners hold little of the government's debt, which may still allow it to postpone a bond-market panic. Thus both the pace of economic deflation and the risk of financial implosion seem to have gone up a notch or two lately. But neither of these threats is new. And, even if the risks are now higher, Japan might still find a way to muddle through and delay any real crunch—as it has managed to do for most of the past ten years.

Even those onlookers who still downplay the situation are fretting, however, for a third reason. Unlike most previous bouts of panic over Japan, they fear, this one has far more potential to cause trouble in the rest of the world. With much of East Asia still in recession, and an American recovery still shaky and uncertain, an implosion of what is still the world's second-biggest economy could seriously damage the global economy. Japan remains a big trader, investor and lender, so any collapse would affect all its counterparties. And even if Japan pursues mild efforts to avoid it, its trading partners, especially in the rest of Asia, will still share its pain.

The most visible sign of this risk is the yen, which began sliding towards the end of last year. It has recently settled down, hovering around 133 to the dollar (see chart 4). But even that has prompted outcries from Japan's East Asian neighbours, as well as from the United States. America's big car makers petitioned Mr Bush, apparently with little success, to put their troubles with Japanese rivals on the agenda of his meeting with Mr Koizumi. Last month America's treasury secretary, Paul O'Neill, also delivered a mild rebuke while he was in Tokyo, by urging Japan not to drive its currency down at the expense of other "reforms".

Reform, reflate or both

Mr O'Neill thus plunged headlong into a contentious and confused debate that has plagued Japan for years: reflate first and reform later? Or vice versa? Or just reflate? A simple dispute over this is hardly the crux of the problem. Vested interests—among the bureaucracy, the politicians of the ruling Liberal Democratic Party (LDP) and the disproportionately powerful voting blocks that back it—are clearly the prime culprits. These groups benefit in some ways from Japan's malaise, especially from the fiscal gravy train that has rattled along unhindered throughout the slump. Just as important, these factions are perennially battling each other, over which of them should bear the shame and financial costs of fixing the problem.

Japan's vested interests do not merely frustrate reform through unpopular votes in the Diet, Japan's parliament. They also command much of the machinery through which ideas are evaluated and turned into legislation. If a prime minister wants to challenge them, he has little chance of even bringing a good alternative up for a vote. That makes it harder for the Japanese voters to vet recovery plans clearly, and make their wishes known. When combined with backroom dealing, lacklustre mass media and the cacophony of factional battles, this had made it all but impossible for any plan to achieve a consensus.

And, when there is no consensus, Japan tends to revert to auto-pilot.

Politically, therefore, Japan would find it hard to recover even if disinterested experts could agree on what it should do. Yet, even without worrying about who wins and loses, economic analysts continue to bicker among themselves over the answer. All agree, however, on Japan's need to inflate its way out of trouble. Its private and public debts are enormous. Falling prices make almost everything worse. Any effort to tackle Japan's numerous other problems will require much more borrowing or take another big chunk out of domestic demand. There is no realistic way forward, therefore, without steps to get Japanese prices rising, preferably by several percentage points a year. This would not only boost nominal demand, but would lower the public and private debt burden in real, inflation-adjusted, terms.

Unfortunately, a collapsed asset bubble followed by years of inaction have made it hard for Japan to achieve inflation, since expectations of flat or falling prices are so entrenched. With short-term interest rates at zero, the Bank of Japan has tried to loosen things further through "quantitative easing", making more funds available to banks. But that has done little to boost broad-money supply; bank lending has been falling inexorably for four years.

Technocrats debate ways to fix this problem. One approach is to get the banks to finance Japan's fiscal deficit directly, bypassing the bond markets. Another is to print yen and use them to buy up foreign bonds. But most economists agree that, if Japan is to achieve inflation, the yen will have to fall much further, perhaps to between 180 and 200 to the dollar.

What about structural reform? Should it wait for inflation or be done in parallel? Various groups are juggling different reform plans to fix Japan's "structural problems" and help restore growth. There is certainly a risk that harsh supply-side reforms would, on their own, make things worse, rather as they did in America in the 1930s; Japan's chief problem is shortage of demand, even though some demand may be suppressed by supply-side problems. So the most sensible option is to work in parallel with inflation, to the extent that Japan can achieve it. The prime candidates for reform are Japan's insolvent banks, along with their mirror reflections, overly indebted companies.

Along with slumping demand, Japan is now beset by overcapacity in many industries, such as construction and retailing. Many of these companies can never be profitable, but because the banks continue to prop them up they can avoid going bust. As they continue to cling on, meanwhile, the walking dead drive down prices and capture business from healthier rivals.

Looked at in isolation, this competition seems good for consumers, since everybody must cut prices. But when you step back and look more carefully, say structural-reform advocates, far from promoting "market competition" in Japan, the corporate zombies are perpetuating the deflationary spiral. Take over the banks and let these companies go bust, say the reformers, and you will help arrest deflation by eliminating much excess capacity.

It does not matter so much exactly how the government does this. It could nationalise the banks, and use its control to deny credit to hopeless debtors. Or it could single out the most in-debted companies and find some way to drive them into receivership, perhaps by simply publishing a list and letting suppliers and lenders do the job. Either way, the effect would be the same. It would also be helpful to cut off the fiscal tap to sectors such as construction, and perhaps channel more public money towards the workers who will be laid off after structural reforms.

Koizumi's conundrum

How has all this affected Mr Koizumi's calls for reform? The basic, abridged, version is that Mr Koizumi, a longstanding LDP insider with a funky hairstyle and a gift for plain talk, persuaded the party's grass roots that he was more eager for change than his rivals in the LDP leadership, and that this was a good thing. The party rank-and-file propelled him to the top last April, after the previous prime minister, Yoshiro Mori, bumbled himself out of the job.

Mr Koizumi started off well, promising to clean up the banks, restrain government borrowing and derail the gravy train through "structural reform without sanctuary". The wider public adored his brisk style of speaking, and his promises to inflict pain for the sake of future gain. When teamed up with his combative foreign minister, Makiko Tanaka, who promised to expose corruption and insubordination in her ministry, Mr Koizumi achieved strong public approval, with more than 80% of Japanese voters, at the high points, saying that they backed his government.

But three developments have helped to pull Mr Koizumi to earth. First, he could not reform much since he does not really run Japan. The despised "resistance forces" in the LDP and the bureaucracy have watered down all his plans and slowed their passage, depriving Mr Koizumi of both momentum and results.

Second, these forces, having bought time, have cashed in on the recession by persuading people that Japan needs to pursue "anti-deflation" (by which the LDP means more public spending) before structural reforms (which would cut off the tap). This put pressure on Mr Koizumi to push his own budget, which at least has better priorities than his opponents'.

But then he botched his response to the third development: Ms Tanaka's battle with the bureaucrats and the LDP old guard. In order to ease the passage of his budget, Mr Koizumi sacri-

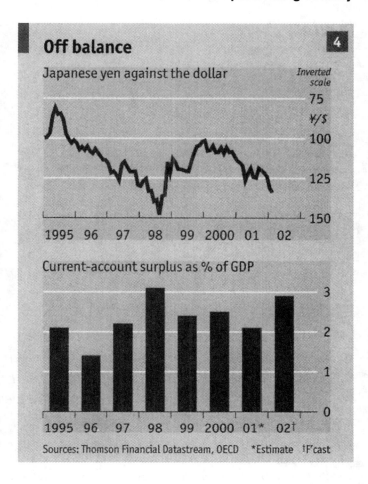

Off balance　　　4

Japanese yen against the dollar　　*Inverted scale*

75
¥/$
100

125

150

1995　96　97　98　99　2000　01　02

Current-account surplus as % of GDP

3

2

1

0

1995　96　97　98　99　2000　01*　02†

Sources: Thomson Financial Datastream, OECD　*Estimate　†F'cast

ficed Ms Tanaka, foolishly provoking a backlash and losing his only real asset, his popularity.

What happens now? Many of Mr Koizumi's reforms seem less likely than ever to happen. If asset prices continue to slide, the government may have to deal more actively with the banks' bad debts. More likely, it will keep muddling through, announcing just a few measures to prop up the banks, without solving their underlying problems. A mildly lower yen might, in the meantime, mildly boost exports; and Japan may get a boost in May and June when it co-hosts soccer's World Cup. Alas for Mr Koizumi, and for Japan, the real crisis that would force an acceptance of reforms could still take longer to arrive.

From *The Economist,* February 16, 2002, pp. 24-26. © 2002 by The Economist, Ltd. Distributed by the New York Times Special Features. Reprinted by permission.

THE GAINS AND PAINS OF FREE TRADE

Two world wars have been the driving force behind European integration.
Khaled Diab *analyses whether an integrated trade solution might also aid the prospects for peace in the Middle East.*

The successful launch of the physical Euro has fleshed out Europe's aspirations for economic integration, and many hope it will pave the road towards political integration. Meanwhile, an increasingly divided Middle East slips a notch closer to war as one 'bloodiest week' in the Israeli-Palestinian conflict replaces another.

Although international diplomacy has so far proven powerless to arrest the evolution of the bloody cycle, the EU is hoping the quiet diplomacy of trade will have a long-term stabilising effect on the region.

European diplomats hope a Euro-Mediterranean free trade area (FTA), as set out in the 1995 Barcelona Agreement, will achieve its declared aims of creating peace, stability and prosperity in the area. Although partially operational, the FTA will take another decade to become a full reality.

"We want to inject new life into the Euro-Mediterranean process and use it to help resolve conflicts in the region, in particular the Middle East," European Commission Presi-

dent Romano Prodi said in a recent speech.

"Europe's recent past highlights the potential advantages of a Euro-Mediterranean FTA," a negotiator at the European Commission, who wished not to be named, said, noting that the lessons of two world wars have been the driving force behind European integration.

Although the Barcelona Process is more than a trade pact, encompassing basic human rights standards, as well as social and political reforms, European diplomats are quick to point out it is not a substitute for the resumption of the Middle East peace process.

"We have long held that the Barcelona Process isn't the right vehicle for trying to address the Middle East peace process," said another European Commission diplomat, noting that the gradual move towards inter-regional trade and investment could, nonetheless, act as an indirect incentive to peace.

In the seven years since the ambitious idea of creating a Euro-Mediterranean trading bloc was floated,

the Barcelona Process has, as one diplomat put it, reached "critical mass", although it will probably miss its target date of 2010 by a few years.

Europe and its Mediterranean partners are gearing up excitedly for the advent of the free trade area

Cyprus, Malta and Turkey already have what are called first generation association agreements that date back to the 1960s and 1970s. The earliest MENA region signatories: Tunisia (1995), Morocco (1996), Israel and the Palestinian Authority (1995) also have functioning agreements.

However, the arduous process of ratification by the parliaments of both the partner country and all 15 EU members has caused delays in enforcing subsequent deals. The Jordan agreement, which was signed in 1997, will only come into full force in May. MENA's largest market, Egypt, signed its agreement last summer, while Algeria and Lebanon initialled theirs in December and January.

Of the EU's 12 Mediterranean partners, only Syria remains without a deal. A pact with Syria, isolated for decades from the global marketplace, awaits the implementation of a series of wide-ranging reforms to prepare its sheltered economy for the open market.

Libya, which currently enjoys observer status, has never been part of the Barcelona Process, which began while the country was still under UN sanctions, but diplomats do not rule out it joining the pact at a later stage.

Europe and its Mediterranean partners are gearing up excitedly for the advent of the free trade area and the vast new export markets it will undoubtedly open up. Although Algeria aspires to become Africa's gas hub to Europe, it also hopes to diversify its petro-chemicals-based economy by attracting more foreign direct investment. Lebanon hopes to restore its pre-war entrepreneurial heyday as the Switzerland of the Middle East, while Egypt hopes to become a major clothing and agricultural exporter to the EU, as well as an IT subcontractor.

Ahmed Galal, an Egyptian economic analyst, envisions a 'bonanza' for his country's exporters who will be able to better utilise economies of scale as they tap into the vast EU market of some 350 million consumers.

Despite urgent calls by the EU for legislative reforms to promote investment, the Lebanese are no less upbeat. "Our dynamic private sector and highly educated workforce will carve out a prominent role for Lebanon in the Euro-Med area," a Lebanese diplomat said.

Nevertheless, concern has been voiced that local industries will have trouble competing against their larger European rivals.

The resolution of the Israeli-Palestinian issue is of paramount importance to the future of the Euro-Mediterranean FTA

"If we wait until our economy is ready for competition, we will never do it," Galal said at a recent conference, maintaining that free trade will force Egyptian industry to modernise and become more competitive. "The Egyptian automobile industry has been in its infant stage for 40 years: when is it going to grow up?" he demanded, citing a convincing example against protectionism.

"The Barcelona Process does involve opening up local industry to tough European competition, so it's important that Mediterranean countries prepare themselves," the European Commission diplomat said, referring to EU-funded reforms being implemented by Mediterranean countries.

One preparation that is lagging behind is inter-regional free-trade pacts, which MENA countries need if they are to trade freely with one another, as well as the EU. Although a string of bilateral trade agreements have recently been signed between Arab countries, only one currently looks set to go beyond ink on paper. Egypt, Morocco, Tunisia and Jordan plan to launch the Mediterranean Arab Free Trade Area (MAFTA), which other Arab countries are free to join later, to complement their agreements with the EU.

Although many MENA governments regard the human rights and political aspects of the Barcelona Process as an excuse for the EU to meddle in their internal affairs, civil society has criticised the EU for not going far enough. Five human rights groups, including Amnesty International, recently urged the EU to bring pressure to bear on the Tunisian government for its handling of opposition figures.

For its part, the European Commission has gone to some pains to highlight, particularly since 11 September, the human rights and cultural aspect of the Barcelona Process, saying it has set itself three new priorities, which include strengthening political and cultural dialogue in the region.

Nevertheless, thousands of European, Arab and Jewish peace activists held a protest march in Brussels at the end of February, calling on the EU to suspend its association agreement with Israel until it resumes peace negotiations with the Palestinians.

"The resolution of the Israeli-Palestinian issue is of paramount importance to the future of the Euro-Mediterranean FTA," said one MENA analyst.

Other analysts and diplomats, however, dismiss the possibility that the current volatility in the Middle East might derail or disrupt the fruition of the Euro-Mediterranean free zone.

"Stalemating one process doesn't necessarily stalemate the other," the EC negotiator said. "There is too much at stake for the parties involved and they stand to benefit too much."

Some analysts maintain that the free zone is a win-win situation for everyone and the attractive prospect of European Union membership for some or all Mediterranean countries might one day be on the table.

"The question isn't whether the Euro-Mediterranean free trade area will hold together. More recently, discussion has been opened on the possibility that some Mediterranean countries, e.g. Israel and the Maghreb states, might join the EU in the long-term future," Eberhard Rhein, a senior policy adviser at the European Policy Centre, a Brussels-based think-tank said.

From *The Middle East*, April 2002, pp. 26-27. © 2002 by The Middle East Journal.

Free Markets and Poverty

Since 1980, as the world has deregulated its markets, income gaps have widened. Why is this record heralded as a success?

BY CHRISTIAN E. WELLER AND **ADAM HERSH**

FOR BETTER THAN TWO DECADES, THE ORTHODOX RECIPE FOR global growth has been embodied in the so-called Washington Consensus. This approach, advocated by the United States and enforced by the World Bank and the International Monetary Fund (IMF), holds that growth is maximized when barriers to the free flow of capital and commerce are dismantled and when individual economies are exposed to the discipline, consumer markets, and entrepreneurs of the world economic system. Proponents of this view have contended that the free-market approach to development will also alleviate poverty, both by raising overall growth rates and by bringing modern capitalism to the world's poorest.

Evidence is overwhelming that income inequality is rising in industrializing countries.

Yet the actual experience since 1980 contradicts almost every one of these claims. Indeed, the free-trade/free-capital formula has led to slower growth and more vulnerability for poor countries—and to greater income disparity among individuals. In 1980 median income in the richest 10 percent of countries was 77 times greater than in the poorest 10 percent; by 1999 that gap had grown to 122 times. Progress in poverty reduction has been limited and geographically isolated. The number of poor people rose from 1987 to 1998; in many countries, the share of poor people increased (in 1998 close to half the population in many parts of the world were considered poor). In 1980 the world's poorest 10 percent, or 400 million people, lived on the equivalent of 72 cents a day or less. The same number of people had 79 cents per day in 1990 and 78 cents in 1999. The income of the world's poorest did not even keep up with inflation.

Why has the laissez-faire approach worsened both world growth and world income distribution? First, the IMF and the World Bank often commend austerity as an economic cure-all in order to reassure foreign investors of a sound fiscal and business climate—but austerity, not surprisingly, leads to slow growth. Second, slow growth itself can mean widening income inequality, since high growth and tight labor markets are what increase the bargaining power of the poor. (Economists estimate that poverty increases by 2 percent for every 1 percent of decline in growth.) Third, the hands-off approach to global development encourages foreign capital to seek regions and countries that offer the cheapest production costs—so even low-income countries must worry that some other, even more desperate workforce will do the same work for a lower wage. Finally, small and newly opened economies in the global free market are vulnerable to investment fads and speculative pressures from foreign investors—factors that result in instability and often overwhelm the putative benefits of greater openness. All of these upheavals disproportionately harm the poorest.

CAPITAL AND TRADE

Because capital controls were reduced or eliminated virtually everywhere over the past 20 years, the flow of capital to developing countries increased rapidly, from $1.9 billion in 1980 to $120.3 billion in 1997 (the last year before the global financial crisis). Even in 1998, in the wake of financial crisis, the flow of capital remained remarkably high at $56 billion (although a substantial share of this money consisted of short-term portfolio investments).

Unfortunately, faster capital mobility in a deregulated environment means an increase in speculative financing and, thus, greater financial instability. Under such conditions, the poor are unlikely to escape poverty through economic growth because they are ill equipped to weather the macroeconomic shocks.

Moreover, higher-income people can protect themselves more effectively from the fallout of a crisis. They have capital that they can move overseas. At the same time, in the IMF/World Bank formula, a crisis invariably calls for a reduction in public spending—at precisely a moment when the poor are more dependent on social safety nets. So on both counts, laissez-faire widens the gap between rich and poor.

Trade liberalization—the complement to deregulated capital markets in the global deregulation agenda—also plays a significant role in expanding inequality and limiting efforts to reduce poverty. It induces rapid structural change as well as a decline in real wages, working conditions, and living standards. It also gives teeth to employers' threats to close plants or to relocate or "outsource" production abroad, where labor regulations are less stringent and more difficult to enforce—thus undermining workers' attempts to organize and bargain for improved wages and working conditions. This trend fuels a race to the bottom in which governments vie for needed international investment by scrambling to offer employers the cheapest body of laborers.

The connection between rapid trade liberalization and inequality is reflected in downward wage pressures and rising inequality in industrializing as well as industrialized economies. A 1997 report by the United Nations Conference on Trade and Development, for instance, found that trade liberalization in Latin America led to widening wage gaps, falling real wages for unskilled workers (often more than 90 percent of the labor force in developing countries), and rising unemployment.

Poverty lines often fail to reflect the true hardships that people face in meeting the necessities of life.

E VIDENCE IS OVERWHELMING THAT INCOME INEQUALITY IS rising in industrializing countries. But there is also a broad consensus— even among laissez-faire cheerleaders—that income inequality has risen in developed nations as well since 1980. In a 1997 paper for the *Journal of Economic Literature*, Peter Gottschalk and Timothy M. Smeeding found that "almost all industrial economies experienced some increase in wage inequality among prime-aged males"

How to Downplay Poverty

THE WORLD BANK TRIES TO DIVERT ATTENTION FROM RISING inequality by emphasizing its analyses of poverty reduction. It argues that because of greater globalization, "the [long-term] trends of rising global inequality and rising numbers of people in absolute poverty have been halted and perhaps even reversed." But the facts contradict this purported success: Relative poverty shares remain high in may parts of the world—and in many regions, they are on the rise.

One problem with the World Bank's assessment of poverty is its use of an international "poverty line," which—compared to other measures—tends to understate the share of people living in poverty. Poverty lines often fail to reflect the true hardships that people face in meeting the necessities of life.

For instance, a recent study conducted by Heather Boushey, Chauna Brocht, Bethney Gundersen, and Jared Bernstein of the Economic Policy Institute showed that 29 percent of working families did not earn enough in 2000 to afford bare necessities. At the same time, the official poverty line showed only 10 percent of working families to be poor. This discrepancy suggests that a better approach to understanding poverty may lie in measuring household budgets.

Another problem with the World Bank's analysis: Even the poverty-reduction gains it does find are small and geographically isolated. In 1998 the industrializing countries' share of the world's impoverished population was estimated to be 32 percent (using a relative poverty line). Although that percentage was down from 36 percent in 1987, the actual number of people living in poverty increased from 1.5 billion to 1.6 billion. In 1998 the share of the population in poverty remained very high in some regions: more than 40 percent in South Asia and more than 50 percent in sub-Saharan Africa and Latin America. Since 1987 the share of the poor has stayed relatively constant in sub-Saharan Africa and Latin America, but it has more than tripled in Eastern Europe and Central Asia.

Poverty remains a large and widespread phenomenon in less-industrialized countries. The World Bank's claims to the contrary may be supported by its own research, but its method of measure is faulty—and its data, skewed.

in the 1980s and early 1990s. Further, data from the widely respected Luxembourg Income Study show that among 24 such countries, 18 experienced a rise in income inequality, only 5 experienced a decline in inequality (Denmark, Luxembourg, the Netherlands, Spain, and Switzerland), and 1 (France) saw no change. While a widening gap between the rich and the poor within countries is not universal, it appears to have occurred in most countries and is affecting most of the world's population.

PROBLEMATIC POSTER CHILDREN

The World Bank's conclusion that the lot of the poor has improved during the era of increasing trade- and capital-liberalization relies substantially on data from China and India. But both countries are anomalies. In reality, the facts in India and China undermine the case for a connection between greater deregulation and falling poverty and inequality. While in China the percentage who are poor has fallen, there has nonetheless been a rapid rise in inequality—most notably, from 1985 to 1995, between rural and urban areas and between provinces with urban centers and those without them. Also, a large number of China's workers labor under abhorrent, and possibly worsening, slave- or prison-labor conditions. This not only means that many workers are left out of China's economic growth; it also makes China an unappealing development model for the rest of the world. Thus, improvements in China are not universally shared and leave many workers behind, often in deplorable conditions.

DISTRIBUTION OF WORLD INCOME
Ratio of top 10 percent to bottom 10 percent

	1980	1990	1999
By countries			
Ratio of average incomes	86.2%	125.9%	148.8%
Ratio of median incomes	76.8	119.6	121.8
By population			
Ratio of average incomes	78.9	119.7	117.7
Ratio of median incomes	69.6	121.5	100.8
By population, excluding China			
Ratio of average incomes	90.3	135.5	154.4
Ratio of median incomes	81.1	131.2	153.2

Note: Distributions are based on per capita GDP in current U.S. dollars (IMF data). Source: Authors' calculations based on IMF data.

Using India to illustrate the benefits of unregulated globalization is equally problematic, since the country achieved its progress while remaining relatively closed off to the global economy. Total "goods trade" (exports plus imports) was about 20 percent of India's gross domestic product in 1998, or 10 percentage points less than in China and only about one-fifth the level of such export-oriented countries as Korea. Moreover, the IMF views India as something of a laggard in deregulating its economy. IMF reports regularly recommend further liberalization of India's trade and capital flows—the only large developing economy for which this is the case.

More broadly, to use India and China as poster children for the IMF/World Bank brand of liberalization is laughable. Both nations have sheltered their currencies from global speculative

pressures (a serious sin, according to the IMF). Both have been highly protectionist (India has been a leader of the bloc of developing nations resisting WTO pressures for laissez-faire openness). And both have relied heavily on state-led development and have opened to foreign capital only with negotiated conditions. The Heritage Foundation, in its annual *Index of Economic Freedom*, ranks India and China as tied for spot 121—among the least economically open nations in the world. Yet by letting in foreign capital in a limited and negotiated way, India and China have benefited from investment without totally sacrificing economic sovereignty. There may be a larger lesson here.

A BROADER PERSPECTIVE

The World Bank's assertion that "between countries, globalization is mostly reducing inequality" seems to contradict the IMF's assessment that "the relative gap between the richest and the poorest countries has continued to widen" in the 1990s. Given this confusion, it is useful to take a global perspective that looks at the distribution of world income across all countries and across all people.

If China is excluded, there is an unambiguous trend toward growing income inequality across the remaining world population in the 1980s and 1990s.

Distribution among countries unambiguously worsened in the 1980s and 1990s. In other words, rich nations have gotten richer and poor ones have gotten poorer. The median per capita income of the world's richest 10 percent of countries was 77 times that of the poorest 10 percent in 1980, 120 times greater in 1990, and 122 times greater in 1999. The ratio of the average per capita incomes shows an even more dramatic increase.

World-income distribution across people (rather than countries) witnessed equitable improvement to some extent in the late 1990s, after a dramatic rise in inequality during the previous years. While the richest 10 percent of the world's population had, on average, incomes that were 79 times higher than those of the poorest 10 percent in 1980, their incomes were 120 times higher in 1990. That ratio dropped to 118 in 1999. The improvement in equality was somewhat more pronounced in terms of median incomes; yet even under this measure, income distribution was remarkably less equitable in 1999 than in 1980.

The few gains in the 1990s come solely from rising incomes in China. If China is excluded, there is an unambiguous trend toward growing income inequality across the remaining world population in the 1980s and 1990s. But since income distribution in the People's Republic has become substantially less equitable in the 1990s, the inclusion of China's per capita GDP in the distribution of world income across all people exaggerates improvements in the world's income distribution in the 1990s. Put simply, inequality is a bigger problem at the end of the nearly 20-year experiment with unregulated global capitalism than it was before deregulation became the rule.

Despite official claims to the contrary, the evidence clearly shows that the laissez-faire era has been one of slower growth and greater inequality. And the apparent improvement of that trend in the 1990s is the result solely of rising per capita income in China, where the enormous population tends to distort world averages. Even so, income inequality within countries is also growing. Success in reducing poverty has been limited.

The promises of more-equal income distribution and reduced poverty around the world have failed to materialize under the current form of unregulated globalization. It is time for multinational institutions and other international policy makers to develop a different set of strategies and programs to provide real benefits to the poor.

CHRISTIAN E. WELLER *is a macroeconomist at the Economic Policy Institute, where* ADAM HERSH *is a research assistant.*

Reprinted with permission from *The American Prospect,* Winter 2002, pp. A13-A15. © 2002 by The American Prospect, 5 Broad Street, Boston, MA 02109. All rights reserved.

Empires without umpires

Asia's business culture is good for tycoons, not shareholders

MEET Robert Kuok, the quintessential Asian tycoon. Ethnically Chinese, Mr Kuok spent several of his eight decades collecting bitter memories of abuse by the Malay majority in his native Malaysia. So Mr Kuok, like most of South-East Asia's *huaqiao*, or overseas Chinese, early on made it his aim in life to build a better future for his children. This meant amassing wealth, spreading it across countries and industries to reduce risk, and above all keeping quiet about it.

He began in the 1950s and 60s by cornering the markets for flour, palm oil and sugar in Malaysia. He then branched out into practically everything, from manufacturing to property, from hotels to media. Today, he commands a sprawling empire, managed by sons, nephews and in-laws. Its headquarters have been, at various times, in Malaysia, Singapore, Indonesia and Hong Kong. To protect himself, he likes to be everywhere in the region and nowhere; exposed to every industry and reliant on none.

Table 1. **Punching above their weight**

Overseas Chinese:	Share of Population, %	Share of market capitalisation, %
Indonesia	3-4	73
Malaysia	30	69
Philippines	2	50-60
Singapore	78	81
Thailand	14	81

Source: Economist Intelligence Unit

Gregarious and chatty, Mr Kuok nonetheless ensures that virtually nothing of substance is known about him. A few years ago, a big international investigative agency probed deeply into the Kuok empire and produced a report that included this profile of the patriarch: name—Robert Kuok; political affiliation—unknown; adversaries—none identified; litigation—nothing known; ambitions—not known.

His Confucian management style is equally legendary. At a recent lunch he hosted, one of his guests put a question to Mr Kuok's

fortysomething, western-educated son Ean, who runs Hong Kong's main English-language newspaper. But just as Ean started to answer, his father noted that it was time for another helping of garoupa, Mr Kuok's favourite fish, and sent his son out of the room to order more. The incident left little doubt about who did the talking in the family.

Mr Kuok embodies "Asian values" in business just as Lee Kuan Yew, Singapore's senior minister, who coined the term, does in politics. Culturally, Asia's tycoons feel Confucian, with all that implies about hierarchy, authority and loyalty (see box). They disdain market research; instead, they act with legendary speed on gut instinct. For information, they turn to their "bamboo network" of other *huaqiao*, or to local politicians. They much prefer to do business with other members of this network, and seal their deals on trust, not contracts. Reflecting both their sense of political insecurity and their origins as traders, they also tend to approach business one transaction at a time.

For decades, this corporate culture appeared to produce tremendous results. Were it not for the Asian financial crisis, it might still be held up as a model in business schools across the world. Although the *huaqiao* are minorities in most South-East Asian countries, they control the majority of their host countries' wealth and stockmarket capitalisation (see table 2). And although these economies have suffered badly in the crisis, the share of the *huaqiao* has barely changed.

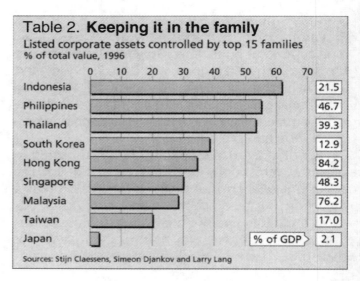

Table 2. **Keeping it in the family**

Listed corporate assets controlled by top 15 families
% of total value, 1996

	% of GDP
Indonesia	21.5
Philippines	46.7
Thailand	39.3
South Korea	12.9
Hong Kong	84.2
Singapore	48.3
Malaysia	76.2
Taiwan	17.0
Japan	2.1

Sources: Stijn Claessens, Simeon Djankov and Larry Lang

But there was a snag. The conglomerates of the *huaqiao* (and the tycoons from the ethnic majorities who imitated them) evolved to suit their environment. The resulting business cultures were optimal for a first-generation founder to establish a decent-sized family business. At a certain point, however, further expansion required outside capital. And here the problems started, because outside capital, whether debt or equity, has a side-effect: the dilution, and perhaps loss, of family control. For a founding family, ceding control is always painful. For most of South-East Asia's *huaqiao*, it was simply unacceptable. Protecting their families, after all, was the whole point of their businesses.

Larry Lang and Leslie Young, two finance professors at the Chinese University of Hong Kong, and Stijn Claessens of the World Bank, have analysed the resulting corporate structures in a study entitled "Dividends and Expropriation". For many *huaqiao*, they found, the answer lay in "pyramids": extraordinarily complex and opaque structures of private holding companies, layers upon layers of subsidiaries, as well as cross-holdings and informal links with yet more companies. Almost always, the pyramids included at least one bank with a licence to take deposits, and several publicly listed subsidiaries that could issue shares in the open market.

The purpose of these pyramids was to draw outside capital into the family group while retaining control over the use of this capital within the family. South-East Asia's corporate conglomerates, in other words, aimed to "internalise" the capital markets that discipline companies in the West.

To see how this works, picture a pyramid at the top of which sits a private holding company owned by the patriarch and his family. It owns 51% of subsidiary A, which owns 51% of subsidiary B, which owns 51% of subsidiary C, which owns 30% of company D. Separately, the family also has another (wholly-owned) vehicle, F, which owns 21% of D. In terms of voting rights, the patriarch and his family therefore control 51% of company D. At the same time, the family can claim only 25% of company D's profits (51% times 51% times 51% times 30%, plus 21% through company F).

This discrepancy between the family's voting rights and its share of profits in the company at the bottom of the pyramid is crucial. It creates an opportunity, and indeed an incentive, to expropriate the outside investors in company D and its parents. How? One way is for the controlling family to make company D pay miserly dividends. Better still, the family could make company D sell an asset to company F at an artificially low price, or make company D buy an asset from F at an inflated price. For example, D might be a construction company in Thailand that buys land and concrete from F, paying $100m more than the market value. The family would lose $25m through its ownership of D, but gain $100m through company F, netting $75m. Meanwhile, minority investors in A, B, C, and d would all lose out.

In practice, though, the transactions tend to be more complex, and therefore harder to trace. Consider, for instance, the business affairs of Lucio Tan, probably the wealthiest *huaqiao* tycoon in the Philippines and a close friend of Joseph Estrada, the former president. Mr Tan has interests in airlines, banking, breweries, tobacco, property and much else, and holds these interests in several extremely complex pyramids. Near the bottom of one of them is the Philippine National Bank (PNB). In 1999, the Philippine government owned 46% of PNB, and Mr Tan and other investors had minority stakes. When the government decided to offer new shares, some of them were bought by Mr Tan direct, and the rest were acquired by four special-purpose companies that were financed, it turns out, by loans from banks linked to Mr Tan. As collateral for the loans, the four companies assigned 93% of their voting rights to none other than Mr Tan.

Suddenly PNB became a very different bank. In November 1999, it disclosed that all of its outside directors had resigned from

The ancient art of making money

NEVER mind, for now, that many of Asia's *huaqiao* are Christian, and that the mainland Chinese are—nominally—Communist and nothing else. Most westerners doing business with the Chinese are convinced that they are confronting inscrutable mentalities. Western capitalism has clearly been influenced by thinkers such as Max Weber and his ideas about the Prostestant work ethic. Has the orient's way of doing business been shaped by eastern philosophies?

The usual suspect is K'ung Fu Tzu (Confucius), an itinerant teacher who lived around 500 BC. Master K'ung codified what he saw as the crucial relationships—those between ruler and subject, father and son, husband and wife, elder and younger brother, and friends—and defined clearly who was to obey whom.

An irony that may have escaped Asian tycoons who take him as their model is that Master K'ung himself would have held them in disdain. The profit motive, the Master felt, was highly suspect. In fact, all the commercial classes were to be treated with extreme caution, since they were not tied to any one place and were therefore hard to tax, rule and—yes—trust.

The relevance of Confucian ethics in modern business is limited, however, for a simple reason: Master K'ung did not have much to say about interactions with strangers, which is what suppliers, customers, minority shareholders and creditors tend to be. This gap is elegantly filled by Sun Tzu, a contemporary of Master K'ung, whose opus "The Art of War" has become required reading at many western business schools. Sun's philosophy consists of a great many ingenious stratagems for outwitting an opponent. Sun's is the eastern philosophy that western businessmen are most afraid of encountering—and try hardest to employ themselves.

Another of China's giant thinkers is Lao Tzu, whose philosophy became known as Taoism. Lao stressed the importance of action through inaction (*wu wei*), of letting go and not resisting nature's way of achieving balance. Taoism chimes well with a free-market economy, and even offers a way of explaining Asia's bust after the boom.

One way of pinning down the philosophical differences may be to consider what the West has that Asia does not. In transcendental monotheism, an abstract and authoritarian ruler lays down the law in negative terms ("Thou shalt not..."). As a basis for, say, contract and securities law, this works well. Since business dealings by their nature involve a clash of interests, it is useful to have recourse to a set of universal principles.

By contrast, many Asians find it hard to accept the idea of, say, an external auditor or an independent board director, since he might actually disagree with them. And western hard-headedness puzzles them. After all, a contract was signed in a context. And if that context has changed, has not the contract?

the board and had been replaced by associates of Mr Tan. Mr Tan himself started playing an active role in managing day-to-day operations. Almost immediately, PNB lent $95m to Mr Tan's brewer and his airline, in which he has much higher ownership stakes. Within months, these loans were restructured, with a later repayment date and a lower interest rate. PNB's auditors reckoned that in all probability the loans would never be repaid. The shares dived. In the summer of 2000, Mr Estrada's government decided to sell another batch of shares in PNB to the public. This time there was only one bidder—Lucio Tan.

Variable geometry

To put South-East Asia's pyramids into perspective, finance students at the Chinese University of Hong Kong examined 3,000 East Asian companies, using publicly available information. They discovered huge differences across the region, reflecting the stage of economic and institutional development of the countries concerned. In Japan, fewer than 10% of companies were controlled by a single family—about the same proportion as in parts of Europe. In the next most developed economies, South Korea and Taiwan, just under 50% of companies were under family control. In Thailand and Malaysia, the ratio rose to between 60% and 70% of companies, and in Indonesia and the Philippines, the least developed in this group, even higher. In these countries only ten families controlled over half of their countries' total market capitalisation.

Even more important, however, are the differences in the "visibility" of family control. Mr Young, for instance, discovered that listed companies in which the founding families have fairly large and traceable stakes pay higher dividends; they are under surveillance from the capital markets. By contrast, companies whose ultimate ownership is unclear paid unusually low dividends, suggesting that minority shareholders are indeed being exploited. The proportion of "visibly" family-controlled listed companies in South-East Asia is not that different from, say, France or Italy. But the share of companies where ultimate control has been disguised is five times higher in South-East Asia, says the study. And that takes in only those companies that were still recognisable despite the disguise. Allowing for those that hide successfully, the real ratio is probably much higher.

What, if anything, about all this is peculiarly "Asian"? It is not the presence of family businesses on the stockmarket, since this can also be found in continental Europe (though less in the "Anglo-Saxon" equity cultures of America and Britain). Nor is it the temptation of founders to dole out senior management positions to family members, or to take outside investors for a ride—again, magnates in Europe yield to both from time to time.

Instead, the main difference appears to be that in western countries the capital markets have had time to catch up with the tricks of family businesses. Regulators, lawyers and judges pay close attention, and creditors and shareholders demand to be represented on the board. All the institutions of mature capitalist systems have evolved to check the power of controlling shareholders and protect the rights of minority investors. Asian capitalism, too, needs to grow up. But how long will it take?

From *The Economist*, April 7, 2001, Survey, pp. 4-6. © 2001 by The Economist, Ltd. distributed by The New York Times Special Features. Reprinted by permission.

Hype at the end of the tunnel

Hollywood uses it; so did the Nazis. **Ziauddin Sardar** on the world's most potent drug

Hype kills. Hype devastates societies. Hype strangles politics. Hype annihilates economies. Hype produces wealth for a few undeserving individuals while destroying the livelihoods of the vast majority. Hype has made lies—blatant, malicious lies—the foundation of civil society.

In times of war, the dangers of hype come more to the fore. Think of the hype surrounding the "smart bombs" that are supposed to be so accurate, we can target military installations with pinpoint accuracy and without killing civilians. But somehow the "smart bombs" are never smart enough in reality: they kill women and children, and our own allies, with mundane frequency, as we saw in the Gulf war and see again in Afghanistan.

But it is not just during wars that all sides lie as a matter of course. The underlying layers of our civilisation itself function on hype. The market operates on hype: stocks and shares soar on exuberant projections of potential riches, only to fall back to earth when reality sets in. Think of the dotcom bubble.

Technology evolves by perpetual hype: "must-have" technology is every child's inheritance, a mindset that creates the means for market saturation. The recent spectacular implosion of hi-tech companies, such as Marconi, and airlines, such as Sabena, will have to be the springboard for developing new techno toys—it's the only way this economy knows how to work, and the only hope the now superfluous labour force has of finding another job.

Hype is integral to science. Any discovery is immediately sold to us with visions of unlimited commercial applications, no matter how ridiculous or absurd. Headline-grabbing hype, persuading private companies and public bodies to part with their money, is what makes science possible; thus it determines what science gets done. Consider the hype surrounding the mapping of the human genome. It was sold as the answer to life, the universe and everything. But no sooner was the genome mapped than we were told that what really matters is not DNA but proteins. For all the hoopla, the potential cures and dividends are nowhere to be seen.

Hype is the stock-in-trade of the entertainment industry. The more execrable a Hollywood movie, the greater the hype. Think of the fanfaronade surrounding such banal films as *Star Wars: the phantom menace* and *Pearl Harbor*. Barry Norman, the doyen of British film critics, described the latter as "a classic example of hype gone mad." The film is "rubbish" and everyone involved in it knows it, but the purpose of hype, Norman says,

is "to make people forget it's rubbish, leave their brains at home, and get to the cinemas early."

Yes, indeed, leave your brains at home. The first thing hype kills is the mind.

The origin of the word "hype" is not as straightforward as you may think. The obvious derivation is from "hyperbole," defined by dictionaries as "deliberate exaggeration used for effect." But "hype" is also American slang for a hypodermic syringe or injection. And hype indeed acts like a drug, under the influence of which people come to believe lies.

This point was first made by German intellectuals of the Frankfurt School, who argued that the media "injected" values, ideas and information directly into each individual. A largely passive and atomised audience swallowed the hype uncritically. Today, we tend to look down on such a "mechanistic" and "unsophisticated" model of the media-audience relationship. But members of the Frankfurt School—they included Theodor Adorno, Walter Benjamin and Herbert Marcuse—had seen at first hand the impact of hype in Nazi Germany. They knew it could transform a rational society into a murderous mob.

Indeed, hype achieves its goal largely by generating a mob mentality. Which brings us to the second thing that hype kills: reality. Hype manufactures an inversion of reality that is used to generate mass hysteria. The Third Reich presented the bogeymen of ancient fairy tales as though they were natural phenomena. It recycled the medieval blood libel against Judaism, depicting Jews as rats infesting German cities. It wrapped racism and other phobias in fashionable scientific theories such as eugenics. It converted the peace treaty that ended the First World War into a victimisation of the German people and an act of aggression against them. All this was packaged and sold with the practised skill of modern advertising executives, through all the media where advertising hype thrives: film, radio, newspapers. The synthesised cocktail was injected and it induced pathological hysteria. The pathology may vary but hysteria is the essence of all hype.

A more innocent proof that we are in no way immune to hype is *The Blair Witch Project*, one of the first films fully to exploit the internet's hype capabilities. New technology, same old strategy, same old hype. The film began by explaining that, in 1994, three student film-makers hiked into the Maryland woods to shoot a documentary about a local legend, the "Blair witch." They never returned. The film was supposedly based on footage from the documentary and from the team's video diary.

The producers went to incredible lengths to create a real-world legend of the Blair witch. An internet site manufactured background material, footage and photographs on its 200-year "history." Through colleges and universities, word spread that the film was based on a true story. When the film opened, students and young "experts" on the legend travelled hundreds of miles and queued for hours—generating a self-feeding frenzy that ensured that a laughably bad film was a runaway success.

On a less elaborate level, think of how the television show *Pop Stars* created the group Hear'say, whose "Pure and Simple" became the best-selling debut single of all time.

Tap into the psyche of a generation and watch hype work like crack cocaine. Hitler Youth, Hear'say groupies, greedy dotcom investors, hi-tech manufacturers and the lunatics who queue up to watch the latest hyped rubbish from Hollywood—all operate on the same pathological mob mentality that is incapable of telling pure illusion from any notion of reality.

If you cannot distinguish between fantasy and reality, or just don't care which is which, you are hardly in a position to distinguish between good and bad. Quality is the third thing that hype kills. It puts the mediocre in the foreground and gives common currency to the pestiferous. Any bestseller list will confirm this. Trashy (but glossy) food and cookbooks, autobiographies of pop/sports/fashion stars who have hardly lived and embarrassing accounts of (mostly imagined) childhood wrongs rub shoulders with madcap mythology, tacky romance and the latest film tie-in.

The hip young, say the theorists, are resistant to hype. Alas not. The hip young are fools

---

It is all at about the same level as the home page of Mahir Cagri. Mahir, a Turk, shot to fame in 1999, proving the rule that hype, including self-hype, is successful in direct proportion to its crudeness. When you log on, you are greeted with: "Welcome to my home page !!!!!!!!!!!!! I kiss you." Underneath, we have pictures of Mahir, sporting a flamboyant moustache below a hefty hooter, in everyday poses: playing table tennis, lying on the beach, lounging in leisurewear. Below that, we have the personal details: "I like sport, swimming... I like sex"; "my profession journalist, music and sport teacher, I make psycolojy doctora... I like to take fotocamera (towns, animals, nice nude models and people)" [*sic*]. When the site first opened, Mahir received e-mails and phone calls from women who wanted to correct his English or take him out on a date. Nothing too unusual

in that. But some of his more cunning friends realised that he was a commodity tapping into an insatiable desire. Mirror sites were established, "hits" multiplied, and a legend was carefully constructed around Mahir.

In the Turkish press, he was hyped as an innocent man chased by oversexed white women. Hype fed upon hype. *The Guardian* and other newspapers ran profiles; CNN put Mahir on air; advertisers, at first local and small-scale, later corporate and international, bought space on his sites; critical theory specialists deconstructed his narrative; presidential candidates sought his endorsement. A simple internet search will now reveal some 25,000 Mahir sites selling Mahir products, promoting Mahir's style, analysing Mahir's impact—there are even parodies of his sites. And perhaps the Mahir phenomenon is itself just a parody of the way we allow ourselves to be duped, deluded and diverted.

The postmodern audience is supposedly alert to hype. Media studies courses in Britain and the US claim that we have all become media savvy. The hip young in particular, according to the theorists, are resistant to hype. Alas, they are not. On the whole, the hip young are fools. Give them a meaningless buzzword and see them lap up the hype like ice cream from a cornet. A couple of years ago it was "ultra"—ultra experiences (as in white-knuckle rides), ultra toothpaste and ultra bras. Now it's "extreme"—sports (bungee jumping, now a megacult), extreme travel (such as a celebrity going to the Arctic Circle, the ultimate in television hype), extreme endurance (as in reality shows such as *Boot Camp, Survivor* and *Castaway*), extreme animals and, no doubt soon to make its appearance, extreme sex. "Max" is on its way; "mega" has been there; no doubt, "severe" is looming somewhere on the future horizon. Indeed, the youth of the globalised world have been so infected with hype that simply labelling plain old H_2O "Aqua" generates a new trend in drinking water.

The more savvy youth are caught by anti-hype. But that is just hype in disguise. Ironic anti-advertising or self-parodying anti-hype is designed to play "we know, you know" games. Think of the copy line from *The Spy Who Shagged Me*: "If you see one movie this summer, see *Star Wars*." The clothing manufacturer Diesel made a name for itself by giving ironic, backhanded compliments to other brands for improving the lives of consumers. Sales of Guinness went through the roof with the ironic and surreal Rutger Hauer advertisements, which associated the product with the young, funky and anti-hype.

If something can be a critical talking point, or better still a source of study in the academy, it is guaranteed to be hyped up as anti-hype. Benetton, with its posters of dying Aids patients, black and white angels and newborn babies, and Wonderbra, with its outrageously sexist advertising, have been very successful at this. Film studios now often set up websites to criticise and abuse their own productions in order to drum up the kind of word-of-mouth hype that so benefited *The Blair Witch Project*.

It is hardly surprising that hype-injected youth don't have any time for politics—for the real struggle to change the world. Politics is the fourth victim of hype. When people would rather vote on which members to expel from the *Big Brother* house than on who should be their MP, we know that politics has entered a terminal stage.

Hype kills trust, confidence and hope and thus chokes community

---

New Labour spin has been widely blamed for voter apathy. But new Labour did not invent spin. In Britain, Margaret Thatcher was the real pioneer of hype. It was Thatcher who transformed party political broadcasts from talking heads to Saatchi & Saatchi advertisements for a political brand: think of the 1979 election campaign and the poster that showed a dole queue with the slogan "Labour isn't working." Later, Thatcher's government led the way in taking hype in to public information films. The chilling Aids campaign advertisements—one with a gravestone, the other with icebergs crumbling in the sea—established the standard. Whether she was fighting an election or a threatened epidemic, Thatcher used panic-ridden hype as her standard-bearer. It worked brilliantly for her successor, John Major, who won the 1992 election by terrifying the public with largely unfounded stories of Labour tax rises.

New Labour's achievement is the transformation of hype into a natural, organic phenomenon. Think of Tony Blair delivering, at the death of Diana, the "people's princess" speech: eyes wet, voice on the safe side of emotion, pauses calculated to be half-a-heartbeat, hands skilfully demonstrating spontaneity. Or the other potent symbol: Blair emerging from the official car in tight, faded blue jeans flashing his cute buns, carrying in one hand his battered guitar case and in the other a battered red box. This is spin at its best, invisible rather than transparent, seemingly accidental and spontaneous rather than stage-managed— much better than kissing babies or donning a hard hat for touring a riot-ridden city.

Finally, hype kills trust, confidence and hope and thus chokes community. We are aware of hype, but completely incapable of seeing how we can extract ourselves from its self-perpetuating cycles. When illusion is marketed as reality, how can we get back to solid ground? Castles in the air generate wealth, employment, and the service-driven world of post-industrial society. What happens to affluence and its consumerist idyll if we should decide to try less profligate lifestyles, more responsible ways of living? That way, we think, lies utter ruin for everyone.

So cynicism is all we have left, and we dignify it as art, the highest accolade of our creative imagination. Today, we are our own art forms, the ultimate expression of all that can be expressed. When everything is hype, we can trust only ourselves, even if we are merely following the rest of the mob. We know we see through it; we cannot be sure anyone else does.

When cynicism rules, and trust is a relic of distant antiquity, when we can be confident only that we are being sold a bill of goods, community suffocates on mob hysteria. To stand against the tide of the unreal, to demand an end to the manufacture and manipulation, is to threaten everyone's investment in a self-sustaining delusion. We may wish to talk about the need to rescue ourselves from this invidious spiral, but all forums of debate— art, media, politics—are centres for hypercreation. A world of glitz, glitz, glitz is bleak, bleak, bleak.

Hype, as the theatre critic Robert Gore-Langton once noted, is a form of passive smoking. But while Gore-Langton thought it was something we ultimately reject, I would argue that we have become so addicted that we may soon find it impossible to escape. In these supposedly post-ideological times, hype has become an ideology to beat all the ideologies of history. Like its predecessors, though more effectively, it acts as a pathogen on society. The dread words of the patron saint of political spin return to haunt us: perhaps there really is no alternative.

In his Turner Prize entry, an installation entitled *227: the lights going on and off*, Martin Creed has captured the essence of hype. We move towards the hyped light but the moment we try to capture it, it goes off. There is nothing behind hype; and ultimately our hype-based civilisation is little more than an empty, dark room.

Ziauddin Sardar's A to Z of postmodern life *was published by Vision paperbacks in February 2002.*

From *New Statesman*, November 19, 2001, pp. 27-29. © 2001 by New Statesman Ltd.

Chile's Democratic Challenge

We believe that all of the decisions linked to development need to be made democratically. That's not the way that things are being decided under the neoliberal model.

An Interview with Sara Larrain

Sara Larrain is the executive director of the Sustainable Chile Program (SCP) in Santiago, Chile. SCP is an inter-institutional program sponsored by the Institute for Ecological Policy, the National Environmental Network and the Bolivarian University.

Multinational Monitor: What does "sustainable" mean for you?

Sara Larrain: Sustainable development or sustainability is a way of development that is linked, first of all, with social equity. Proponents of neoliberal policies and trade liberalization emphasize the importance of economic growth. But there is no guarantee that this economic growth will benefit the population.

In the last 17 years in Chile, we have had an annual growth rate of 7 percent, with the exception of the last two years. But one in four Chileans lives in poverty. So social equity is key for us.

The second goal is environmental sustainability. Economic growth in developing countries like Chile has been achieved mainly through the exploitation and export of natural resources. In the case of Chile, 44 percent of our exports are copper; 13 to 15 percent are forest products; about 15 percent fish meal and other fish products. A large portion of the rest consists of agricultural products. If you look at these figures, you see that more than 80 percent of our exports are natural resources. Most of this 80 percent is raw materials. So we are exporting our natural capital.

At the same time, we are not creating jobs. So Chile is receiving minimal social benefit in exchange for the exploitation of our natural resources.

Chile is also externalizing the environmental costs of the country's economic activity. We have a huge internal ecological debt in terms of spent natural resources and major pollution problems.

The last component of sustainable development for us is public participation. We believe that all of the decisions linked to development need to be made democratically. That's not the way that things are being decided under the neoliberal model. It's worse in the case of globalization where nation-states have less and less flexibility and ability to make decisions in line with the needs of their populations.

The economy can be sustainable in Chile and other countries in Latin America with a growth rate of probably around 3 or 4 percent. But the economies of the northern countries can probably grow sustainably at a rate of only about 1 percent or zero percent. So sustainability is more complex than sustainable economic growth. Economic growth is a semantic and economic trap that corporations put before the United Nations and others who look at sustainable development. Development centered around the goal of economic growth has impeded the implementation of sustainable development strategies around the world.

From 1997 until 2000, Sustainable Chile built an alternative development project for the country. We analyzed all the social, environmental and political problems and highlighted the more critical problems of equity, environmental sustainability and problems in politics because we have had an incomplete transition to democracy. Then we put forward a package of reforms to reorient Chile's development model towards sustainability. We have a 500-page program which shows, sector by sector, the main changes we have to make to reorient the development of the country towards sustainability.

MM: What are the main environmental problems in Chile?

Sara Larrain: First, we have the over-exploitation of natural resources; we are expending our natural capital.

This is most serious in mining. The tax system in the mining sector provides no funds for development in the regions that have been devastated by the extraction of non-renewable mineral resources.

The second problem is with forests. All the studies we have from the central bank and other institutions conclude that, if we continue exploiting our native forests at the current rate, in 10 years Chile will not have any native forests except for the protected national parks.

Fisheries are also over-exploited. At this time, the government says that 80 percent of commercial species are over-exploited.

These are the three main areas where there is over-exploitation. The second main environmental problem is pollution, which is a consequence of the externalization of environmental costs.

The pollution problem is a serious public health problem. The city of Santiago, where 45 percent of Chileans live today, is saturated with pollutants. The city is under a cleanup plan, but the government has no money to implement the plan. According to government estimates, 1,000 people die annually because of the pollution.

The mining sector in Chile does not create much employment. We are exporting 100 percent unprocessed copper. We are asking the government to require the companies to include processing of the mineral inside the country and not export raw materials.

A second pollution problem in Chile comes from the mining industry. All the main mining sites are considered saturated zones because of the pollutants. In some of the cases the government set clean-up plans. In other cases, for instance in Chuquicamata—the biggest copper mining site in the world—they decided to relocate the people instead. At this moment they are dismantling the village and relocating all the people to the city, because the conditions there do not support human life.

MM: In your alternative plan, what would you like to see done in, say, the mining sector?

Sara Larrain: First, we need to change the system that regulates the mining sector. Mining companies pay fewer taxes in Chile than all the other industrial sectors. So our proposal is to increase mining taxes, to bring them up to the level of other sectors—about 15 percent. This would provide the government with more money to enforce the law. For example, right now we have only four or five people to monitor all of the mining activities in the entire country. That makes it impossible to regulate the industry.

We are also asking for a 1 percent sales tax on the mining industry to be used to create a recovery fund. That would allow the regions that have lost their natural capital to have money for development alternatives, including tourism, agriculture and so on.

We also recommend that mining investments be linked with the previous evaluation of water resources. Mining activities are mainly in the northern region of the country, which is a highlands desert with few water resources. The companies use all the existing water, they ask the government for the water rights and leave the indigenous communities without water resources. So you have a huge relocation of indigenous communities because they can't continue their agricultural activities or feed their livestock. We've collapsed a lot of villages and cultures because of the mining investment. So we need an evaluation of water conditions before mining begins, and we need to impose conditions on the projects to make sure they properly recycle water and use water-efficient technologies.

The last recommendation relates to employment. The mining sector in Chile does not create much employment. We are exporting 100 percent unprocessed copper. The mining sites are increasingly mechanized and unemployment is increasing year by year, so the destruction of natural resources is not creating much social benefit. We are asking the government to require the companies to include processing of the mineral inside the country and not export raw materials, like unprocessed copper.

Multinational Monitor: What mining companies are involved?

Sara Larrain: Compania del Cobre (CODELCO) is the main national. Some of the main multinationals involved include BHP (Australia), Rio Tinto (UK), Exxon Coal

(U.S.), Phelps Dodge (U.S.), Sumitomo (Japan), Outo-kumpu (Finland), Placer Dome (Canada), Cominco (Canada), Nippon Mining (Japan), Mitsubishi (Japan), Rio Algum (Canada), Falcon Bridge (Canada) and Anglo American (South Africa).

We have no post-closure plans for mines in Chile. We have more than 100 mining waste sites. These all have tailings ponds. The government has to figure out what to do with these because the companies have no responsibility for their waste. Right now we have no regulation of what happens after they're done extracting the minerals.

Multinational Monitor: What are some of the shifts you hope to achieve in the broader political economy?

Sara Larrain: We had a long period of dictatorship. During the transition period, our political leaders promised to advance a plan to end the conditions that existed under the dictatorship, and to link it with solutions for poverty, democratization, changes in labor laws, the creation of environmental laws and the creation of indigenous law (before we had no legislation to defend indigenous rights). That did not happen.

After all these years of economic growth, we have the same level of distribution of income that we had during the dictatorship. So there's no democracy in terms of income distribution inside this country.

After the first phase of the plan and after the second, nothing very structural changed.

After all these years of economic growth, we have the same level of distribution of income that we had during the dictatorship. We are a little better off in terms of poverty. Before, we had more or less 35 percent of the population in poverty. Today it is 20 percent. But if you look at the distribution of income you have really poor people and rich people—essentially the same level of distribution that existed during the dictatorship. So there's no democracy in terms of income distribution inside this country.

During the transition, for instance, we did not reform the labor law. The labor law was set during the dictatorship, when we didn't have unions, we didn't have political parties and we didn't have a congress. So you can imagine who discussed the labor law. After 10 years of transition to democracy we have the same labor law.

In terms of natural resources, we pushed and we pushed and in the last months of President Aylwin's government at the beginning of 1994, they passed the environmental law. We then spent three years until 1997 asking for regulations to implement this law. But if you look at the sectoral laws governing forests, water resources or mining, we really have the same codes as dur-ing the dictatorship, despite the work of all the organizations asking for new natural resource codes. We really are administrating the same economic model that was set during the dictatorship. This is the structural problem that we have in Chile, and means that we have advanced very little during the transition to democracy.

The Sustainable Chile program was born as a blueprint for the country developed by civil society so that we don't continue working only in a reactive mode—only saying "no" to their programs for mining, water, social programs.

To have democratically elected officials administering the same economic model and the same political structure established during the dictatorship—by the 1980 constitution—is really amazing. We still have all the political problems that we had from the 1980 constitution, which was created by Pinochet. Pinochet designed a political constitution that doesn't allow the people to easily re-write the rules of the country in terms of labor law, water law, mining law, indigenous law, investments and the privatization of pension funds, health and so on. So in the transition period we are under the same economic rules and institutions by all these sectoral laws. We have practically the same political code.

Progressives have asked the government to ask the Congress to change the constitution, to call a plebiscite. They make excuses such as "we don't have a majority." But for the majority of the population, it would be better if the democratic government put the reforms to the Congress and lost than it is to do nothing. At least you would begin to create the spectacle and the fight, and put into concrete terms what democratization means and show that the opposition (the right-wing parties) are an obstacle to change.

Because the democratic authorities don't put these reforms before the Congress, the people are becoming disoriented and confused. The right-wing coalition now wins almost as many votes as Concertacion [the center-left coalition which has run the government since the transition from dictatorship]. The people no longer know what change means. The message of the right-wing candidates is "change." And the message of the Concertacion is "no change."

The Sustainable Chile program was born as a blueprint for the country developed by civil society so that we don't continue working only in a reactive mode—only saying "no" to their programs for mining, water, social programs, etc. We want to say "no," but we also want to be able to articulate how we want things to be. We think we cannot as citizens take political initiative if we don't have our own agenda for the country. So the Sustainable Chile program and the 500-page book we put together is really a blueprint that gives civil society the political initiative for a new country project, including the mechanisms, the laws, the timelines by which we need to change.

Multinational Monitor: How does the distribution of income and wealth compare now to the period of dictatorship?

Sara Larrain: In 1987, when Chile's Ministry of Planning officially began to study income levels, the poorest 10 percent of the population received 1.5 percent of the overall income while the richest 10 percent received 41.3 percent. The last official count in 1996 shows that the poorest 10 percent of the population still received only 1.5 percent of the income and the 10 richest percent received 41.3 percent. The same.

Between 1992 and 1994, we had a decrease in poverty, but more or less the distribution gap remained the same. This is completely contradictory with a democracy. In Latin America, Brazil has the worst distribution of income. Chile is the next worst. Chile is the model of Latin America in terms of economic growth and modernization, etc., but it's really the second worst, socially, in terms of distribution of income. The situation is unacceptable.

Multinational Monitor: Why does the Chilean government want to enter into a free trade agreement with the United States?

Sara Larrain: Maintaining the dictatorship broke relations with a lot of countries. The dictatorship's political strategy was to open the economy and legitimize the country via economic development.

Chile was the first Latin American country to unilaterally open its economy. The dictatorship liberalized trade and investment, and privatized sectors—health, pensions—in ways that were unimaginable in other countries. By 1988 and 1989 tariffs rates in Chile were completely different from other Latin American countries.

In 1994, Clinton signed the NAFTA. The Clinton administration saw Chile as the first country to which NAFTA could be extended, because of its low tariffs. Chile saw being in the NAFTA as a chance to get ahead of other countries in the region and increase its status in negotiations with the European Union.

We have no comparative advantage with our neighbors in term[s] of natural resources, so we have the opportunity to export industrial products, and begin to aggregate value to our natural resources and through this create jobs.

When the U.S. Congress refused to pass fast track, Chile asked to join Mercosur (the Common Market of the Southern Cone) because the government knew that the European Union was beginning talks with Mercosur to construct an agreement. At the same time, the government continued to negotiate a free trade agreement with Canada modeled after the NAFTA, including with the environmental side agreements.

The idea of prioritizing the signing of an agreement with the United States is to take advantage of the export of natural resources before Chile's competitors, Argentina and Brazil.

For the United States, Chile is key because tariffs are very low. There is a lot of investment here, but not a market on a scale that would be of much interest to the United States. The political interest of the United States involves approaching Chile through the NAFTA framework and therefore legitimizing the NAFTA for the FTAA negotiations. They don't want the FTAA just for trade, they also want rules on investments included. Chile is very useful for the U.S. strategy of implementing the NAFTA model inside the FTAA because Brazil doesn't want the model for the region.

Multinational Monitor: What would you like Chile to be doing within the Mercosur and the region?

Sara Larrain: The Mercosur is a bloc where we can continue expanding the export of our processed products and not only natural resources. We have no comparative advantage with our neighbors in term[s] of natural resources, so we have the opportunity to export industrial products, and begin to aggregate value to our natural resources and through this create jobs. If we really began to have an exchange in services, industrial products and so on, we have the opportunity to decrease the exploitation of natural resources.

Mercosur is more an integral agreement and is not just focused on trade. You have a better opportunity for cultural exchange, services exchange and so on.

This is not the case with our bilateral relationship with the United States. The comparative advantage we have with the United States is mainly in natural resources—mining, fisheries and agriculture (fruit). At the same time, we have a lot of dangers in terms of a flood of imported manufactured and agriculture products.

Multinational Monitor: What are the principles that you would like to see guiding the evolution of Mercosur so that you have the development of a sustainable regional arrangement?

Sara Larrain: We think that some of the processes guiding the European Union's integration process would be more appropriate in terms of looking at all sectors at the same time, and not just under the umbrella of trade. Looking at all sectors through the lens of trade economizes everything.

The EU has a lot of problems, but what is good about the European process is that it involves parallel efforts for economic, political and cultural integration.

In the case of Mercosur, there is an opportunity to prioritize social and environmental concerns because tariff reduction is just beginning and proceeding very slowly. For example, Brazil is very careful as to how it decreases tariffs because they don't want to create social problems inside the country. This is a correct position. It's important to look at the social and environmental conditions. It's important to apply the precautionary principle—to make a social and environmental evaluation before signing the treaty. This enables you to pursue different measures to decrease the impacts or have mitigation measures to avoid harmful development impacts or real social crises. Mercosur should apply the precautionary principle within the paradigm of integration and not only within the trade paradigm.

Any integration needs to be put into a framework of existing agreements. Integration should occur within a framework of respect for international labor standards, multilateral environmental agreements and human rights standards.

What is happening today is that the goal of trade is the economic growth of the region. So economic growth became the dogma that drives all the integration process through trade. This has begun to create human rights, environmental, social and labor problems—not to mention what is happening with the investment regimes such as Chapter 11 of the NAFTA.

From *Multinational Monitor*, April 2001, pp. 22-26. © 2001 by Multinational Monitor. Reprinted by permission.

Government

Progress Against Corruption

Efforts accelerate to make governments more transparent and accountable.

Corruption in governments throughout the world used to be considered a fact of life: undesirable, but not especially harmful. Now that attitude has changed, according to Peter Richardson, a board member of Transparency International, a corruption-fighting organization.

"High levels of corruption are no longer regarded as inevitable. Consensus now exists that corrupt behavior reduces economic growth and can destabilize governments," writes Richardson in his contribution to *Managing Global Issues,* a collection of essays about global governance.

Corruption erodes respect for the law and deters honest people from entering public service. It results in over-invoicing and substandard work by contractors and reduces tax revenues. Corruption also undercuts environmental regulations and building code regulations, discourages foreign direct investment in developing countries, and facilitates other crimes, such as drug trafficking, according to Richardson.

Corruption scandals in the 1990s (in France, Brazil, Japan, Pakistan, and elsewhere) demonstrated that corruption is widespread, even in democracies. In recent years, government leaders and nongovernmental organizations have developed a variety of strategies to expose corruption and counter its effects.

Transparency International, a global organization with 80 chapters, builds anticorruption coalitions with governments, business people, and representatives of civil society. The World Bank

and the International Monetary Fund focus on introducing reforms in developing countries to address the demand side of bribery. In cases where a country has high levels of corruption and a government that is not instituting reforms, international financial institutions may reduce or eliminate aid. In 1996 the UN General Assembly approved a code of conduct for public officials and called on member states to make bribing public officials a crime.

Corruption reform programs have had success in exposing government bribery by conducting national surveys and publishing "report cards" that detail specific instances of corruption. "Big Mac Indexes," which reveal suspicious cost differences in a country for similar commodities, such as a school lunch or a bottle of aspirin, can be especially effective, according to Richardson.

"Transparency International/Argentina conducted a Big Mac survey, which revealed that a school lunch in Buenos Aires cost the equivalent of $5. A comparable lunch in Mendoza, which had been implementing anticorruption measures, cost the equivalent of 80¢. Within days of publication of the survey's results, the cost of a school lunch in Buenos Aires was more than halved," Richardson writes.

Transparency International also publishes two annual reports that put pressure on governments tolerating high levels of corruption.

• **The Corruption Perception Index** ranks countries according to

The Bribe Payers Index		
Rank	Country	Score
1	Sweden	8.3
2	Australia	8.1
	Canada	8.1
4	Austria	7.8
5	Switzerland	7.7
6	Netherlands	7.4
7	United Kingdom	7.2
8	Belgium	6.8
9	Germany	6.2
	United States	6.2
11	Singapore	5.7
12	Spain	5.3
13	France	5.2
14	Japan	5.1
15	Malaysia	3.9
16	Italy	3.7
17	Taiwan	3.5
18	South Korea	3.4
19	China (including Hong Kong)	3.1

Source: Transparency International, www.transparency.org.

Sweden ranked least corrupt on the Bribe Payers Index, maintained by Transparency International, a group that monitors corruption around the world. Transparency ranked 19 leading exporting countries on their propensity to bribe senior public officials, based on a 1999 survey of 770 respondents from 15 emerging market countries. A score of 10 indicates a perception of negligible bribery, while 0 represents very high levels of bribery.

levels of corruption revealed by a composite of 14 surveys of business people, academics, and country analysts.

- **The Bribe Payers Index** focuses on the supply side of corruption by ranking countries according to how many bribes are offered by their international businesses.

Putting a media spotlight on corruption helps to raise public awareness of the issue and can be an effective tool in combating corruption in developed countries. But attacking government corruption in the developing world will require reforms that curb the opportunities and incentives for bribery and extortion, increase the risks that corrupt behavior will be detected, and hand down severe penalties for bribery. However, many developing countries lack one or more components of the infrastructure needed to combat corruption:

"The prerequisites for anticorruption reform include governmental checks and balances, a respect for the rule of law, in-dependent judiciaries, competent prosecutorial capabilities, financial disclosure standards, free and independent media, and an expectation that bribery is not necessary in business relations," writes Richardson.

One pragmatic approach to corruption reform can produce rapid results by severely prosecuting and punishing bribery in particular places. These "islands of integrity" may focus on a single city, a large building contract, or an industry segment such as power generation. For instance, all bidders on a contract are required in writing to adopt a code of conduct, provide financial reports, and submit to monitoring. Breaches of the agreement can result in legal action or international arbitration. In recent years, the "island of integrity" approach has been applied to a refinery rehabilitation project in Ecuador, a subway construction project in Argentina, and a telecommunications privatization plan in Colombia.

Although reducing worldwide corruption is no longer viewed as a quixotic undertaking, considerable obstacles remain—governments too disorganized to mount reform efforts, lax enforcement, and the resourcefulness of those who benefit from corruption. In order to be effective, reform efforts will require much time and many strategies.

"Silver bullet solutions are a recipe for disaster. Building coalitions and mixing options are a slow and often frustrating way to make a difference, but for many global challenges, it is often the only effective way," write P. J. Simmons and Chantal de Jonge Oudraat of the Carnegie Endowment for International Peace.

—*Dan Johnson*

Source: *Managing Global Issues: Lessons Learned,* edited by P. J. Simmons and Chantal de Jonge Oudraat. Carnegie Endowment for International Peace, www.ceip.org.2001. 771

Originally published in the March/April 2002 issue of *The Futurist,* pp. 12-13. Used with permission from the World Future Society, 7910 Woodmont Avenue, Suite 450, Bethesda, Maryland 20814. Telephone: 310/656-8274; Fax: 301/951-0394; http://www.wfs.org.

Serving up the Commons
A Guest Essay

By Tony Clarke

THE SMOKE AND PEPPER SPRAY had barely lifted from the streets of Seattle when the World Trade Organization (WTO) began a new set of global trade negotiations. Although efforts to launch a new round of worldwide comprehensive trade talks collapsed in Seattle, one of the built-in agendas which the WTO inherited from the Uruguay Round of the GATT was a commitment to expand global rules on cross-border trade in services through the General Agreement on Trade in Services (GATS) regime. In February 2000, the WTO launched what has been labeled as the GATS 2000 negotiations.

The GATS negotiations are designed to provide multinational corporations with the power tools they need to take control of much of what remains of the 'commons' on this planet. Every service imaginable is on the table, including a wide range of public services in sectors that affect the environment, culture, energy and natural resources; plus drinking water, health care, K-12 education, post-secondary education, and social security; along with transportation services, postal delivery, prisons, libraries and a variety of municipal services. By phasing out all governmental "barriers" to international trade and commercial competition in services, the GATS regime is designed to apply to virtually all government measures affecting trade-in-services, from labor laws to consumer protection, including regulations, guidelines, subsidies and grants, licensing standards and qualifications, and limitations on access to markets, economic needs tests and local content provisions.

If the proposed set of GATS rules are adopted, they will radically restructure the role of government regarding public access to essential social services worldwide, to the detriment of the public interest and democracy itself.

The existing GATS regime of the WTO, initially established in 1994, is already comprehensive and far reaching. Currently, the GATS rules apply to all modes of supplying or delivering a service including foreign investment, cross-border provisions of a service, electronic commerce and international travel. The current GATS features a hybrid of both a "top-down" agreement (where all sectors and measures are covered unless they are explicitly excluded) and a "bottom-up" agreement (where only sectors and measures which governments explicitly commit to are covered). What this means is that presently certain provisions apply to all sectors while others apply only to those specific sectors agreed to.

The new GATS negotiations are designed to adopt new GATS rules, and to extend them to all service sectors. Besides compelling governments to grant unlimited market access to foreign service providers, without regard to the environmental and social impacts of the quantity or size of service activities, the proposed expansion of the WTO regime on services will:

- Impose new and severe constraints on the ability of governments to maintain or create environmental, health, consumer protection and other public interest standards through an expansion of GATS Article VI on domestic regulation. A proposed "necessity test" would require governments to show that their laws and regulations affecting service industries are the "least trade restrictive," regardless of financial, social,

IN THEIR OWN WORDS

Critics are ringing alarm bells about the potential impact of an extension of World Trade Organization rules over the services sector.

The expansion of the General Agreement on Trade in Services (GATS), they say, would entrench privatization and deregulation worldwide, largely for the benefit of U.S. and European multinational corporations. Expanded GATS rules would impose profound, permanent constraints on democratic policy-making. For citizens of the North, valued public services and regulations are at risk. Citizens of the South, they warn, are facing the prospect of having IMF/World Bank-style structural adjustment locked in place for all time. The idea of the GATS itself, and proposals for GATS expansion now being debated in ongoing GATS negotiations (known as GATS 2000), are largely the creation of multinational service corporations, they claim.

Supporters largely agree.

Andre Sapir, an adviser at the Directorate-General of the European Commission, writes that the very idea for a trade agreement covering services originated 20 years ago with a small group of U.S. multinational corporations. WTO Director of Services David Hartridge said in 1997 that the GATS would never have even been signed in 1994 if it had not been for pressure from American Express and Citicorp. The Coalition of Service Industries, the key U.S. corporate lobby group on services, including companies from AT&T to Citigroup, brags that it had a major role in shaping the original GATS agreement.

John Irwin, chair of the International Association of Drilling Contractors, says that the GATS is the world's first multilateral agreement on investment. Pierre Sauve and Christopher Wilkie of the OECD (Organization for Economic Cooperation and Development) agree, adding that GATS has the political advantage of not attracting as much NGO attention and not being as easy to oppose as a whole new set of negotiations on investment.

Industry Canada (Canada's Department of Commerce) says that the GATS is first and foremost an instrument for the benefit of business. Dean O'Hare, chair of the Coalition of Service Industries, told a U.S. Congressional committee that the GATS can encourage more privatization, particularly in the field of health care. The European Commission says in a guide to the GATS that the agreement reflects WTO members' basic belief in deregulation.

Although WTO officials deny that proposals in the new GATS will require wholesale deregulation, they do acknowledge that GATS 2000 would constrain government's regulatory authority. "The GATS imposes constraints, however, on the use of unnecessarily restrictive or discriminatory requirements in scheduled sectors," says a 1997 paper, "Economic Effects of Services Liberation," published by the WTO Secretariat. "Governments may thus be required to complement market-opening measures with a review of domestic regulation."

The WTO Secretariat also agrees that commitments to privatize and deregulate under GATS are nearly irreversible. In the Secretariat's words, "bindings undertaken in the GATS have the effect of protecting liberalization policies, regardless of their underlying rationale, from slippages and reversals."

—Ellen Gould
is a Vancouver researcher
and GATS analyst

technological or other considerations. This matches existing WTO rules related to the trade in goods.

- Restrict further the use of government funds for public works, municipal services and social programs. By imposing the WTO's national treatment rules on both government procurement and subsidies, the new negotiations seek to impede governments from making public funds available only for public services, to the exclusion of foreign-based, private service corporations.

- Accelerate the process of providing service companies with guaranteed access to domestic markets in all sectors—including education, health and water— by permitting them to establish their commercial presence in another country. These rules would hold that, since provision of a service may require an in-country presence (as contrasted to goods, which can always be shipped), foreign service corporations must be permitted to invest and open shop in GATS member countries.

THE INDUSTRY LOBBY

The chief beneficiaries of this new GATS regime are a breed of corporate service providers determined to expand their global commercial reach and to turn public services into private markets all over the world. Service corporations view health, education and water each as trillion-dollar-plus annual markets.

Driving the GATS agenda are powerful lobby machines like the U.S. Coalition of Service Industries (USCSI), which specifically claims credit for establishing the agenda for GATS 2000. The USCSI is composed of major corporate players with vested interests in securing global markets for their service products including electronic entertainment and telecommunications giants AOL Time-Warner, AT&T and IBM; energy and water enterprises like Enron and Vivendi Universal; financial empires like Citigroup, Bank America and J.P. Morgan Chase; investment houses like Goldman Sachs and General Electric Financial; health insurance companies like the Chubb Group; management and consultant firms like KPMG and PriceWaterhouse Coopers; and express delivery services like United Parcel Service and Federal Express.

The USCSI is further fortified in its lobbying actions by both the European Services Forum and the Japan Services Network, which represent similar corporate service providers who want access to global markets. The European big business coalition is comprised of 47 corporations providing for-profit services in several key sectors. These include major banking institutions like Barclays PLC and Commerzbank AG; telecommunications giants such as British Telecom, Telefonica and Deutsche Telekom AG;

water giants including Vivendi and Suez-Lyonnaise des Eaux; health insurance companies like the AXA Group and CGNU (CGU plus Norwich Union); financial consultants/accounting firms such as Arthur Andersen Consulting and PriceWaterhouse Coopers; publishing and entertainment conglomerates like Bertelsmann; plus brand name empires such as Daimler-Chrysler Services and Marks and Spencer PLC. The head of the newly formed Japan Services Network is the CEO of the Mitsubishi Corporation.

If these big business coalitions get their way, the GATS 2000 agenda will amount to a frontal attack on the collective and individual rights of people that are enshrined in the United Nations Universal Declaration of Human Rights and its accompanying Covenants and Charters. Not only will foreign-based, for-profit corporations be able to access public dollars to take over public hospitals and schools, but regulations on health and education standards will be undermined by global trade rules under the WTO. Chains of foreign-based, for-profit corporations will be able to invade the child care, social security and prison systems in all WTO member countries. Foreign-based corporations will gain rights to bid for municipal contracts for construction, sewage, garbage disposal, sanitation, tourism and water services.

For many Third World countries, this invasion of peoples' basic rights is not new. During the past two decades or more, the structural adjustment programs of the International Monetary Fund and the World Bank have been used to force many governments in the South to dismantle their public services and allow foreign-based healthcare, education and water corporations to provide services on a for-profit basis. Under the proposed GATS rules, developing countries will experience a further dis-

mantling of local service providers, restrictions on the buildup of domestic service providers, and the creation of new monopolies dominated by corporate service providers based in the North.

The WTO will convene a stocktaking session at the end of March 2001 to clarify the negotiating positions of the member countries along with the rules and guidelines for the GATS negotiations. Following this stocktaking session, formal negotiations are expected to begin and continue for roughly another two years or so.

WTO chief Michael Moore has been issuing public warnings in Washington, D.C. and the capitals of other major industrialized countries about the dangers of the GATS becoming the target of a citizen campaign. As civil society groups begin to mount their campaigns to "Stop the GATS Attack," the WTO is calling on member governments and their corporate allies to become vigorously engaged in publicly defending the GATS.

As the chair of the U.S. Coalition on Services, Dean R. O'Hare (who is also CEO of the Chubb health insurance consortium), put it in his presentation to a European Services Forum conference on GATS 2000: "We have to do more to counter those who have distorted the issues and threaten to roll back the benefits of freer trade. As we saw in Seattle, and at the IMF meetings in Washington and Prague, ... those opposed to open trade are strongly mobilized. We can't any longer expect to be able to win our case in private closed meetings with governments. We have to convince wider publics."

Tony Clarke is the director of the Polaris Institute in Ottawa, Canada. He is the co-author (with Maude Barlow) of Global Showdown: How the New Activists Are Fighting Global Corporate Rule.

From *Multinational Monitor*, April 2001, pp. 14-16. © 2001 by Multinational Monitor. Reprinted by permission.

ANALYZING AND MANAGING COUNTRY RISKS

Uncertainty can't be eliminated from the business environment,
but as this author points out, it can be managed
by transforming it into planned uncertainty.

BY DAVID W. CONKLIN

Evaluating country risks is a crucial exercise when choosing sites for international business, particularly if investment is to be undertaken. Certain risks can be managed through insurance, hedging and other types of financial planning, but other risks cannot be controlled through such financial mechanisms. Some of these latter risks may be measured in a risk-return analysis, with some countries' risks requiring higher returns to justify the higher risks. The study of country risks is also necessary in order to develop alternative scenarios: Uncertainty may remain, but it can be transformed into planned uncertainty, with no surprises and with contingency plans in place.

Each corporation confronts a unique set of country risks. As a result, this article does not prescribe a common formula. Rather, it discusses the many issues and analytical frameworks a business should examine as it develops its own evaluation of country risks and creates its own strategy to manage the uncertainties those risks entail. Fortunately, a great deal of relevant information is available on the Internet, and this article points to a number of helpful Web sites.

POLITICAL RISKS

Prior to the 1990s, the political risks associated with interventionist governments were considerable. They included government expropriation, regulations that imposed inefficiencies, and foreign-investment restrictions. Many countries pursued the goal of economic self-sufficiency through extensive tariff and non-tariff barriers to both trade and investment. Bribery often influenced government decisions. In many countries today, such political risk has been reduced and replaced by a new acceptance of free markets and a belief that international trade and investment are the bases for economic growth. Nevertheless, political risks still remain. The Index of Economic Freedom ranks countries according to the impact that political intervention has on business decisions, while the Corruption Perception Index indicates the extent of corruption in each of 91 countries. To the degree that a government has the power to regulate and intervene in matters that affect businesses, bureaucrats may be tempted to provide the desired approvals in return for bribes. As a result, these indexes can be closely related.

The Index of Economic Freedom, which must be considered in a risk-return analysis, points to the various ways in which a government may take away potential profits. The Corruption Perception Index warns that doing business in certain countries will require clear corporate practices for bribery, ranging from enforcing a zero-bribery policy, to permitting specific types of "gifts," to authorizing a local partner to undertake certain "assistance" activities for those in power. Canadian and U.S. legislation on foreign corrupt practices must be considered. Furthermore, new control and audit practices may have to be implemented to operate in a culture where corruption is common, and where employees may therefore

Index of Economic Freedom

see www.fraserinstitute.ca, *and* heritage.org/index

"The index comprises 23 components designed to identify how consistent institutional arrangements and policies in seven major areas are with economic freedom. The seven areas covered by the index are: 1) size of government, 2) economic structure and use of markets, 3) monetary policy and price stability, 4) freedom to use alternative currencies, 5) legal structure and security of private ownership, 6) freedom to trade with foreigners, and 7) freedom of exchange in capital markets.

Areas 1 and 2 are indicators of reliance on markets rather than the political process (large government expenditures, state-operated enterprises, price controls, and discriminatory practices) to allocate resources and determine the distribution of income. Areas 3 and 4 reflect the availability of sound money. Area 5 focuses on the legal security of property rights and the enforcement of contracts. Area 6 indicates the consistency of policies with free trade. Area 7 is a measure of the degree to which markets are used to allocate capital. Reliance on markets, sound money, legal protection of property rights, free trade, and market allocation of capital are important elements of economic freedom captured by the index."

Corruption Perception Index (CPI)

see www.transparency.org

"This year's index, published by the world's leading non-governmental organisation fighting corruption, ranks 91 countries. Some of the richest countries in the world—Finland, Denmark, New Zealand, Iceland, Singapore and Sweden—scored 9 or higher out of a clean score of 10 in the new CPI, indicating very low levels of perceived corruption. But 55 countries—many of which are among the world's poorest—scored less than 5, suggesting high levels of perceived corruption in government and public administration. The CPI, which Transparency International first launched in 1995, is a poll of polls, this year drawing on 14 surveys from seven independent institutions. The surveys reflect the perceptions of business people, academics and country analysts."

not automatically adhere to the standards of honesty expected by the corporation.

For natural resource sectors, in particular, political risk may still be a showstopper, since the risk of nationalization, special taxes or new regulations is particularly severe. Managers in these sectors must consider whether the risks may be too high to justify investment. It remains helpful to seek the views of local political experts. One technique involves circulating a questionnaire to these experts, compiling the results, and returning them to the respondents for further commentary. This "Delphi" technique facilitates the development of a consensus view on the political risks that a potential investor faces.

Home-country political risks

Analyzing and managing political risks has become important even when doing business in one's home country. It is not automatically true that country risks are greater abroad than they are in Canada. Inco's experience with delays in its Voisey Bay project—the result of environmental objections, the advocacy of aboriginal rights and the issue of government taxes—has involved consider-

able difficulties compared with the relatively easy approval for mining projects in many less developed countries. When the question of Quebec's secession is added to these political risks, many Canadian corporations may conclude that political risks in Canada exceed those in many other countries. In this respect, certain less-developed countries may offer a competitive advantage.

Managing political risks

International investment agreements attempt to limit political risks. Both Canada and the United States have signed investment agreements with many other countries that promise financial compensation for corporations based in Canada or the U.S. if their assets are expropriated. These agreements promise that the amount of compensation will be determined in a fair and just manner. Under NAFTA's Chapter 11, corporations can sue a NAFTA government on the grounds that they have been denied "fair and equitable treatment" in a way that is tantamount to expropriation. However, it is not clear how far Chapter 11 or other investment agreements go in protecting corporations from new government regulations that increase costs or restrict prices. The Enron dilemma in India illustrates the potential seriousness of political risks.

Political risk insurance may be purchased as additional protection against specific outcomes such as capital repatriation difficulties, expropriation, or war and insurrection. Canada's Export Development Corporation offers credit insurance for many such risks.

Economic risks

Economic risks may be particularly important in regard to exchange rates, economic volatility, industry structure and international competitiveness.

Exchange rate risks

In recent years, the risk of foreign exchange rate movements has become a paramount consideration, as has the risk that a government may simply lack the economic capacity to repay its loans. Many countries have been experiencing ongoing fiscal deficits and rapid money-supply growth. Consequently, inflation rates remain high in these countries, and devaluation crises appear from time to time. A devaluation of one country's exchange rate automatically creates pressure for devaluation in other countries' exchange rates. Competitive domino devaluation pressures are intensified because of the reliance of many countries on primary product exports and their price volatility.

The Enron Dilemma

Enron invested heavily in the construction of a power plant in India where its sole client was the Maharashtra State Electricity Board (MSEB). Enron believed that its contract with MSEB outlined a clear agreement for determining the rates that it could charge. When Enron completed the plant and began to sell electricity, the MSEB refused to pay Enron's rates. The position of MSEB has been that the rates are much higher than those charged by other power producers. At this point, Enron is attempting to gain the support of the U.S. government in arguing that these price restrictions are tantamount to expropriation.

Recent crises—especially the Asian crisis of 1997, the Mexican devaluation of 1994, and the Russian crisis of 1993—have created a new risk of heightened foreign exchange volatility for some countries. Today exchange rates may be maintained at unrealistically high levels as a result of considerable inflows of foreign capital. Yet, these capital inflows may slow or even reverse abruptly. Foreign investors now recognize these risks of foreign exchange volatility. In the future, capital flows will be more sensitive to changes in each country's financial system and general economic conditions than they have been in the past. Future surges in capital flows may translate into increased volatility of foreign exchange rates for some countries.

Competitiveness Ranking

see www.imd.ch/wcy

"The World Competitiveness Yearbook 2001 (WCY), measures the extent to which countries provide an environment that sustains companies' competitiveness. The analysis covers 49 countries. Of the 286 criteria, which are covered by the WCY, many are structural and thus evolve slowly over time. The development of technological infrastructure, the efficiency of government administration, the quality of education or the productivity of the workforce are competitive factors that cannot be altered overnight. It can safely be argued that the dynamic competitive relationships between nations are less volatile than individual national economic performances.

The 2001 edition has been improved with a simplified organization of the 286 criteria into four factors: Economic Performance, Government Efficiency, Business Efficiency and Infrastructure."

But how can foreign investors protect themselves from these exchange rate risks? Hedging mechanisms offer some hope for reducing foreign exchange risks, though generally not without some cost. Here are some other ways managers can cope with these country risks:

1. Consider the timing of your investments. Investors should restrict capital transfers to a country to those times when the foreign exchange rate is in equilibrium. The theory of "Purchasing Power Parity" provides a guide to likely exchange rate changes. Compare a country's cumulative inflation over a number of years with the cumulative inflation rate of its major trade partners. If the difference in cumulative inflation rates exceeds the percentage change in the foreign exchange rate, then devaluation is a real possibility. For example, this calculation would suggest that the Mexican peso is currently substantially overvalued.

2. Borrow domestically to do business domestically and avoid foreign exchange rate exposure. Keep in mind that this approach does expose the business to the possibility of interest rate increases as a result of a central bank's response to foreign exchange rate devaluation. For a foreign-owned financial institution, this approach also involves the possibility of a "run" on deposits, as the depositors seek to withdraw funds in order to transfer them abroad.

3. Focus on the devaluation risk when choosing among countries as investment sites. From this per-

spective, Chile is currently a less risky region for investment than Argentina or Mexico.

4. Consider the amount of capital required by those activities that are being developed in a country subject to devaluation risk. The significance of a foreign exchange risk may be relatively low for a business that requires little capital investment, like one in the service sector or fast-food industry; it may be high for a firm in the manufacturing and natural resource sectors, where considerable capital is required.

5. Spread the purchase price over as long a time period as possible. This allows domestic currency to be purchased at a lower cost if devaluation occurs. Alternatively, gear the purchase price to a weighted average of the exchange rate over future years, with projected future payments adjusted in accordance with the exchange rate.

Risks of economic volatility

Economic stability depends upon a strong banking sector; without it, a foreign exchange crisis may have a particularly severe impact. An ongoing challenge for financial institutions everywhere is that the time profile for liabilities is not the same as the one for assets. Banks borrow short-term from depositors and lend long-term. This exposes the banks to the risks that fixed assets may fall quickly in price and that depositors may make sudden withdrawals. With dramatic reductions in land and stock prices, bank loans made on the security of real estate and stocks suddenly may be at a major risk of default, further exacerbating the effects of a foreign exchange crisis, and transforming it into a general crisis in the economy.

Industry risks

Managers must analyze the domestic situation for industry risks such as the strength of competitors, the potential for substitutes, the capabilities of suppliers and customers, and the risk of new entrants. It may be helpful to determine the risk level by developing a matrix in which each industry risk is evaluated as minor, serious or "show-stopping," and in which the various ways of mitigating each risk are analyzed. For many foreign corporations, one example of industry risk may be the difficulty in finding suppliers who can offer the required level of quality and service. Public utility disruptions may also be risky, especially for firms dealing in perishable commodities. (In some countries, for example, electricity outages are common.) For some Canadian corporations, one solution has been to encourage other Canadian or U.S. suppliers to open a business in the same locality. For others, the construction of one's own utilities, such as power supply, is a solution to the risk of electricity outages. Such actions may serve to strengthen

a corporation's domestic competitive advantage. Further, the process of developing a matrix of industry risks leads to strategies and solutions unique to each country and, indeed, to regions within countries as well.

Competitiveness risks

It will always be necessary for managers to consider a country's competitiveness factors when making investment decisions. For example, Latin American countries continue to rank poorly in international surveys of such factors; labour-intensive export facilities should likely be located in other regions of the world, despite Latin America's lower wage levels. Findings in the World Competitiveness Yearbook provide some critical data on the competitiveness factors of 49 countries.

Intra-country economic risks

Managers would do well to consider risk differences within each country. Many countries contain a high-growth region with strong competitive attributes. For some industries, Mexico's U.S. border region and Monterrey could be regarded as a part of the U.S. economy rather than the Mexican economy, since a major portion of trade and investment is cross-border.

LINKING POLITICAL AND ECONOMIC RISKS

In many countries, bank loans have been granted as favours to political leaders and their friends, often without due diligence. The 1997 Asian foreign exchange crisis revealed that a very high percentage of bank loans were non-performing. As a result, many Asian banks had a negative net worth and financial systems were in disarray. A democratic political system generally does not experience the spread of a foreign exchange crisis to its financial sector and its general economy, since politicians are accountable to the public. Both the opposition and the media bring bank loans that have been given for political affiliation to the public's attention. For some countries, this has not been the case. Unless there is a basic shift in the political paradigm, such financial-sector disasters may occur again. Economic reform requires political reform.

The Asian economies may again become precarious if the difficult situation faced by China's banks worsens, the result of large political loans to now-suffering state-owned enterprises. The development of alternative financial instruments could result in a reduction in deposits at domestic Chinese banks. Hence, the liberalization of the Chinese financial sector, combined with the growth of the stock exchange and the expansion of foreign banks, could lead to the collapse of the country's domestic financial sector. Here, a change in the political system with new fi-

Economist Intelligence Unit: Country Risk Assessment

see www.eiu.com

"The Country Risk Service's risk ratings methodology examines risk from two distinct perspectives: 1) broad categories of risk grouped under the headings of political, economic policy, economic structure and liquidity factors; and 2) risk exposure associated with investing in particular types of financial instruments, namely specific investment risk. The latter includes risk associated with accepting foreign-exchange exposure against the U.S. dollar, foreign-currency loans to sovereigns and foreign-currency loans to banks. The model operates by asking the EIU's country expert to answer a series of quantitative and qualitative questions on recent and expected political and economic trends in the relevant country.

Four types of general political and macroeconomic risk (political, economic policy, economic structure and liquidity) are assessed independently of their association with a particular investment vehicle. The factors in each risk category are given a letter grade. These scores are the basis for compiling an overall score and rating for the country. This overall country risk assessment can be used for making a general assessment of the risk of a crisis in the country's financial markets, where foreign investors may have exposure. It is also useful for investors wishing to obtain a quick view of the generalised risk of investing in the country or for those investing in the country in an investment vehicle which is not expressly covered in our specific investment risk categories."

Opacity Index

see www.opacity index.com

"PricewaterhouseCooper's Global Index measures the impact of business, economic, legal and ethical opacity on the cost of capital around the world.

The first Opacity Index report looks at the impact of opacity from two perspectives—firstly, its impact as a form of hidden corporate tax, and secondly as a risk premium when countries borrow through sovereign bond issuance. Looked at from the tax perspective, for example, the impact of reducing Colombia's opacity score to the level of Singapore's would have the same effect on domestic and international investment as a 25 per cent cut in corporate tax rates.

Expressing opacity as a risk premium on sovereign borrowing is equally compelling since countries with more opaque practices generally need to reward investors by paying them a premium over what the United States (the benchmark) pays."

nancial accountability for state-owned enterprises is necessary before a sound financial system can emerge.

Many commentators have argued that future growth in Japan and Korea will depend on the restructuring of corporate organizations, with a breakup of the conglomerates that have dominated many Asian economies. Only with such a dismantling of huge organizations will entrepreneurial initiative and innovation be released. Closing businesses that are suffering ongoing losses or even restructuring such businesses will require clearer lines of responsibility and ownership. Furthermore, bankruptcy laws will need to be rewritten in order to achieve such restructuring.

Changes in trade and investment agreements can substantially change the economic conditions under which a corporation operates. A notable example today is China's entry into the WTO, which will require the country to cut its tariffs significantly and to eliminate many of its restrictions on foreign ownership. Foreign corporations that invested in China prior to WTO membership may suddenly face much less expensive import competition; those required to accept a joint venture partnership with a state-owned enterprise will face competition from new foreign wholly owned subsidiaries. In managing country risks that involve linkages among various political and economic forces, a particularly helpful Web site is the Economist Intelligence Unit. The site offers analyses of broad categories of risk as well as risk exposure associated with specific types of investment.

COUNTRY RISK STRATEGIES

For corporations that are searching for foreign suppliers and customers, as well as those that are evaluating investment opportunities, the analysis of country risks has attained a new importance and a new complexity. More careful differentiation among countries and business sectors is now required. For example, instead of viewing Southeast Asia as a group of tigers that have been involved in an economic miracle and subsequent downfall, it is now necessary to carefully analyze the situation that each individual country faces.

Managers should prepare themselves accordingly with an analysis of interest rates and stock prices, the country's balance of payments, projections of probable macroeconomic policies, and fiscal and current-account deficits. It is important to examine alternative potential scenarios and projections, and assign probabilities to each scenario in order to determine the risks and rewards connected with particular business opportunities. PricewaterhouseCoopers has developed an index that indicates how one may quantify the impact of country risks in terms of equivalent tax rates and rates of return.

The events of September 11 and the subsequent conflicts have added another dimension to country risk. How to preserve the personal security of employees has gained new prominence in corporate strategies. Here, significant differences exist among countries, as some appear to be experiencing a heightened antipathy towards foreigners. Specific plans for protection and exit must be based on an analysis of each country.

The relative significance of various country risks differs from one corporation to another, depending on features such as the type of business activity, experience in managing a certain risk, and financial strength. Hence, each corporation has to develop its unique country risk strategies. In the context of globalization, the New Economy and the changing role of governments, the analysis and management of country risks is now of paramount importance.

DAVID W. CONKLIN IS THE JAMES D. FLECK PROFESSOR OF INTERNATIONAL BUSINESS AT THE RICHARD IVEY SCHOOL OF BUSINESS.

From *Ivey Business Journal*, January/February 2002, pp. 37-41. © 2002 by Ivey Management Services. Reprinted by permission.

NAFTA

THE HIGHEST COURT YOU'VE NEVER HEARD OF

Do NAFTA judges have too much authority?

When a Mississippi jury slapped a $500 million judgment on Loewen Group, a Canadian funeral-home chain, in 1995 for breaching a contract with a hometown rival, the company quickly settled the case for $129 million but then decided to appeal. But instead of going to a U.S. court, the Canadians took their case to an obscure three-judge panel that stands distinctly apart from the U.S. legal system. And that panel's decision cannot be appealed.

Thanks to some fine print in the 1994 North American Free Trade Agreement, the case of *Loewen Group vs. the U.S.* is just one of two dozen wending their way through a little-known and highly secretive process. The panels, using arbitration procedures established by the World Bank, were supposed to ensure that governments in the U.S., Mexico, and Canada would pay compensation to any foreign investor whose property they might seize. U.S. business groups originally demanded the investor-protection mechanism, noting that the Mexican government had a history of nationalizing its oil, electricity, and banking industries, including many U.S. assets.

But even some of NAFTA's strongest supporters say that clever and creative lawyers in all three countries are rapidly expanding the anti-expropriation clause in unanticipated ways. "The question in a lot of these pending cases is, will the panels produce a pattern of decisions that the negotiators never envisioned?" says Charles E. Roh Jr., deputy chief U.S. negotiator for NAFTA, now a partner at Weil, Gotshal & Manges LLC Some of the early indications, he says, "are troubling."

In one case, a NAFTA panel issued an interpretation of the Mexican Constitution, an authority the NAFTA negotiators hadn't intended to give the panel. In the dispute, a California waste disposal company, Metalclad Corp., was awarded $16.7 million by a NAFTA tribunal after the governor of the state of San Luis Potosi and a town council refused the company a permit to open a toxic waste site. The company had asked for $90 million in damages, insisting that the state and local governments had overstepped their authority.

The majority of the cases are yet to be decided, but the NAFTA panels are controversial nonetheless. For one thing, they are already pitting environmentalists and federal, state, and local government regulators in all three countries against multinationals. The basic disagreement: Business groups want to include NAFTA's strongest investor-protection provisions in all future free-trade agreements, while many environmentalists would like to scrap the entire procedure as an impediment to government regulatory action. The cases are also complicating efforts to negotiate free-trade agreements with Chile and the hemispheric, 34-nation Free Trade Area of the Americas.

Washington's problem: While such panels may favor U.S. businesses abroad, foreign plaintiffs would enjoy the same such privileges in the U.S. And that could end up giving them protections against regulations far beyond those domestic companies enjoy in their own courts. What's more, states and municipalities have also warned that their ability to govern is being compromised by "a new set of foreign investor rights."

In some cases, the NAFTA suits seek damages for government decisions that are clearly legal but can be questioned under vague notions of international law. For example, a Canadian chemical company, Methanex Corp., bypassed U.S. courts to challenge California's ban on a health-threatening gasoline additive, MTBE, that has been polluting municipal wells and reservoirs. In its $970 million claim, the Canadian company said California Governor Gray Davis had been influenced in his decision by a $150,000 campaign contribution from U.S.-based Archer Daniels Midland Co., the maker of a rival gasoline additive. The campaign contribution was legal, but Methanex' lawyers argued that the Davis decision was "palpably unfair and inequitable" because of ADM's influence. Such an argument wouldn't likely work in a U.S. court.

A GROWING CASELOAD

A sampling of the NAFTA panel's docket

UPS OF AMERICA VS. CANADA
UPS claims that Canada Post, the state-owned postal system, uses its monopoly on letter mail to gain an unfair advantage in parcel deliveries

LOEWEN GROUP VS. U.S.
Canadian funeral home chain says a Mississippi jury erred in awarding $500 million to a local funeral home operator in a contract breach case

METHANEX VS. U.S.
The Canadian manufacturer of a gasoline additive sued after California found the health-threatening chemical had contaminated water, and banned its use

METALCLAD VS. MEXICO
U.S. company sued after it obtained permits from the Mexican federal government for a waste disposal site, then localities denied a permit to operate

Data: *BusinessWeek*

No laws can be overturned by the panel, but the cost of defending against a NAFTA lawsuit may run so high that it could still deter agencies from imposing strict regulations on foreign companies, critics charge. They point to a decision by Canada not to restrict cigarette marketing after Ottawa was threatened with a NAFTA case by U.S. tobacco companies. In another potentially intimidating move, United Parcel Service Inc. is seeking $160 million in damages from Canada, arguing that the state-owned Canadian postal system, Canada Post, maintains a monopoly on first-class mail and delivers parcels with private Canadian partners.

But right now, the Loewen case is the one in the spotlight. The Mississippi trial was so theatrical that Warner Bros. Inc. and film director Ron Howard have acquired the movie rights, according to attorneys in the case. Canadian funeral chain founder Ray Loewen was vilified as a foreigner, a "gouger of grieving families," an owner of a large yacht, a racist, a customer of foreign banks, and greedy besides, according to the transcript. Yet the State Supreme Court refused to waive the appeal bond, which had been set at $625 million—to be posted in 10 days. (The largest previous verdict in the state had been $18 million.) Loewen filed for bankruptcy protection in 1999 but is hopeful that the imminent NAFTA ruling will revive the company.

Although many of the current cases raise questions, business groups insist that NAFTA-like panels are needed in all trade deals because so many developing nations have poor judicial systems. But they allow that the process may still need some tweaking. "Of course, if I look at the filed cases so far, I could write a pretty scary story," says Scott Miller, a Washington lobbyist for Procter & Gamble Co. And Eric Biehl, a former top Commerce Dept. official, who supports NAFTA, wonders, "how does some mechanism on a trade agreement that no one ever thought much about suddenly get used to open up a whole new appellate process around the U.S. judicial system?" That's a question a lot more people may soon be asking.

By Paul Magnusson in Washington

Reprinted from the April 1, 2002 issue of *Business Week,* pp. 76-77 by special permission. © 2002 by the McGraw-Hill Companies, Inc.

EUROPE

THE WORLD ACCORDING TO MONTI

Europe's competition czar isn't afraid to take on
U.S. giants like Microsoft—or the Justice Dept.

Mario Monti—judge, jury, and executioner all rolled into one. That's how many bosses of American multinationals view the courtly Italian who heads the European Union's Competition Commission. Europe's antitrust chief rocked the industrial world last summer when he shot down the proposed $42 billion merger between General Electric Co. and Honeywell International Inc. But that could just be a warm-up act for Monti, who now has his sights set on another American behemoth, Microsoft.

Mario Monti
BORN
Mar. 19, 1943, in Varese, north of Milan.
ACADEMIC LIFE
Earned degree in economics and management from Bocconi University in 1965. Appointed professor of monetary theory in 1971, rising to rector and president. Studied economics at Yale University in 1968–69.
REFORMER
Helped draft Italy's first law on competition and was a key player in banking reform.
EU POSTS
Commissioner for Internal Market, 1995–99; Commissioner for Competition, 1999–2004.

Data: *BusinessWeek*

Yes, even if the U.S. Justice Dept. finally pushes through a settlement of its four-year-old case against Microsoft Corp., Monti is prepared to jump in this summer with his own ruling on a similar case. And the Brussels regulator packs plenty of punch. If he finds that Microsoft

gouges customers or stiffs rivals, he can fine the software giant up to 10% of annual revenue—or $2.5 billion—or even force the company to hand over the keys to the source code of its Windows operating system. Add it up, and not only is Monti ready to blast away at American icons, he does not shrink from battles with the Justice Dept.

EU PARLIAMENT
Monti wields more brute influence than most elected officials

But to put an American slant on Monti's moves is far too simple. Yes, the formal, soft-spoken Italian arguably wields more brute influence than any elected politician in Europe. But here's the twist: Monti is the closest thing in Europe to a free-market zealot. He praises the "greater dynamism" of the U.S., and he's busy using his formidable power to push Europe along the same path.

In truth, Monti wreaks far more havoc in the Old World than in the New with his push for reform. Just ask German Chancellor Gerhard Schröder. In late February, Monti pushed Schröder to dismantle Volkswagen's takeover defenses—a move the Chancellor vows to resist. Days later, Monti and his fellow commissioners used the EU's national governments, which are bucking Brussels' mandates to cut state subsidies. And last year when he found DaimlerChrysler guilty of price manipulations, he fined the car company $65 million.

Monti's case is piled high with paradox. The 59-year-old Italian, for decades an economics professor at Milan's Bocconi University, favors free enterprise. But he pushes for it by using the biggest of big governments, a Brussels bureaucracy that operates largely by decree. He regularly dispatches investigative hit squads to make dawn raids on companies he's investigating for overcharging consumers, from cell-phone giant Vodafone Group PLC to Coca-Cola Co. Search warrants? A signature from Monti will suffice.

What's more, Monti has never held elected office and claims disdain for partisan jostling. Yet he finds himself at the heart of two vital political dramas. One involves nothing less than establishing a central government in Europe. In the other, he's working to make Europe's role as a referee for global antitrust equal to that of the U.S. Both jobs require political smarts and a knack for dealmaking. Yet the upright Monti, who associates negotiations with the sly nods and winks of politics in his native Italy, runs the other way. "It's his reluctance to negotiate that gives him such a scary reputation," says Alec Burnside, a partner at the Brussels office of Linklaters & Alliance, a London law firm. Adds a leading Italian CEO: "He acts like a high priest." Monti's political greenness, and some priestly inflexibility, may have gotten him into trouble in the GE case. The result was a rift between the U.S. Justice Dept. and Monti's European team.

Washington's Worries—and Monti's Defense

WASHINGTON COMPLAINT: Monti favors competitors over consumers.

MONTI: *That's a false dichotomy. More competition is good for consumers.*

WASHINGTON: While Washington must prepare every antitrust case for court, Monti can rule by fiat, with few checks and balances.

MONTI: *The Competition Commissioner has to convince other commissioners and member states. And the European court has teeth, though it takes up cases years after the decision.*

WASHINGTON: Monti's staff is packed with zealous career regulators who have never worked in the private sector.

MONTI: *Yes, but they're smart, they're pros, and—with the exception of GE-Honeywell—they've worked harmoniously with Washington.*

WASHINGTON: Monti wants to hijack global antitrust, establishing European standards.

MONTI: *Nonsense. The heritage of antitrust is American, and despite occasional differences, Europe is moving toward the U.S. norms.*

WASHINGTON: Monti is anti-business.

MONTI: *Preposterous. From his university post in Milan, he was long a leading advocate of free markets in an Italian economy dominated by the state. He has served on the boards of leading companies, from Fiat to Generali.*

WASHINGTON: Monti ignores economic analysis, tending to fall for worst-case scenarios.

MONTI: *Why would an economist ignore economics? True, the analysis came out differently in GE-Honeywell, but in 98% of the cases, Washington and Brussels agree.*

Data: *BusinessWeek*

The commissioner, of course, rejects any notion of such political calculations. What's more, he insists that he got the GE case right. He ruled that by leveraging its broad portfolio, which extends from finance to jet engines, the combined company could have achieved a dangerous dominance in Europe's market. This so-called portfolio theory is widely dismissed in America. But Monti stuck to it, and impassioned arguments by GE CEO Jack Welch failed to sway him.

Now, even some Monti admirers say that the commissioner got locked into a theoretical corner by eager staffers, and then lacked the savvy to extricate himself. "He's very moderate and thoughtful, which made it all the more surprising that he blew up the GE deal," says Robert Pitofsky, chairman of the Federal Trade Commission under Clinton. A Brussels lawyer adds: "He regrets the GE decision every day."

Monti denies this. But his frustration is all too clear. It was GE-Honeywell alone that established his reputation as a maverick, one who was willing to embrace ideas long discredited among the antitrust Establishment in America. "Ninety-eight percent of the time, we agree [with the U.S.]," Monti says. "If you have the most respected CEO in the world complaining vociferously, it's hard to get a balanced picture." The question now is whether, with the Microsoft case, he's willing to stir up another transatlantic storm.

It's true, as Monti notes, that the European case is slightly different from the American one, which focused largely on Internet browsers. Brussels, by contrast, is investigating whether Microsoft is illegally using its dominance of desktop systems to extend into network software and multimedia systems, two pillars of the Internet. Microsoft denies the charges, and argues that rivals such as Sun Microsystems are simply targeting Microsoft in Brussels, where court and administrative costs are low.

For now, Monti appears eager to smooth relations with Washington. He has proposed changes in Europe's competition rules to bring them closer in line with Washington's. The guessing in Brussels is that the Commissioner, eager to get to work on the European economy and reluctant to lock horns with U.S. regulators, may swerve from a head-on collision over Microsoft. What might work?

Perhaps Monti will force Microsoft to share design work earlier, or hit Microsoft, which has $38 billion in cash, with a fine. The case should be closed by summer.

Fact is, reforms in Europe are far closer to Monti's heart. He's threatening Europe's phone companies to slash mobile roaming fees and to open up their phone lines to competitors. He's looking into beer sales and sports television contracts. He may take a giant Electricité de France in his push to open Europe's energy markets.

More than two decades ago, Monti as a young free-market economist traveled to London for a private audience with Margaret Thatcher. Now, until his term ends in 2004, he has a chance to extend a Thatcher-like jolt to all of Europe. And the speculation that Monti would return home to Italian politics? Get serious! After this high-voltage tour in Europe's capital, for Mario Monti even the top job in Italy would probably feel like a demotion.

By Stephen Baker in Brussels, with Gail Edmondson in Milan and Dan Carney in Washington.

Reprinted from the March 25, 2002 issue of *Business Week,* pp. 48, 50 by special permission. © 2002 by the McGraw-Hill Companies, Inc.

International Alliance Negotiations: Legal Issues for General Managers

Élise Campbell and Jeffrey J. Reuer

Let's negotiate a strategic alliance. For the sake of simplicity, let's create a hypothetical equity joint venture (JV) between two partners of different nationalities and with roughly equal bargaining positions. The vehicle we shall use for this collaboration is to be a new business entity in which both partners take equity positions. We shall assume that the two partners have already agreed to go ahead with the alliance and have widely considered the strategic and financial implications of doing so. Their agreement currently exists in outline form only, possibly as a Memorandum of Understanding (MOU) or based on an oral understanding and a handshake. The partners have agreed to put into place a contract to cover the details of the alliance, and this contract is to be negotiated and drafted with the assistance of lawyers.

All strategic alliances are not alike. But many of the legal aspects of negotiating them are. From picking a partner to the final handshake, know the ins and outs.

In establishing the JV, key clauses are to be negotiated that set out the scope of the agreement and the partners' obligations to each other. Major establishment issues to be considered include initial discussions, setting up the JV, the parties and framework of contract, performance clauses, restrictions on the partners, and liability. Following establishment of the JV will be contractual changes, dispute resolution, share disposal, and alliance termination. Here we shall discuss all of these issues, as well as explore the negotiation process itself by considering the identity and role of negotiators and the interaction between managers and their lawyers.

Several caveats should be kept in mind from the outset. First, many of these same considerations would also apply to nonequity alliances, except for such issues as those surrounding the disposal of shares and so on. And even though the presence of more than two partners increases the complexity of the deal structure and the negotiations, the basic principles are nonetheless similar.

Second, the issues and views contained here are not a substitute for legal advice. Naturally, opinions differ among lawyers, and the legal and negotiation issues to be laid out here are introductory and illustrative in nature rather than being exhaustive or applicable in all alliance contexts. Rather, the intention is to raise general managers' awareness of some of the salient issues and concerns that arise during the course of alliance negotiations.

ESTABLISHMENT ISSUES

There are two main aspects of initial discussions or approaches to potential partners that could have legal implications. The first is that, though not always effective in practice, a confidentiality agreement or nondisclosure agreement (NDA) may be desirable for protecting both companies. This could be combined with "lockout" provisions that prevent one of the companies from conducting parallel negotiations with a competitor.

The second aspect concerns the need to ensure that a legally binding contract is not accidentally entered into at too early a stage. An MOU and even simple oral discussions can be legally binding, unless clearly agreed that they are not and that they are "subject to contract." It may be advisable to involve lawyers, at least behind the scenes, before any document, including an MOU, is signed. Even if not legally binding, outline terms agreed to at the outset can be commercially difficult to retreat from at a later stage.

Setting Up the Joint Venture

It is not always the case that a separate JV company is formed with both partners taking shares in it. However, this setup will often be preferred if the collaboration is large in relative terms and involves multiple functional activities or projects, or if partners desire the control and performance incentives provided by equity JVs. Establishing a separate company for the collaboration is also a method of limiting the liability of the new venture as well as facilitating the exit of one partner or the sale of the JV in its entirety at some future time. If the single company has not yet been formed, the agreement needs to address who will take on this responsibility and at whose expense. Below are some key issues related to the establishment of the JV.

Shareholdings. If the partners' financial and other inputs to the venture are not equal, the control structure and shareholdings may reflect this inequality. However, a partner's agreed-upon control and its ownership of the venture need not be equivalent. For example, at least in the UK, the ownership percentage of the shares, the voting percentage, and the dividend percentage can all be dealt with differently by establishing different classes of shares. Perhaps the trickiest of these is the control issue. It is relatively straightforward if one partner is to have clear control over the venture and a majority shareholding. Yet even in such circumstances the other partner may wish to include provisions to protect its minority position. In such cases, governance provisions might include the obligation to obtain the minority partner's consent on key decisions. If the partners do provide input on an equal basis, a 50/50 split of ownership and control may be the most equitable. However, this structure can give rise to deadlocks on crucial decisions, so partners that elect to use this structure may also need some provision to break potential deadlocks.

Board of directors and staffing. The initial directors and managers for the JV may be named in a schedule to the alliance contract. The agreement may also deal with the power of appointments and dismissals. Unless otherwise agreed, in the UK a controlling shareholder can appoint and dismiss board directors, and the board directors can appoint and dismiss managers. However, the partners may wish to agree on such issues as whether a certain number or proportion of managers should come from each company, what their minimum qualifications should be, whether the other partner has a right to object to any individual, and/or what the level and source of remuneration should be.

Articles of association. Legally required for establishment, articles of association (or their equivalent outside the UK) essentially amount to an agreement between the shareholders on such matters as passing resolutions, share issuance, transfer and disposal of shares, appointment of directors, and so on. The articles may either be kept short and simple, letting the JV agreement deal with all the details, or they can deal with these matters themselves. The most important thing is that the articles and the JV agreement do not conflict with each other.

Place of incorporation and advisors. The partners need to consider where the JV should be established based on fiscal, operational, and strategic considerations. Lawyers, accountants, and other advisors also need to be agreed upon. They may be independent of the two contracting partners' advisors, or both partners may wish to agree on their appointment or replacement.

Parties and Framework of Contract

The parties to the contract may seem obvious—the two companies that plan to be involved in the JV. However, this may not be the end of the matter. If the JV company has already been established, it may also need to be a party to the contract, because the agreement is likely to cover the duties of the JV itself. Moreover, other relevant parties such as guarantors (a bank, a parent, or other associated companies of the negotiating partners) may need to be included. As an example, if a partner has set up a new subsidiary to enter into the contract and take shares in the JV, the new company may have few assets and will therefore offer little comfort of legal recourse to the other partner should a dispute arise. Another reason why the parent or other associated companies of a partner may need to be made a party to the agreement is that they may also have obligations stated in the agreement (such as in a country other than the JV's location). In such circumstances, their obligations may not be legally enforceable unless that company is also a party to the contract or the JV partner has effectively taken responsibility for procuring the company's performance.

A sample index from an actual international JV agreement appears in **Figure 1** to illustrate the number and complexity of clauses partners negotiate into their alliance agreements. In more general terms, the broad framework of the agreement is often roughly as follows:

- identification of the parties;
- recitals (introductory paragraphs) setting out, usually in a general manner, the purpose of the agreement and the role of the parties;
- the main body of the agreement, setting out the obligations and restrictions on the parent firms;
- "boiler plate" clauses—the standard clauses dealing with a variety of issues, such as notifications, variations in writing, dispute resolution, waivers and exemptions, and governing laws;
- the signature and date clauses; and
- schedules that provide more detail on elements of the agreement.

The main point here concerns what is and is not included legally within the agreement. Any document referred to can, depending on the context, be brought in its entirety into the legally binding alliance agreement. For this reason, it can be inadvisable, say, to refer to sales documents or even letters or the MOU that were not originally drafted from a legal perspective and therefore may contain dangerously broad or vague promises. This is also why the agreement will usually include an "entire agreement" clause to the effect that no other documents or oral agreements form part of the enforceable contract between the parties.

Let's say one partner, a supplier of services, has sent a sales document describing its sales personnel as "the best in their field" and indicating that they will provide the services "immediately." The agreement should not accidentally incorporate that sales document by saying that the services are "as set out in the sales document dated xxx." If that is done with no further comment, then the partner has agreed, literally, to supply the best people in the field who will provide services immediately, rather than as soon as reasonably possible.

Conversely, if a document is intended to be part of the contract, it should be clearly incorporated by reference within the agreement. Simply attaching it at the back and labeling it "Appendix 1" may not be sufficient.

Performance Clauses

Performance clauses represent the main content of the agreement and will normally set out the duties and obligations of the partners and the timing of any performance. If one partner is to supply raw materials to the JV, the exact mechanism of that supply and the timing may be spelled out in the contract, or the agreement could refer to a separate supply contract. Warranties or minimum service levels may also need to be negotiated and included if the JV will be relying on the goods or services provided by one partner.

At this point, the question that naturally arises is whether the negotiators should strive to be comprehensive and attempt to identify all contingencies and the appropriate resolutions to them. It may well be that, in the interests of flexibility, partners' duties are not defined exhaustively at the outset. However, one partner may later think its "understanding" was that the other partner would perform a particular duty, but unless this obligation is included in the agreement there may be nothing to prove it in the event of a dispute. On the other hand, too much detail can make the agreement overly complex and could eliminate the flexibility that partners seek in entering into an alliance in the first place. There is also a danger that the list of duties, if it is very long and detailed, could be seen as exhaustive, which it clearly never can be. Partners will therefore often refer to other duties that tend to be more vague, and a balance needs to be struck between the conflicting concerns of wanting to include everything that has been agreed upon at this stage and maintaining flexibility and simplicity. However, with appropriate clauses for review and changes in the contract, the flexibility partners seek can be largely retained.

Restrictions on the Partners

The partners may wish to include certain restrictions on each other that relate to their businesses and the JV's operation. Legal advice is usually needed because there may be competition law or other regulatory concerns with such restrictions, particularly if the partners are large multinationals. Within these limits, the partners can consider clauses to help ensure

Figure 1

Table of Contents of an Actual International Joint Venture Agreement

that they do not compete directly with the JV (noncompetition), do not offer employment to each other's staff (nonsolicitation), do not use information or assets from the JV for their individual projects (confidentiality), and so on. Restrictions on the partners may include a time period after the JV is terminated for any reason, but again regulatory constraints may make it difficult to implement such restrictions.

"One possibility is that all liability is excluded and neither partner will bring a claim against the other. At the opposite extreme, full liability could remain as it would under law."

Confidentiality is an issue the partners should probably deal with in advance. These obligations will normally be mutual and should be noncontentious at the negotiation stage. However, even though many companies do cover keeping the information from the other contracting partner confidential, this may not be sufficient. Other considerations include confidentiality of material from the JV itself, confidentiality of the agreement terms, and ongoing confidentiality obligations after termination. The partners may also wish to agree that any statements or press releases relating to either the formation of or ongoing business of the JV needs to be subject to both parties' consent.

Although not strictly a restriction, a related issue that will often be the subject of negotiation is the ownership and licensing of intellectual property rights (IPRs), especially when the JV boasts technology or innovation. For example, the IPRs of anything supplied by one partner could stay with that partner and be licensed to the JV, or they could be transferred to the JV. The IPRs of anything created within the JV may stay with it. However, in this case, it is important to agree where ownership of those rights will lie if the JV is terminated. Without prior agreement, the partners run the risk of deadlock, particularly at the termination stage. They also risk losing some of their own IPRs in unclear situations, such as when an employee works for a parent firm as well as the JV. If one partner or the JV itself owns IPRs in software, for example, and another party needs to use the software, then the terms for licensing the software can be set out in the alliance agreement or in a separate license document.

Liability

The partners will usually wish to consider the matter of liability. The JV is likely to be a limited company, so its liability will be limited to the amount of its capital in most circumstances. However, a more difficult issue concerns the liability of the contracting partners, such as when one partner is negligent or causes the JV to perform poorly. One example is when a partner for whom the JV is less important fails to provide the appropriate personnel to ensure that sales leads are generated.

As a result, consideration should be given as to how the partners would like to deal with such occurrences. One possibility is that all liability is excluded and neither partner will bring a claim against the other. At the opposite extreme, full liability could remain as it would under law. Between these two extremes, a compromise could be reached so that either partner's liability is limited to a certain agreed amount of money in total, or so that any liability for indirect losses or loss of profit is excluded. These clauses could be made one-way, particularly if one partner's contribution is mainly performance-related while the other partner mainly provides funds. However, negotiation may be easier if the same limitation of liability applies to both partners.

A related situation concerning liability is that of *force majeure*, which arises when an external event or catastrophe such as war, riots, fire, or flood precludes one partner from performing as expected. It is common to agree that in such circumstances the partner affected will not be liable for failing to perform its duties. What may also need to be considered is what the partners should do if they find themselves in such circumstances. For example, there may be a dispute if the nonaffected partner wants the JV to switch to a third party to perform some duties and such a switch is against the wishes of the affected partner. By discussing such issues in advance, partners can agree to appropriate actions and time frames for how long a partner has to be affected before being "replaced" for those duties or before the JV is terminated altogether.

POST-ESTABLISHMENT ISSUES

Once our joint venture's establishment has been spelled out, negotiating parties need to consider several key post-establishment issues. The notorious instability of JVs and their generally short life spans provide ample motivation for explicitly considering contractual changes, disputes, and the possibility of termination before the venture is operational. Each of these issues is discussed below.

Changes to the Contract

The partners may wish to agree in advance on how they will deal with any contractual changes. This can be particularly important if the agreement is fairly lengthy or detailed, but also if there are still areas of uncertainty at the time of negotiations—which is more often the case than not. It is common to include a clause stating that any variation to the contract must be in writing and signed by both partners. This prevents any informal or oral changes that could be difficult to keep track of and could lead to difficulties in the event of a future dispute.

One method of enabling simple changes in the contract is to agree in advance to a "change control procedure" and set it out in detail, usually in a Schedule. This approach can specify what level of management within the companies can agree to contractual changes, and can include a simple form legally incorporating it within the main agreement and subsequently varying it. As part of these discussions, the partners might also agree in advance to a minimum number of formal meetings in which managers from a certain level meet to review any issues or concerns surrounding the JV. They can update each other on its performance, review the ongoing strategy of both partners, and consider any potential changes needed in the alliance. Although these parts of the negotiation should be noncontentious and do not have to involve lawyers, they can form a useful basis for the partners to appreciate the need for adaptability of the JV and the agreement that documents it.

A further change the partners may wish to consider in advance is the assignment or transfer of the agreement and the obligations within it. One partner may be able to transfer the agreement to another of its group companies (due to corporate restructuring or other factors), but transfer to an outsider will rarely be acceptable.

Dispute Resolution

It may seem awkward for soon-to-be collaborators to broach the topic of disputes before any have actually arisen, much less before the negotiations are completed. However, even when disputes seem unlikely, it is sensible to put in place an efficient and equitable means of resolving them should they occur anyway. Often it may be worthwhile to specify an "escalation procedure," whereby a dispute is first referred to the operational managers of the two partners, then passed up to senior management if unresolved, then to an outsider for assistance if still unresolved. If a fourth stage is needed, the partners could agree to mediation or arbitration for resolution.

"However, even when disputes seem unlikely, it is sensible to put in place an efficient and equitable means of resolving them should they occur anyway."

In any event, the issue of court proceedings still remains, since many countries' laws allow referral of contractual disputes to courts despite anything agreed upon regarding other resolution methods. Particularly when partners are from different countries, they should agree which courts will have jurisdiction over the agreement and any disputes, as well as whose laws will govern the agreement (usually the same country). Without such agreement, there could be an expensive battle on this jurisdictional issue before any court action takes place on the substantive dispute. A partner whose country is not chosen should bear in mind the costs of getting the agreement evaluated by foreign lawyers prior to signature and the additional legal and other expenses in the event of any court action.

Share Disposal

There are many issues relating to the shares held in the JV that deserve consideration. No matter what the initial share-holding, the partners will often wish to agree on the circumstances in which new shares should be issued—especially if there are different classes of shares—and to whom. This need not be particularly elaborate, but it can be more complicated if an initial public offering (IPO) of the JV becomes possible and could therefore dilute the partners' shareholdings.

The main issue to be discussed will often be the transfer of shares between the partners or to an outside party. A simple agreement is that neither partner can transfer its shares to anyone without the consent of the other. However, many other alternatives might be considered, such as preemption rights, sales to outsiders, transfers to group companies, put options, call options, and tag-along and drag-along rights. Some of these rights are described in **Figure 2**.

If the JV itself is allowed to establish subsidiaries, further complications will need to be dealt with. These may include whether it is to conduct business in several countries and whether subsidiaries will be established in each country. Because the original partners will not directly own shares in those subsidiaries, they may need to discuss what should happen if one of them needs or wants to exit from one particular country. This could be accomplished by spinning the subsidiary off from the main JV and transferring the shares directly to the main partners before transferring the shares of the one that is exiting.

The agreement might also specify that all the shares of each partner must be dealt with in a block. Otherwise, one partner could exercise its rights over just part of its shares and the original JV agreement may no longer be workable (such as when a partner sells half of its shares to a third party). Given that the identity of the shareholder is often important to the JV's operation, negotiators usually agree to fairly onerous restrictions on both partners when it comes to the transfer of shares to outsiders. Usually the shares must be offered first to the other partner. If agreements on transfers are made, the partners may also want to deal with how the shares are to be valued. Alternatives include: call or put options with pre-specified exercise prices; shotgun or Russian roulette clauses enabling one firm to name a price and allowing the other party to buy out or sell off the venture at that price; and appraisals by impartial external experts. Partners can also agree to circumstances that trigger the transfer of shares, such as when one firm acquires the other. If one partner transfers its shares in the JV entirely to another company, then the agreement may continue on, with the new partner signing a Deed of Accession that binds it to fulfill the obligations of the exiting partner.

Termination

One of the more difficult clauses to discuss in advance can be the end of the JV. However, it will no doubt come to a planned or unplanned end at some point, so the aim is to avoid problems in the final stages of collaboration and

---

Figure 2

Transfer of Shares

Each of the rights below could apply equally to both partners or be one-sided. They could even be extended to apply to shares of the contracting partners themselves. Thus, there are many possibilities and combinations, and the ones set out below are merely examples.

Right	Description
Preemption rights	If one partner wishes to sell its shares, it must first offer them to the other partner.
Variations on preemption rights	Each partner could be prevented from even discussing a sale to an outsider without having first declared a wish to sell and offering the shares to the other partner. Alternatively, both partners could be allowed to agree on a sale and price with an outsider in principle, but have to offer the shares first to the other partner for the same price.
Call options	One or both partners could have the right to force the exiting one to sell its shares in the JV to the remaining one. Issues here include: (a) the valuation of the shares, or a mechanism for the valuation; and (b) the circumstances and timing for excercise of the call option.
Put options	The flip side of call options. One partner has the right to force the other to buy the shares in the JV from it.
Drag-along rights	One partner (usually the majority shareholder) can arrange a sale to an outsider and then force the other partner to sell its shares as well (usually at the same price and on the same terms). This can be a way to ensure an exit.
Tag-along rights	The flip side of drag-along rights. In circumstances in which one partner has arranged (as allowed by the agreement) the sale of its shares to an outsider, the remaining partner (usually the minority shareholder) can prevent the sale unless its shares are also bought by the outsider at the same price and on the same terms.
Initial Public Offering (IPO)	If an IPO of the JV is a possibility or could be an exit strategy, the partners may wish to agree in advance on the circumstances (such as a certain profit level or need for financing) in which they will accept an IPO.
Transfer to group companies	The partners may allow the transfer of shares to group companies, particularly when there is a restructuring. But they will want to ensure that the new partner is as reliable as the old one in terms of obligation fulfillment, and that a Deed of Accession is executed so that the new partner takes on all the old one's liabilities and obligations.

beyond. Naturally, termination can result from many different causes and can be either positive or negative for one or both of the parent firms. For example, the alliance's stated, limited purpose may be fulfilled, or its agreed-upon time span may expire. One partner may have sold out its stake in the venture to the other partner or to an outsider, perhaps earning large capital gains. A severe or lengthy situation of *force majeure* could trigger termination. The partners may have agreed on a "change of control" provision wherein one of them can terminate the JV if the other is bought out (especially if bought by a competitor). During a review process, partners may simply agree that the alliance is not working out as anticipated and it is time to cut losses. A more difficult end to a JV stems from a partner's breach of the agreement.

Aside from the share disposal issues mentioned above, two main termination issues need to be resolved. The first is the circumstances under which the agreement can be terminated including what constitutes a breach serious enough to lead to termination. Often this will be a material or significant breach of duties or a repeated breach that is not corrected. Other circumstances could include events referred to above or the insolvency of either partner. The second issue relates to the consequences. Even when a termination is not acrimonious, partners can benefit from specifying what will happen to IPRs, personnel, assets, and the JV's ongoing contracts and obligations.

THE NEGOTIATION PROCESS

Although lawyers play an important role in negotiating and drafting alliance agreements, no clear dividing line exists between so-called legal and business issues, and the commercial managers will often need to be involved in making decisions on the legalities mentioned here. For this reason, commercial managers may wish to consider some of their alternatives in advance so they know where they stand on the issues to be covered in the agreement and decide which proposals (partner restrictions, transfer of shares, and so on) they wish to put forward for negotiation. It can happen that the partner who takes control of the negotiations earliest—such as by having its lawyers prepare the first draft agreement—is better able to meet its objectives in the deal. This is because negotiators often tend to proceed on the basis of what is already in a draft rather than having a completely new one written out.

Clearly, a decision needs to be made on what issues to address and in how much detail. From the perspective of legal clarity, the more that is included of what has been agreed upon and the more detail, the better. However, firms also want to avoid protracted and expensive negotiations, maintain good relations with the other partner at this early stage, and avoid an inflexible or overly complex agreement. Difficult issues such as limitation of liability, potential disputes, or termination will therefore be handled carefully. It is on these issues that managing the roles of the negotiators can be most useful.

Negotiations normally involve at least two participants per partner—one commercial representative and one lawyer. Some companies prefer to have more representatives from different business areas, and often the lawyer will have at least one junior colleague involved. The more complex the JV, the more negotiators are likely to be involved. If more than two partners are entering into the alliance, negotiations become more complex, with representatives and lawyers of each partner needing to agree over the terms of the contract.

Commercial and legal representatives bring unique skills and perspectives to the negotiation process. The ideal commercial representative is usually someone who understands the companies and the strategic alliance, has the authority to make decisions without referring back to others, is of a level to match the representative from the other company, has prior experience and skills in similar deals, and has the time available to commit to potentially lengthy negotiations and meetings.

An argument can be made for involving the managers who will actually be running the JV. Such inclusion will ensure that their concerns are addressed and that they will thoroughly understand the alliance agreement and be able to ensure the fulfillment of what is being negotiated. However, a counter-argument is that it may be better for JV managers not to take part in case the negotiations become protracted or acrimonious on specific contractual elements—which can happen even when the partners are in broad agreement and there are good relationships among company representatives. To avoid tainting the ongoing working relationship for JV managers, it may be better to shield them from these disputes at the early stages if this occurs.

The choice of lawyers can be equally important in alliance negotiations. Ideal legal representatives are competent and experienced lawyers in the field who have a good knowledge of the company as well as the circumstances and goals of the alliance, can represent the company accurately—both in the stance taken on issues and in style—and understand how to conclude the negotiations effectively and amicably in order to lay the foundations for the ongoing relationship. It may not be helpful to involve lawyers whose negotiating style is known to be aggressive or adversarial when the aim is to establish and build a cooperative relationship with the other firm. The personality and negotiating style of the individual lawyers (not just their firms) will be important in representing each company entering the alliance. Similarly, if the lawyer does not understand the business or the logic of the alliance, it will be more difficult to conduct the negotiations smoothly.

The roles of the negotiators will usually be fairly clear. The lawyers will take responsibility for technical or legal issues and generally deal with noncontentious or boiler plate clauses. However, when the lawyers cannot agree, the commercial managers will need to be involved to make decisions and resolve issues that arise. The business or strategic input will often be a combination of the lawyers and the managers. Purely commercial negotiations and prices will often be left to the managers. Lawyers can be called upon to address contentious issues, such as clauses dealing with disputes or termination. Some commercial managers may "blame the lawyers," having them insert sensitive clauses while maintaining a positive relationship with their counterparts.

Managers designing strategic alliances can become more effective by raising their awareness of some of the basic legal and negotiating aspects of collaborative agreements. They need to recognize the relevance of both the content of strategic alliance agreements and the process of negotiations. The key establishment and post-establishment issues laid out here generally form part of such negotiations. Heeding those issues, as well as the roles of commercial and legal representatives and their interactions, can help bring about a more complete and equitable agreement and ensure an easier time of it when sitting down at the negotiating table.

Élise Campbell was a lawyer and international negotiator before becoming UK Managing Director for Result, a global Internet/new media accelerator based in London.
Jeffrey J. Reuer is an assistant professor of strategy and management at Ohio State University in Columbus.

Reprinted with permission from *Business Horizons*, January/February 2001, pp. 19-26. © 2001 by the Board of Trustees at Indiana University, Kelley School of Business.

UNIT 5

How Management Deals With Environmental Forces

Unit Selections

Key Points to Consider

- What are some of the things that a corporation can do to manage customers more effectively in an international setting?

- In the 1950s "Made in Japan" meant junk. Today, it means quality. Do you think a national image can have an impact on the quality image of a product?

 **Links: www.dushkin.com/online/**
These sites are annotated in the World Wide Web pages.

Business Policy and Strategy
http://www.aom.pace.edu/bps/bps.html

Harvard Business School
http://www.hbs.edu

International Business Resources on the WWW
http://globaledge.msu.edu/ibrd/ibrd.asp

Managers of international organizations have to deal with a changing and varied global environment. To be successful, managers cannot just sit back and wait for things to happen. Rather, they need to be proactive in their approach to the problems and opportunities associated with doing business on an international basis, and to find partners who can help them. Each country's manager will find his or her own way of doing things, and while the American economy may be leading the way, the way they do business in Brazil or France or Japan will be a little different, according to the article, "Does Globalization Have Staying Power?"

One of the major tools that managers have to help their organizations become successful on the global stage is marketing. Marketing analysis managers need to realize that while all markets have certain similarities, they are all different in their own way, and each can pose different problems. Many practices are different and many hurdles exist, but "International Growth Patterns Remain Strong" for many. In sales, communicating with customers can be difficult and demanding, even in an "integrated" market such as Europe. The speed of communication is going to have a tremendous impact on the way business is conducted.

An easy way for a firm to get into international business is through import/export channels. Often, when a small firm first starts to engage in international trade, it is not due to any deliberate decision of its own. Instead, the firm may place an advertisement in an industrial magazine, or have a booth at a trade show, or be featured in an article in the news. As a result, one day it happens to get an order from someone outside its domestic market. It may be a very small order that merely says, "Send us one of these. We would like to look at it." That first small order is then frequently followed by a much larger order, and the small domestic firm suddenly finds itself doing business abroad. This can happen on either side of the equation, as an importer or an exporter. As time passes, the company's foreign business grows at a faster rate than does the domestic business, especially if it involves one of the more rapidly developing economies, and soon, a significant amount of business is being done overseas. This growth in international sales is significant for American firms and the American economy, as well as others.

China, Eastern Europe, and the former Soviet Union have been especially difficult areas for firms. Certainly there is great opportunity in these markets, but there is also great risk, as seen by the recent developments in the Pacific Rim and with the Chinese military forcing down American military observation aircraft. Many people in these societies simply do not know how to operate in a developing capitalist system. Commercial laws have not been developed, and an understanding of the fundamental aspects of capitalism has not been achieved by much of the population, including important government officials, as well as quasicapitalists such as factory managers. International managers must be prepared for setbacks and disappointments before they will be able to experience success. The relationship between the West and these countries will be difficult in the coming years, but not impossible. Some of the problems and opportunities are discussed in "Post–Cold War International Relations: Trends and Portents" and "The Russian Approach to Human Rights Intervention."

The monetary problem has always been of particular concern in international trade. Currency trading and fluctuation cause managers sleepless nights and terrible days. Some currencies of the developing world, in particular, are difficult to deal with. The rewards can be very high, but unfortunately, so can the risks. Managers who engage in world trade need to develop a strong financial management system to deal with the financial aspect of their global business if they are going to be successful.

An additional factor that needs to be considered is that of production. A world economy means not only worldwide customers, but worldwide production. To be competitive, organizations must be able to produce worldwide and to coordinate production for the greatest advantage. With the introduction of the North American Free Trade Agreement (NAFTA), firms in North America are not just American, Canadian, or Mexican, but North American, with an entire continent as their backyard. Production is global and rapidly becoming the business of global organizations, in spite of the War on Terror, with the Internet playing a growing role, as seen in "Redefining the Business Case for Offshore Outsourcing."

Organizations that are going to produce, distribute, and sell overseas must realize that they cannot do this without workers, the people who perform the necessary tasks for the organization's success. Generally speaking, labor relations are very different outside the United States. The relationship between union and management in Germany, for example, frequently involves a highly cooperative arrangement. On the other hand, in some less developed countries child labor is common, and a living wage, let alone benefits, is as rare as a union organizer, as outlined in "Comrades Are on the March Again" and "Unions Forming Global Contract." This does not mean that organizations from developed countries encourage these types of activities in the developing world, but some of them turn a blind eye to them.

International managers must learn to combine all these parts of the new global business environment. They must plan strategically to make good use of marketing, production, finance, and labor. They must learn to control this highly diverse and sometimes contentious brew by using the most modern management technologies available, as discussed in "The Incredible Shrinking World" and "Has Strategy Changed?" Controlling a business on an international scale is certainly not easy, and new systems will be needed in the future for managers to be successful. Things are changing and, perhaps, management needs a new paradigm to deal with the changes coming in the new international environment.

In conclusion, there are many challenges facing managers in the international environment. But, fortunately, they have at least some of the tools they need to deal with these challenges. The task will not be easy, and new problems and opportunities are certain to arise in the future. Managers will have to develop the necessary new tools to solve the problems and grasp the opportunities for success in the ever-changing international business environment. For the past 10 years, the American economy has done very well, while much of the rest of the world has not. This is going to change, however, because the rest of the world is starting to catch up with the United States. People are starting to question some of the basic assumptions of world trade. Countries are making the changes they need to be successful, and American firms are going to find it more difficult than in the past. Globalization has been the watchword for many firms for the past decade. But they are now starting to meet resistance, and "Reforming Globalization" is going to have to be put on the agenda with people challenging what they feel are "Globalisation's Misguided Assumptions" if international trade and business is going to continue to grow and prosper. This means opening the process to a more democratic environment, educating people on the benefits of globalization, and helping people to recover from the dislocations caused by globalization and the changes that are then necessitated in their lives.

Putting branding on the map

Branding a country has outgrown its corporate roots to develop positioning insights that are world-class.

Creenagh Lodge

Branding a country differs expansively and subtly from branding a corporation and is different in almost every respect from branding a product.

It is beginning to develop its own rules and approaches and, as practitioners gain experience of the phenomenon, the similarities with the principles of corporate branding are fading and new thinking has started to emerge.

The greatest difference between country and corporate branding is in the two classic marketing elements of positioning and proposition.

Countries that need branding often have little to differentiate them from their competition: similar beaches, same sort of investment offer, and one apple is not much different from another apple. The art of positioning countries is not yet very sophisticated, yet positioning is often the biggest problem the brand must seek to remedy if the country in question is to pull itself out of 'the wrong set' geographically. This is illustrated by the great quote from Mexican president Porfirio Diaz: "Poor Mexico, so far from God, so close to the United States."

Positioning has to be exact yet imaginative: exact to be credible; imaginative to remedy the problem. There are several repositioning strategies possible.

For New Zealand it was geographical: 'Orchard of the South Pacific'. For Ireland it was political/cultural: a unintessentially European (not British) country. For Spain it was conscious sophistication: the Espana logo and the iconic Guggenheim building.

The proposition for a country is an enormous task: to give a vivid and compelling reason to the world to buy everything it can offer. It has to be all-encompassing yet focused; based on credibility yet aspirational; have the wit or sophistication to attract the world's attention and persuade it to buy; and be acceptable to the indigenous population.

Public money

That acceptance by the population is crucial. In branding nations, there is no 'client'. Or rather there is, but not one that marketing people find easy to manage. Governments or their development agencies may be the instigator and paymaster, but a country does not have the tight, hierarchical authority lines found in a commercial organisation. And the people of a country are neither as accessible nor as controllable as employees. Government money is public money.

Ultimately the inhabitants are the paymasters and the brand must connect with them instantly and intuitively if it is to please and therefore to work.

Marketing is not generally reckoned to be a government's key competency. Spin-doctoring maybe, but the principles and idiom of strategic marketing are not particularly well developed.

Increasingly, however, countries recognise that they need to think and act competitively if they are to succeed; and while they may not be familiar with the concept of disproportionate impact, they quickly get the idea because of its good sense.

This is very good for classically trained marketers: it forces us to abandon our assumptive jargon and re-present marketing's basic principles to intelligent people unversed in the discipline.

Values, always important in a corporate brand, take on new significance for a country. Branding is more urgently needed for under-performing countries than successful ones and for those overshadowed by economically heftier neighbours.

In these cases, the brand has to be rooted in an economic strategy (in New Zealand's case, low volume quotas into the EC dictated high margins).

This, almost by definition, will be highly aspirational and new to the main mass of the population. But if the brand strongly reflects values identified by the people, then the strategy will not only be comfortable but inspirational as well.

This is particularly potent when the values are recognised with equal force by the country itself and the outside world.

Scotland is immensely fortunate in having not only an unrivalled visual and sonic equity (the sight of the kilt, the sound of the pipes) but admirable and attractive values as well. These are acknowledged by both Scots and outsiders to be more evident in Scotland than practically any other country.

The four key Scottish values of integrity, inventiveness, tenacity and spirit are not Scotland's only values.

However, these were selected when the country was rebranded to help cover the key strategic issues: how to reconcile commerce with culture (technology with tourism; people with products) and how to balance the remote, romantic Scotland of the past with the lively Scotland of today.

There was marked agreement on the values between the Scots in the research and the rest of the world (though the Japanese did say "if Scotland invented broadcasting and telecommunications why are we, the Japanese, laughing all the way to the bank and not the Scots?").

But it was the recognition of the values by the Scots themselves that was impressive ("our legal system really is the fairest in the world"). In other words, because they can recognise themselves they are willing to participate in the strategy.

As with corporate brands, country brands tend to be rooted either in competency—'what we do'—or attitude—'what we stand for'. Scotland used to be competency-based, essentially engineering, but this was lost when the last great shipyard closed down in the 1970s. It is fortunate in having attractive and widely known values, which now allow it to become an attitude-based brand.

New Zealand was quite the reverse. Twelve years ago, when it began a branding project, New Zealand had no profile to speak of. The British hitherto the major market, tended to be disparaging; Kenny Everett was quoted everywhere: "70 million sheep, three million people, need I say more?"

But what was going unnoticed was not only lamb, but apples, pears, kiwi fruit, cheese and, best of all, remarkably fine wine. Thus New Zealand's brand could be competency-based. An attitude-based brand stance was tried, found worthy, but not very persuasive.

Export promotion

And just as Scotland is fortunate in its values, New Zealand is fortunate in its core competency—agriculture/food—because of the way this impacts so positively on the three key 'products' all countries seek to sell to the world: inward investment, tourism and exports.

The New Zealand strategy focused on exports; but inward investment and tourism needed to be included in the overall New Zealand proposition as well. For inward investors a successfully managed food export programme implies good management and sustainability, two important influences on investment.

For tourists, especially Europeans, the presence of good food and even finer wine suggests a civilised country to visit; and the presence of exotic fruits (like the tamarillo) evokes an exotic landscape, even more inviting.

And focus on exports has, independently of these virtues, other interesting benefits. Recent benchmarking studies in Wales have shown that money spent on promoting exports has a disproportionate impact on a country's GDP. And the Scottish research showed that export success builds a country's self-esteem in a way that inward investment triumphs and tourism performance do not.

'Far and away the finest', New Zealand's proposition worked because it reflected the strategy, made a very bold claim and persuaded the people of New Zealand that they could deliver that claim in full. The current proposition, '100% Pure New Zealand', continues to reflect the original strategy—and the enormous confidence the country has gained. And you'll have noticed that the jibes about sheep have entirely ceased.

Creenagh Lodge is chairman of Corporate Edge, which has worked with New Zealand and Ontario and is currently working with Scotland, Wales and Ghana on their brands.

From *Marketing*, March 14, 2002, p. 17. © 2002 by Marketing. Reprinted with permission of Haymarket Magazines Ltd., London W6 7JP, England.

DOES GLOBALIZATION HAVE STAYING POWER?

Global business expert John Quelch looks at marketing in a post-Sept. 11 world.

John A. Quelch

Many questions about global business are being debated in the boardrooms of U.S. corporations. For instance, how has global marketing evolved in the last 20 years? Are there any truly global brands? Are the forces of globalization increasing or decreasing? Perhaps the most telling perspective on any of these questions revolves around post-Sept. 11 attitudes. In a new era, how do companies organize their international marketing activities and how will this affect the global strategies of companies who are already in global markets—as far as security, distribution, promotion, and advertising strategies?

To get the latest thinking on these issues, we contacted global marketing expert John A. Quelch, senior associate dean and Lincoln Filene Professor of Business Administration at Harvard Business School. Quelch serves as the senior non-executive director of WPP Group plc, a marketing service company. He also is a non-executive director of easyJet plc and a founding non-executive director of Reebok International Ltd. Quite apropos to the times is his most recent book, Business Strategies in Muslim Countries (Prentice-Hall, 2001).

Conducting our interview with John Quelch was Sevgin Eroglu, professor of marketing at the Robinson College of Business, Georgia State University. Eroglu's research and teaching interests are focused on international marketing and global retailing. She brings excellent academic credentials to the table with a BS from the Middle East Technical University and an MBA and PhD from Michigan State University. She also is a native of Turkey and as such is tuned into the issues at play in the Middle East, Muslim cultural dimensions, and alternative views of globalization from an international perspective.

MM: There is a great deal of speculation about the effects of globalization today on companies and the global economy. If you were to pick out the most important points of discussion, where would you begin?

The impact of Sept. 11 on globalization might be a good place to start. It will likely moderate the enthusiasm of multina-

tional companies to proclaim their global virtues. I think it will result in further emphasis on what Douglas Daft, CEO of Coca-Cola Co., has called a "think local, act local" strategy. This is a very interesting statement from the CEO of what must be the most global brand in the world. What explains it? In any national market—for example, carbonated soft drinks in Germany or Brazil—there's a market segment that's willing to pay a price premium for the global brand over local alternatives. Coca-Cola has conquered this segment in almost every country in the world. There are some markets that are still dominated by Pepsi, but not very many. Now Coca-Cola is finding it increasingly difficult to penetrate further with its global brand. Therefore, there's a need to localize Coca-Cola brand marketing to increase its appeal in each country market. In addition, over the last 10 years, Coca-Cola has been acquiring local soft drink brands, which now account for around 10% of company sales.

When you say they are going to think "local," beyond adaptation of the product, distribution, promotion, and so forth, what other corporate practices and processes will be influenced by this strategy?

More new product development will be locally driven. Obviously, Coca-Cola has hitherto used its country organizations to implement a global strategy. So the field has not had the charter for coming up with new products. But, increasingly, Coca-Cola will encourage new product and other marketing initiatives to bubble up around the world much as, for example, Nestle has done. With the benefit of greater creativity at the local level, some of these new products may be robust enough to succeed at the regional or even global level.

Coming back to Sept. 11, some blame globalization, which they claim is actually Americanization that's just called globalization to make it more palatable, with global brands representing a new form of cultural imperialism. However, the penetration of Coca-Cola consumption or McDonald's restaurants in Muslim countries is among the lowest in the world. To somehow blame global brands for poverty in such countries is preposterous. And to suggest Islamic cultures, more than a thousand years old, are being threatened by a few global brands is insulting.

Another reason many global brands have traveled well is that they respond to latent needs common across cultures. Whether or not Coca-Cola quenches your thirst in Pakistan or in France, the fact is that the physiology of the human species is pretty consistent across national boundaries. To blame Coca-Cola for having come up with a product that successfully addresses needs that are common to humanity regardless of culture seems unfair.

But these brands are going to have to be a little bit more humble, respectful, and local in their approach in the future. Though they're not the cause of Sept. 11, a certain percentage of people see globalization of these brands as symbolic of American success (I wouldn't say American imperialism, but American success) and dominance as the world's only superpower. Localization strategies can signal greater humility and still be commercially profitable.

How will companies reflect this humility in their marketing strategies?

Advertising is an obvious area where adaptation is essential. For instance, you can't show a model in a Saudi Arabian advertisement in the way we would show that person in the West. Cosmetics advertising is therefore very different in Saudi Arabia. But the per capita consumption of cosmetics in Saudi Arabia is among the highest in the world. And the fact that religious strictures require women to wear the hijab outside of the home in public places doesn't detract from their natural interest as women in beauty and in cosmetics.

Companies must also attend to whom they assign as managers in Muslim countries. I have asked several CEOs of U.S. multinationals, "How many of your top-50 managers worldwide are Muslims?" After all, one-fifth of the world's population is Muslim and, given the birthrate in Muslim countries, this will rise to one quarter within about 20 years. The answer, of course, is, "Very, very few." We must identify and develop indigenous managers who are able to operate on behalf of American and global corporations within the Islamic world.

Leaving aside Sept. 11, are the forces favoring globalization of consumer brands increasing or decreasing?

First, let's take a step back and focus on what is a global brand. If you consider well-known global brands according to the percentage of their revenues from outside their domestic markets, then there are actually very few global brands. So Coca-Cola would have perhaps 80% of its sales outside the United States; Philip Morris' Marlboro brand about 67%; Pepsi, maybe 42%; Kellogg, 50%; Pampers, 65%; Nescafe, about 50%; Gillette, around 62%. Beyond the top-10 brands, you start slipping very quickly below 50%. From our occasionally myopic perspective, we often think of certain American brands as global in scope when in fact they are not. For example, Campbell's soup only has around about 6% of its sales outside of the United States. There's an opportunity for Campbell's to in-

crease the percentage of its sales from outside the United States and to achieve greater geographical diversity.

At the same time, I believe there's a finite ceiling on the size of the segment in any product-country-market that's willing to buy global brands as opposed to local or regional brands. Of course this segment size varies from one country to another, from one product category to another. In some countries, Coca-Cola has hit a ceiling in the percentage of the market that they're going to persuade to pay a price premium for the global brand. The only way forward then is to increase the per capita consumption of existing brand users rather than to convert the remaining consumers into preferring the global brand.

Should the United States move away from globalization simply for security's sake? Will this post-Sept. 11 thinking influence the strategies of global companies?

Yes, there will be an impact on human resources management. Expatriate American executives and their families aren't going to be as eager to take on international assignments, especially in countries viewed as security risks. As I mentioned previously, this will require more development, training, and recruiting of indigenous Muslim executives, which in the long run should be beneficial to all.

I don't believe the forces of globalization can be reversed. We have more than $1 trillion in financial assets moving across national boundaries every day. There have been significant productivity gains through the global rationalization of supply chains in many product markets. As a result of all the merger and acquisition activity of the '90s, we have cross-border investment levels that are unprecedented. These interdependencies aren't going to be reversed. In addition, more executives have been trained to believe, and I think rightly so, that international experience is critical to their long-term career success. We have more international MBA applicants than ever before. These and other forces increase the frequency of international travel, cross-border migration, and lower communication costs across national boundaries. The advent of the Euro is one of the most significant currency changeovers in world history. (Actually, when Europe was run by the Romans, there was a single currency.)

Whether or not Sept. 11 means globalization will continue at the same pace as previously is debatable. I think it will. In some respects, Sept. 11 is motivating greater cross-border cooperation among national governments on security matters, and this cooperation will reinforce interaction in other areas.

Does globalization represent cultural imperialism?

The globalization as cultural imperialism argument is an insult to the cultures those arguing this point are seeking to defend. Can Islamic cultures, more than a thousand years old, be threatened by a hamburger and a Coke? I remember meeting with Carlos Salinas, the former president of Mexico, prior to the North American Free Trade Agreement and someone in our group asked him, "How are you going to defend your culture if you integrate economically with the United States?" His reply was that the Aztec culture was here a long, long time before anyone ever thought of the United States, and that he was sure

Mexicans would be perfectly capable of sustaining their cultural distinctiveness. The globalization as cultural imperialism argument, which you don't hear being made by too many Muslims, is actually a patronizing argument. It diminishes the strength and longevity of Islamic culture.

The main problem in the Muslim world is its economic performance. Over the last 10 to 20 years, Muslim countries have hardly participated in the benefits of globalization accruing to people in many other emerging markets. The real per capita GDP in most Muslim countries has declined over the last 20 years. Why? These countries have birthrates that exceed their GDP growth rates and, as a result, their per capita GDP drops. There is a population explosion in these countries that's producing a vast number of unemployed young men who have no opportunities commensurate with their education.

This is not the fault of the United States. The United States does not determine birthrates in Pakistan or Saudi Arabia. The United States does not determine that the governments of many Muslim countries refuse to open their borders to foreign competition or foreign investment, to engage in deregulation or privatization of their industries, and to advance the ability of their economies to compete effectively with the Western world. These, to my mind, are the root causes of the economic dissatisfaction. And, again, the notion that a hamburger and a Coke are causing these self-inflicted problems is preposterous.

Would you comment on the appointment of Charlotte Beers, former chairman of J Walter Thompson and the former CEO of Ogilvy and Mather, to the position of assistant Secretary of State for public diplomacy with the mandate of "branding America" (and communicating an American point of view internationally to counter the al Jazeera satellite news channel and other anti-American commentaries on Islamic media)?

This is a creative appointment, and the U.S. media have been giving her an unfair reception as the person who successfully branded Uncle Ben's rice. The communication principles involved are, of course, quite similar. First, identify the perception or image gap in different countries of the world vis a vis the United States, see what U.S. strengths and weaknesses are perceived to be. Next, identify the target markets that we want to communicate with, the messages we want to send to these groups, and the media to effectively communicate the messages to the target markets.

By the way, many other countries regularly track their international images as a matter of course. In the United States, many state governments are involved in marketing and brand building to compete for foreign and domestic direct investment, tourism, and the like. The U.S. government is really exceptional in not having been actively engaged in brand building. Why is that? Well, the U.S. brand is very well-recognized. Top-of-mind unaided awareness around the world of the brand and the flag is close to 100%. So little effort has gone into shaping perceptions of brand USA. Now, we discover that many people hate us and don't understand our core values. They accuse us of cultural imperialism, of throwing our weight around militarily in an unconstructive way rather than engaging in dialogue. Many of these criticisms may be unfair, but in marketing, we all

concede that perception is reality, so I think it's good that Charlotte Beers is doing this job.

Regarding improved communications with the Muslim world, there are three points. First, the Muslim world is not homogeneous; there is as much diversity within Islam as there is within Christianity. At the state level, there are benign expressions of Islam, in Indonesia for instance, vs. much stricter interpretations of Islam, as in Saudi Arabia.

Second, our tendency, and I think this is a weakness, is to want to tell the world how great and good we are rather than listen to what others have to offer us. And I hope therefore that any brand-building effort by the U.S. State Department will aim to encourage a balanced two-way exchange between the Islamic world and the West. I also hope we take the attitude that the Islamic world may have things to teach us as much as we have things to teach them. Without a balanced perspective, we will risk being accused once again of being arrogant.

Third, we need to tailor our messages to particular target groups. There are messages we need to send to opinion leaders in the Muslim world, but there are also messages that we need to send to the youth of the Muslim world. And the youth is especially important because of the exploding birth rate. If we fast forward to 2030, almost 50% of the world's population under age 18 will be Muslims. People just have not caught onto the magnitude of this challenge. We'd better have plans for good information, education, communication, humanitarian aid, and overseas development strategies directed at this particular group.

Major U.S. consumer goods companies have roles to play in this effort. For example, Nike, Coca-Cola, McDonald's, or Gillette could help the Islamic world fund such things as the kind of high school student and teacher exchanges or exchanges of sports teams and journalists that we take for granted between the United States and Europe, and nowadays increasingly with China. Only 2% of total U.S. tourist dollars spent overseas is spent in Islamic countries that represent 20% of the world's population. A cute advertising or brand-building campaign is inadequate to meet the challenge. What's required here is a total cultural exchange strategy that will last decades and focus on building understanding, one citizen at a time.

What inspired you to put together your recently published book, *Business Strategies in Muslim Countries*?

Six years ago, I was teaching the international marketing course at Harvard Business School. At that time, we had no case studies addressing marketing issues in Muslim countries. I came across data regarding the Muslim percentage of the world's population and Muslim population growth projections. It seemed this would be a very important emerging market. I believed we had to go out and develop case studies and establish links with companies and executives in these countries.

One important insight that emerged from the case studies in this book is the large number of outstanding executives running businesses, often against all odds, in many Muslim countries. I'm not talking about the people who are working for western multinationals, I'm talking about local business people. Two of these companies stand out. One is Milkpak in Pakistan, a joint venture between Nestle and a local company called Packages, the Tetrapak licensee in Pakistan. A man named Babar Ali, who is also currently the chairman of the World Wild Life Fund, runs it. Here is a superb Pakistani business person who has not only built from scratch this amazing business that ends up in joint ventures with Tetrapak and Nestle, but who also founded and supported the best business school in Pakistan, LUMS (Lahore University of Management Sciences).

A second example is Said Darwazah, who is the founder of a Jordanian pharmaceutical company named Hikma Pharmaceuticals, a company that not only operates in Jordan, but also has a manufacturing plant in Portugal and a significant drug distribution company in New Jersey.

The prejudice exists that managerial competency and leadership talents are weak in these countries. This is totally untrue. A second myth is that global best practices in business all emanate from the United States and could not possibly be developed in these countries. Again, that's not true. One interesting example concerns Saudi Arabia. The best new technologies in the photo lab business (where you take your film to be developed on a "while you wait" basis) are developed for Saudi Arabia. And why is that? Strict Muslims are not tolerant of strangers seeing images of their spouses or female family members. Therefore, when they need to have film processed, they prefer to be present while this is being done so they can ensure those developing the film don't try to view the photographs they are developing. Obviously, they want to wait in the photo lab for the shortest time possible and as a result advanced technology for rapid photo lab processing as it's developed by Canon, Fuji, and Kodak is tested initially in the Saudi Arabian market. It comes into the United States several years later.

You simply can't appreciate these insights without going to these countries, digging around, and learning how the culture and the religion bear on what's possible or what's necessary in terms of marketing.

Another case we developed examined the Arcelik white goods division of Koc, a Turkish company. With a dominant share of the domestic market, Arcelik wanted to expand outside of Turkey. What could a Turkish company possibly bring to Western Europe? In the United Kingdom, Arcelik identified an unserved niche for small refrigerators that would fit under the kitchen counter. Under the brand name of Beko, they now have almost 20% of the under-the-counter refrigerator market in the United Kingdom just because they identified and pursued this focused, niche market. This is yet another example of a company from an unexpected emerging economy breaking into a developed market.

Are there things you would change if you could rewrite this book today? Would you add or subtract or would you alter the contents of it in any way?

No. The book presents a balanced set of cases, some of which deal with western multinationals confronted with the challenges of marketing in Muslim countries, others which focus on indigenous Muslim-led businesses that showcase best-practice marketing in Muslim countries. In today's climate, the book represents a very strong advertisement for (1) doing business and continuing to engage in the Muslim world despite Sept. 11, and (2) the talents of managers operating in very difficult environments. Hopefully, this will motivate leaders of United States and other western multinationals to seek out, recruit, develop, and retain Muslim managers to help them do a better job of taking their services and goods into Muslim countries in ways that are helpful to the local populations and are culturally sensitive.

John A. Quelch, may be reached at jquelch@hbs.edu.

From *Marketing Management*, March/April 2002, pp. 19-23. © 2002 by the American Marketing Association. Reprinted by permission.

WORLD WITHOUT BORDERS: FRANCHISING'S INTERNATIONAL APPEAL

International Growth Patterns Remain Strong

Solid support from headquarters combined with trusted, knowledgeable local partners have always been essential to successful international expansion of franchise systems. That is still true today—only more so.

By Polly Larson

Despite today's lackluster economy and troubled international political environment, U.S. franchisors have lost none of their enthusiasm for global expansion. It's not that they are oblivious to the obstacles, but that they are confident of their ability to continue to grow in foreign lands and adapt to a climate that sometimes calls for conducting business not-quite-as-usual.

Now, more than ever, it is important to have a strong relationship with a trusted local partner when expanding into a new overseas location. "We need to be smarter about who we partner with," says Chris Joseph, group vice president, international region, Blimpie Subs & Salads. "Do your 'due diligence' checks very carefully, and number one, go and visit with your potential partner in his country. Spend some time, go out to dinner, see their friends, see how the person interacts with their community."

And once you have found that perfect partner, treat him or her well, says Adela Fernandez, international sales manager for Novus Franchising, Inc., which provides automotive windshield repair and replacement, paint restoration and dent repair services. "Recent events have made franchisors rethink the way they do business. We must concentrate on building a relationship with the franchisee now more than ever. Pay attention to the franchisee."

There is no question most of the world still loves U.S.-based franchises. Tricon Restaurants International reports a record-breaking 1,041 new international restaurant openings in 2001 for its KFC, Pizza Hut and Taco Bell brands, according to David Fitzjohn, chief business development officer.

At AlphaGraphics, Keith Gerson, CFE, vice president of global development, reports continued strong international demand for its design, print and digital imaging business service franchises, which currently are in 17 countries, ranging from the United Kingdom to Russia.

And Uniglobe Travel's John Henry, senior vice president, global franchise development, says despite being part of the travel industry, which was the one most heavily affected by the events of last September, Uniglobe's international program is on track. While the travel industry is "suffering from some perception problems at the moment," Henry says. "it is the second sexiest business on earth, every-one wants to travel or needs to travel."

Here, There and Everywhere

In the beginning, it was the fast-food franchise powerhouse franchises such as McDonald's and KFC that filled the appetite for U.S. franchise concepts in overseas markets. Now these pioneers of international franchising are as ubiquitous in many other countries as they are in the United States, and they have been joined by other food concepts as well as by most of the major players in all industries that franchise. For many large franchisors today, the question is not where they do have franchises, but rather where they do not.

Of Tricon's 30,000 restaurants in over 100 countries, nearly 11,000 are outside of the United States. Fitzjohn credits the company's strong joint venture and franchise partner base for its continued success in key growth markets, citing such far-flung franchisee-operated markets as Malaysia, New Zealand, Latin America, the Caribbean and Greece. Tricon's successful joint venture markets include the United Kingdom, Poland, Canada and Japan.

Business Format Franchising Boom(erangs)

Over the past decade, it has become commonplace for U.S. franchise systems to export their concepts to countries around the world. Now the Made-in-America idea of business format franchising has come full circle, as franchise systems indigenous to other nations begin to introduce their concepts here. Just as the first franchises exported from this country to others were restaurants, so are most of those now arriving on American shores from abroad. One notable exception is Pirtek, which now boasts 18 units in this country and counting.

Migrating from Australia in 1996, Pirtek franchises repair and replace hydraulic hoses, a fast-growing market, according to Morgan Arundel, president and CEO of Pirtek USA. "There are hydraulic hoses everywhere—construction equipment, cars, air conditioners, amusement park rides, sign trucks, garbage trucks, to name a few. It's the cheapest form of power," Arundel explains, noting that the industry is expected to grow from $3 billion to $11 billion a year over the next several years.

Pirtek started in Australia more than 20 years ago and expanded to the United Kingdom in 1989. There are now approximately 74 Pirtek Hose Service Centers in Australia and 75 in the U.K., as well as centers in Europe, South Africa, and Singapore.

Just as U.S. franchisors emphasize the importance of carefully researching foreign markets, companies moving into this country must first determine if their concept will work here. "We did a lot of research," Arundel says. "One of the reasons we opened our pilot unit in Minneapolis-St. Paul was because previously we had been in climates that don't have the severe weather we do in the northern tier of this country. We wanted to test the product in a market where you have 20 degrees below zero, which might affect the hoses." As it turned out, the weather was no problem, and the new center set a record for Pirtek during its earliest months.

A market that emphasizes high productivity is essential to Pirtek's success. "Our business merged in here really well because we are keen on productivity in this country," Arundel says, adding that in slower-moving economies, the concept is not appropriate. "We sell time," he explains. "If you get into a country where there is no emphasis on productivity, it wouldn't make much sense."

Pirtek centers are open around the clock in order to respond instantly whenever a call for help comes in. Arundel cites the example of one client, Federal Express, at the Minneapolis-St. Paul Airport. "They told us if they can't load a plane because a piece of machinery with a hydraulic hose on it has gone down, it costs them $500 a minute for every minute that jet stays on the ground."

Pirtek's global reach enables the company to service equipment made all over the world, regardless of where that piece of equipment ends up. "We put a hose tag on every hose we fix, denoting what kind of hose it is, the length and fittings, so somebody can just give any of our centers all over the world that number and we can reproduce that hose exactly and get it out to them," Arundel says.

Pirtek's reputation in other countries is another factor in the imported franchise company's success in the United States. Arundel tells of a call from a person who had recently transferred from Rotterdam to a shipyard in Connecticut, asking if this was the same Pirtek he had bought all his equipment from in Rotterdam. When assured that it was, he quickly replied, "Then, I'll definitely be calling you."

In October, KFC celebrated the grand opening of its 500th restaurant in China with a traditional "Lion Dance" to bring good fortune. Since then another 100 KFCs have opened in China, where, says Fitzjohn, "The Colonel is revered. Customers frequently have their photograph taken with life-size statues of the legendary founder outside our restaurants."

Other franchises, while lacking the celebrity of Colonel Sanders, also have expanded their global reach into countries with strong markets, then reached beyond them into "emerging" economies that are just growing strong enough to support franchise development. While these markets offer unusual opportunities, they often also present special challenges for the franchisor.

Uniglobe's most recent opening, for example, was in India, where Henry describes franchising as the "new kid on the block." "It's not that it doesn't have credibility; it's just that people don't know what it is and don't understand it," he explains. "The franchisee-franchisor relationship is unlike any other relationship, and there is a tendency to be bureaucratic to things fitting into certain boxes. With franchising, we are presenting them with a new box." By choosing a sophisticated master franchisee who already understood franchising, Uniglobe was able to overcome the challenges involved with opening its operation in India.

Considerations for Expansion

In addition to strong local partnerships, international development specialists stress the need for plenty of support from the home office. Blimpie, which began franchising in 1964, is a relative newcomer to international franchising. Most of its 60 units operating in other countries are less than three years old.

"That speaks to our deliberate approach," says Joseph. "Before we launched internationally, we wanted to design and have the infrastructure in place."

He emphasizes the need to build a team oriented to the international marketplace. "A different kind of development is required. Younger markets need more energy. If you are in New York and you say Blimpie, people know what that is, but in Mexico, they don't know. What does the brand stand for? What is the product? We have to create that brand identity."

Focus and resource are the keys to successfully entering foreign markets, according to Tricon's Fitzjohn. "Most companies fail when they are focused on too many things and not properly resourced. Differentiate yourself from the competition," he further advises.

Fernadez says she acquaints herself thoroughly with local culture and customs before introducing the Novus automotive services to a new location.

"Make sure that the person directing the global operations in your company is knowledgeable enough and has the skill to build global relationships," she advises. "In the international market, a company is going to find they have to build the relationship before they close the deal."

Among other considerations for companies expanding internationally are legal and trademark issues. "It's all very well to have your trademark registered around the world, but if you are not using it, it is still at risk," explains Uniglobe's Henry. He notes that, while in cases of trademark violation, the first inclination is to resort to legal conflict, negotiating often can achieve better results.

"Of the four situations we have had, the outcome was always more satisfactory when, after we protected our legal rights, we dealt person-to-person. One of the best reasons for doing this is, once you get into conflict in some countries, particularly emerging countries, the legal processes take two or three times as long."

AlphaGraphics' Gerson describes a specific checklist of considerations his company uses when deciding whether to go into a new foreign territory:

1. ability to protect our trademarks and intellectual properties;
2. "comfort level," i.e., the economic stability and projected growth in the country ("One of the obligations we have as the franchisor is to also make sure that we can effectively support the master franchisee, and so we want to make sure we are not sending our people into dangerous or unstable environments," Gerson explains);
3. taxation rates and stability;
4. recognition of contract law within certain countries;
5. language barriers; and
6. availability of labor in the skill needed.

What Not to Do

Along with the advice to build strong local relationships, respect cultural differences, develop an adequate infrastructure, and research your markets thoroughly, international development experts agree on one big "don't" for companies considering "going global": Don't do it for the license fee.

"You have to be prepared to do the work," Gerson says. "Be prepared to travel, prepared to support, to do what it takes to make your international master franchisees profitable and happy. You can't leave them alone. You have to make sure that they understand the product and that the market is a viable place to do business."

Uniglobe's Henry agrees. "Make sure you are doing it for the right reasons. There are so many companies who expand internationally for the worst reason possible. They need the money. And that is one of the biggest nails in a coffin. A company should expand internationally when they don't need the money, when they have really established themselves in their home market."

Polly Larson is a freelance writer. She was editor of Franchising World *for 14 years and now contributes frequently to the magazine.*

From *Franchising World*, April 2002, pp. 6-8. © 2002 by Franchising World. Reprinted by permission.

The Role of International Trade and Investment

Policymakers in the United States and other nations should heed the lessons from the last great global downturn—the Great Depression of the 1930s.

CLAUDE E. BARFIELD

In combating the deepening worldwide recession, policymakers should heed lessons from the last great global downturn—the depression of the 1930s. The lessons are both negative and positive. That is, they tell us what policies should not be applied, as well as which ones should serve as models in this first decade of the twenty-first century.

Certainly, a key component of any strategy to jump-start national economies will be domestic stimulus packages. They need to be carefully crafted to provide short- and medium-term stimuli (tax cuts and targeted spending increases) without gravely damaging long-term fiscal health or thwarting structural adjustment. But given the advanced state of globalization, U.S. policymakers should give special attention to the role of trade and foreign direct investment (FDI) as a means of restoring noninflationary economic growth.

Here the lessons of the 1930s, particularly of what nations should *not* do, are striking. In 1930, after the stock market crash but before the full onset of the Depression, Congress passed the infamous Hawley-Smoot Tariff Act. Logrolling and the reconstruction of most individual tariff rates caused the average U.S. tariff

rate to rise steeply to almost 60 percent, thereby reducing import volume by 12–20 percent.

Today economists do not argue that Hawley-Smoot caused the Depression, but they generally agree that it was one important factor in precipitating a worldwide trade collapse. The League of Nations argued in 1933 that the U.S. tariff act "was the signal for an outburst of tariff-making activity in other countries, partly at least by way of reprisal." Studies have documented this result in Canada, Spain, and Switzerland; in other nations, purely domestic pressures were deciding factors.

In any case, the international economic scene changed dramatically between 1929 and 1932. Worldwide, trade volume fell 26 percent, and industrial production plummeted 32 percent during these years. Protections in the form of tariffs, import quotas, and foreign exchange restrictions spread like wildfire. The collapse of trade during the 1930s meant that one key engine of economic growth was no longer available to turn around national economies. Thus, while increased protection may not have caused the Depression, it did prolong and deepen it.

Postwar trading program

Those who constructed our postwar multilateral trading system were very mindful of the disastrous international economic experience of the 1930s. Though protectionist sentiment still prevailed in many nations, postwar leaders from North America and Europe established the General Agreement on Trade and Tariffs (GATT) to begin the laborious process of reducing trade and investment barriers.

Over the past 50 years, as a result of negotiations in eight rounds, average national tariffs have gradually been reduced from 55 percent in 1945 to 3–4 percent today. In the Uruguay Round that ended in 1994, the GATT tackled major nontariff barriers behind the borders in such areas as services and agriculture.

The economic consequences of this steady reduction of restrictions, which resulted in more open markets and increased competition, constitute a second positive lesson from the past. Trade and FDI became true engines for economic growth, not only for developed countries like the United States but also for developing countries such as South Korea,

The Legacy of Hawley-Smoot

- The lessons of the 1930s—particularly what nations should *not* do—are striking.

- In 1930, after the stock market crash but before the full onset of the Great Depression, Congress passed the infamous Hawley-Smoot Tariff Act, which raised the average U.S. tariff rate to almost 60 percent, consequently reducing import volume by 12 to 20 percent.

- Today economists do not argue that Hawley-Smoot caused the Depression, but they generally agree that it was one important factor in precipitating a worldwide trade collapse.

- Learning from the mistakes of the past, the Bush administration should give high priority to liberalizing trade and investment as an essential element of its drive to return the U.S. economy to a path of sustained growth.

- A new trade round with lower tariffs would be the most important element of a growth-enhancing international trade and investment strategy.

Singapore, Chile, and, more recently, China, Mexico, and Brazil.

A review of the figures for trade, FDI, and national economic growth weaves a convincing tale of positive synergy. In almost every year from 1945 to 2000, the worldwide growth of merchandise trade exceeded the growth of national output, often by substantial margins. From 1950 to 1963 annually, the average growth in trade volume was almost 8 percent, while national output growth averaged 5 percent. From 1990 to 2000, trade volume grew 7 percent and average output grew 3 percent. Thus, throughout the entire period, international trade exerted a positive, pulling effect on individual national economies, allowing them to exceed their domestic growth potential through commerce with other nations.

During the 1990s, FDI began to enhance growth throughout the world economy, particularly in the United States. The United States was far and away the largest investor in foreign economies, and it attracted the most FDI within its own economy. In 1998, for instance, U.S. FDI amounted to $980 billion, while FDI in the United States reached $812 billion. Directly connected to trade, FDI enhanced the positive "pulling effect" of trade on the U.S. national economy. Forty percent of our merchandise trade and about 60 percent

of our services trade consist of commerce between domestic and foreign affiliates of U.S. and foreign companies.

The payoff from future trade negotiations

Recent trading rounds have liberalized trade and investment, but much remains to be done. Highly respected University of Michigan economists have calculated the potential future gains that would flow from additional trade liberalization. They estimate that a 33 percent reduction of post—Uruguay Round tariffs on agricultural and industrial products, combined with a 33 percent reduction in services barriers, would produce annual world welfare gains of $613 billion, with $177 billion of this total going to the United States, $169 billion to Europe, $124 billion to Japan, and $90 billion to developing countries. (In the United States, a one-third reduction in trade barriers would translate into an additional $2,500 annually for a typical American family of four—just the kind of jump start for consumerism that is needed in a potentially severe downturn.)

Further, about 80 percent of the gains stem from liberalization in the services sectors—areas where the United States enjoys a strong competitive advantage and where increased liberalization would result in often doubling or tripling U.S.

services exports over the short term, further stimulating U.S. job growth.

A plan of action

Given the potential payoffs, the Bush administration should give high priority to liberalizing trade and investment as an essential element of its drive to return the U.S. economy to a path of sustained, noninflationary economic growth.

> **A new trade round is the most important positive element of a growth-enhancing international trade and investment strategy.**

First, do no harm. Harking back to the experience of the 1930s, the initial guideline should be "First, do no harm." This means actively opposing interest groups that want increased protection in such areas as steel and textiles. The Bush administration, unfortunately, has already made some concessions to the steel industry.

But in fashioning a "safeguards" measure to grant temporary relief for steel, the administration should demand that current protectionist antidumping actions be dropped for the duration of government relief. It should publicly pledge that after a short (two- to three-year) period we would open our steel market to all comers.

Such a program makes overwhelming economic sense for it builds upon the reality that steel users contribute tenfold more to U.S. economic and job growth than does the shrinking and uncompetitive U.S. steel industry.

In the same category of "do no harm," the administration should oppose the farm bill that Congress is considering, which increases agricultural subsidies and price supports. Passage of a bill that increases subsidies would inevitably result in greater distortions in the international market for agricultural products and greatly complicate future trade negotiations.

Multilateral liberalization. A new trade round is the most important positive element of a growth-enhancing international trade and investment strategy. Among the areas that could bring the highest economic gains, the following are the most essential:

- Services. Some 80 percent of welfare gains accruing to the United States stem from liberalization of key service sectors such as telecommunication, financial services, energy services, and professional services.
- Agriculture. To achieve substantial world welfare gains in a new round, liberalization in the trade of agricultural products is absolutely essential. Progress here is a prerequisite for obtaining support from developing countries for liberalization in all other sectors.
- Industrial Tariffs. While average industrial tariffs in developed countries are now relatively low (3–4 percent), there are important exceptions. In addition, many developing countries have special exemptions that should be gradually removed in the new round.
- Textiles. As with agriculture, this sector (which is protected in some developed countries by tariffs up to 20–25 percent) is of major importance to the economies of many developing countries. Indeed, the United States should unilaterally reduce textile tariffs starting in 2005 and after.
- Investment. Though the rights of investors to sue governments are controversial, a set of simple, transparent rules for foreign investors should be formulated. Of particular importance would be regulations further restricting performance (export) requirements for foreign investors.
- Environment and labor policies. In return for advances in agriculture and textiles, developing countries should allow the WTO to establish study groups in these areas—without any implication that such activities will result in new rules and sanctions in these areas.

Regional and bilateral agreements. Economically, the two most important agreements for the United States are the Free Trade of the Americas Agreement (FTAA) and the Asia Pacific Economic Community agreement. In both cases, negotiations should be pursued as backups if WTO talks bog down. But all parties to these two agreements should keep in mind that their economic payoffs are much less than with worldwide trade liberalization.

The FTAA, for instance, is estimated to increase world welfare by only $78 billion—$53 billion for the United States and about $25 billion for the rest of North and South America. Bilateral agreements are correspondingly smaller in payoff and introduce additional problems of trade diversion (i.e., increased trade between two countries because of differential tariff rates and not because either is necessarily the lowest-cost producer).

Conclusion

For most of its history, the U. S. economy has operated as an independent, relatively self-contained unit. During the 1930s, even though the global Depression had a negative impact on the U.S. economy, trade (exports plus imports) as a percentage of the total U.S. economy never even reached 10 percent.

Today, matters are dramatically different. The United States is much more affected by international trade and investment disruptions. Exports and imports now represent about one-quarter of the total U.S. economy, and the new importance of foreign direct investment (about 20 percent of the U.S. economy) links the U.S. economy even more directly to the world economy.

Thus, getting it right on international trade and investment policy is an indispensable component of any U.S. strategy to combat the growing menace of recession.

Claude E. Barfield is a resident scholar at the American Enterprise Institute in Washington, D.C.

From *The World & I*, January 2002, pp. 26-31. © 2002 by The World & I, a publication of The Washington Times Corporation. Reprinted by permission.

Article 39

AAEI Conference Highlights:
What Does China's Entry Into the WTO Mean for US Exporters?

At the west coast conference of the American Association of Exporters & Importers (AAEI; www.aaei.org), held in Los Angeles, fully half the export-related programs were devoted to China's accession to the World Trade Organization (WTO) and its implications. Hands-on practical workshops like What China's Entry into the WTO Means for U.S. Exporters, Finding Customers in China, Chinese Customs Requirements and Practices, and Chinese Business Culture: Rules for Doing Business in China gave attending export pros a wealth of valuable information and ideas on how to penetrate this growing—and now more accessible—market.

The significant attention to China by AAEI is not surprising. In 2000, China was the United State's fourth largest trading partner and 10th largest destination for U.S. exports. China is also among the fastest growing export destinations for U.S. goods and services, up 20% for the first nine months of 2001—before China's WTO admission. U.S. exports to China have doubled since 1990, reaching $16.2 billion in 2000 and projected to hit $19 billion for 2001. This is clearly a market U.S. exporters cannot afford to miss.

Whole New Ball Game

One of the conference's keynote speakers, Ambassador Jeffrey Bader, Assistant United States Trade Representative, laid out the scope of the unilateral, market-opening concessions across nearly every market sector that China made to the United States for WTO admission:

- Industrial tariffs slashed. Industrial tariffs on U.S. products will fall from a 25% average in 1997 to an 8.9% average by 2005.
- Agriculture tariffs cut. On key agricultural products, tariffs will drop from a 31% average to 14% by 2004, with sharper drops for some commodities. U.S. firms will be allowed to export and distribute directly within China for most agricultural products, bypassing state-trading enterprises and middlemen.
- Right to import and distribute liberalized. In the past, China severely restricted the right to import and the ability to own and operate distribution networks. Trading rights and distribution services will be phased in over three years and distribution-related sectors (repair and maintenance, warehousing, trucking, air courier services) will be opened up. U.S. firms will no longer have to set up factories in China to sell products through Chinese partners.
- New markets for IT. China will join the Information Technology Agreement and eliminate tariffs on two-thirds of products like computers, semiconductors, and related goods by 2003—and all such products by 2005.
- Telecom, Insurance, Banking. In another "first," China will open its telecommunications sector, expand investment and other activities for financial services firms, and increase opportunities open to legal, management consulting, accounting, and other professional services.
- Joint ventures. Joint ventures with minority foreign ownership will gain full trading rights within one year and joint ventures with majority foreign ownership within two years of WTO accession. All enterprises in China will gain full trading rights within three years.
- Intellectual Property safeguards. Full implementation of the Trade-Related Aspects of Intellectual Property Agreement (TRIPS).
- Trade barriers removed. Importation and investment approvals can no longer be based on the existence of competing domestic suppliers or on performance requirements (such as export performance, local content, technology transfer, offsets, foreign exchange balancing, R&D). China may not use technical regulations, standards and conformity assessment procedures as unnecessary obstacles to trade.
- Taxes. China has committed to ensuring that its national and local laws and regulations relating to internal taxes and charges levied on imports comply with WTO rules and are applied without discrimination.
- Subsidies. China agrees to eliminate all subsidies on industrial goods prohibited under WTO rules,

such as export and import substitution subsidies.

From Agreement to Implementation

As Bader noted, "agreements on paper are one thing, performance is another." Export pros can anticipate an uneven and sometimes frustrating road ahead, however compliance mechanisms are in place:

- Export pros can access both China's Goods and Services Schedules on the WTO Web site: www.wto.org.
- China has established an "inquiry point," with a 30-day response time, to provide information about laws and regulations related to WTO commitments. Inquiries must be made in writing on forms downloaded from the MOFTEC (Chinese agency responsible for trade negotiation and administration) Web site (www.moftec.gov.cn) or fax: 0086-10-65197340, and submitted by fax or mail. China has agreed to translate all such trade laws and regulations into one or more of the WTO languages (English, French, Spanish).
- Commerce's "China Team" monitors implementation of the agreement on a new computer database. Seven new officers have been added to the China Office in Washington, D.C., and four more compliance officers to China.
- Export pros can download the guide, Dispute Avoidance and Dispute Resolution in China from a homepage link on Commerce's new China Web site: www.export.gov/china. The site provides details on China's WTO compliance and export opportunities to China.
- Export pros encountering specific trade problems or trade barriers in exporting to China can contact Commerce's Trade Compliance Center (e-mail: TCC@ita.doc.gov; Web site: www.tcc.mac.doc.gov). Or, report trade complaints at: www.mac.doc.gov/tcc.

From *Managing Exports*, April 2002, p. 1. © 2002 by Managing Exports Report, editor, Chris Horner, 212/244-0360, http://www.ioma.com.

POST-COLD WAR INTERNATIONAL RELATIONS: TRENDS AND PORTENTS

Sharif M. Shuja

Two world wars and the establishment of totalitarian tyrannies have shaken our faith in progress; technological civilization has shown that it possesses immense powers of destruction, for the natural world as well as for the cultural and spiritual environment. The civilization of abundance is also that of famines in Africa and other places. The collapse of totalitarian communism has left intact the evils of the democratic liberal societies, ruled by the demon of money. As the scramble for global wealth unfolds, international banks, transnational corporations are anxious to play a direct role in shaping financial structures and policing economic reforms.

One can find modern societies repellent on two accounts. On the one hand, they have taken the human race and turned it into a homogeneous mass: modern humans seem to have all come out of a factory, not a womb. On the other hand, they have made every one of those beings a hermit. Capitalist democracies have created uniformity, not equality, and they have replaced fraternity with a perpetual struggle among individuals. The collapse of communism and the end of the Cold War have brought neither economic stability nor social democracy to the world. Instead of 'a New World Order', based on democracy, open markets, law and a commitment to peace, we witness a geopolitical disorder.

On the positive side, it has paved the way for the universal aspiration for democracy as the only form of acceptable government because of its vital self-correcting capacity. It is said that we now live in one world, often called a global village. It can be argued that in many ways, particularly in terms of instant communications, of economic value, of a desire to avoid war, of a functional integration, of disease control, monetary and trade policies and so on, we are more of an integrated global community than ever before.

The dynamic transfer of people, information, capital and goods is progressing on a worldwide scale. Globalisation and an expansion of information technology have given rise to a new wave of changes in international relations. In this global era, people from numerous countries and civilizations will be blessed with the opportunity to work together.

While discovering in the next section the general trends in post-Cold War international relations, this article does not deal with how to learn the tricks of international relations. It is rather a reflection on some pretty powerful underlying forces which govern our lives unless we understand and take control of them.

Trends in Post-Cold War International Relations

These general trends can be identified in post-Cold War international relations.

First, on the security front, we have observed the decline in the salience of strategic nuclear weapons. The world is in transition from nuclear to conventional deterrence at the central (global) level. In the Cold War era, the strategic pillar of mutual assured destruction (MAD) made conquest difficult and expansion futile by either camp. The futility of expansion accounted for robust deterrence. Moreover, nuclear deterrence was robust for at least two other reasons: (1) due to the futility of 'overkill', it was possible for the superpowers to reach a weapons parity, and thus equilibrium, bringing stability to the system; and (2) ever fearful of the massive destructive might of nuclear weapons, each superpower had a powerful incentive to constrain its followers, lest a reserve proxy war break out unwittingly.

Thus, on the security front, we recognize that there is a growing trend toward depolarization, with the United States as the sole superpower. With the danger of thermonuclear warfare greatly diminished, the world has become more peaceful. But at the same time, the revival of nationalism, fundamentalism and ethnonationalist disputes in some parts of the world has become a threat to international peace and the integrity of nations. New short and long-term security challenges also have come to the fore, such as the ongoing mid-intensity regional conflicts, the proliferation of weapons of mass destruction, and uncertainties surrounding the reform process in the former Soviet Republics (Commonwealth of Independent States) and in other former socialist countries.

One important aspect is that the concept of security is now broadening to encompass issues, such as national development and economic interdependency, environmental protection and the promotion of democracy and human rights.

Second, on the economic front, there is a continuing trend toward tripolarity, with the European Union (EU), North America, and East Asia as the major poles. Each of them accounts for approximately one-fourth of the world's gross national product (GNP). The importance of economic factors in defining international relationships has grown relative to politico-security factors, and one of the major economic challenges facing us today is, of course, the possibility of increased friction among the three major economic poles.

This perception of tripolar economic alignments, in turn, makes us ask ourselves the following questions: Will the transatlantic security partnership run into trouble? Will transpacific trade friction intensify? Can regionalism and interdependence coexist in such a way as to maintain an open trading system, despite, or perhaps facilitated by, the tripolar economic arrangement?

Finally, on the ideological front, the ideas of market democracy, civil society, transparency and accountability of government, and market economy are becoming universalized.

The collapse of communism left the USA and its allies as the pre-eminent voices in intellectual, policy and scholarly discourse—many of the values that the Soviets espoused have been discredited and generally rejected. Command economies and many of the elements of socialism are in disrepute; market principles, private property and competition are hailed as the essentials of economic health. Communist Party monopoly of power and extensive and intrusive state bureaucracies are rejected; elections, democratic governments and civil society are widely seen as the hallmarks of good governance.

The values and institutions associated with Western societies during the Cold War do not, of course, provide panaceas. They will undoubtedly undergo serious challenges, and modifications. International policies will continue to influence such choices, but will presumably not dominate them to the degree that bipolar politics did during the past half-century. Scholarship will continue to shape and clarify social, political, and economic options, but should operate in an atmosphere of greater openness and flexibility.

These fundamental transformations of international relations have undoubtedly produced profound changes in the Korean Peninsula. First of all, the major foreign policies and relationships of both the South and the North have undergone significant changes. Although Pyongyang seems reluctant to acknowledge these publicly, the tremendous changes that have taken place within its major allies and friends must have produced a profound impact on North Korea. The most obvious example is that North Korea together with South Korea as a Korean team participated in the XXVII Olympic Games in Sydney from 15 September to 1 October, 2000.

The Asia Pacific region is undergoing extensive and unprecedented change and the trend today is towards greater integration, democratization, and deregulation.

Market forces have become the instruments of change and transformation in international relations and nowhere more so today than in the Asia Pacific region. The forces for global change are economic in origin, but they operate within particular political systems and deeply rooted cultures that will modify and condition their effect. The impact of global change upon the many disparate cultures and political systems of the Asia Pacific region is one of the most important issues of international relations today. Is globalisation a set of processes dominated by Western countries to their own advantage? It is not easy to answer, but the implication is that globalisation refers to a complex of changes rather than a single one. No single country, or group of countries, controls any one of them. Economic globalisation, of course, has been and is shaped by U.S. foreign and domestic policy. Globalisation will not have the same effect in the Asia Pacific region as in North America or Europe, and it would be senseless to imagine that the impact would be similar, or that the results of globalisation would be uniform and comparable for all regions and cultures. At this stage we need to look at this globalisation issue more closely.

Globalisation and the Knowledge Divide

There is every indication that globalisation will increase. Western powers and the Western-based NGOs are likely to continue to promote the universalisation of values, rules and institutions. However, the pressure for homogenisation will intensify the struggle for diversity, autonomy and heterogeneity. Dr Samuel M. Makinda of Murdoch University's School of International Politics argued in 1998, in Current Affairs Bulletin (April/May), that:

The question of how to reconcile differences with uniformity, universalism with particularism, and globalisation with fragmentation, will remain central to policy makers at the national, regional and global levels. Political leaders will continue to determine policies that facilitate or frustrate globalisation, taking into account domestic and external pressures. But, at the same time, transnational forces will continue to lobby the states, regional organisations and the UN to try to influence those policies. It is this inter-subjective relationship between the policy-makers and the transnational forces that determines the character of globalisation.

However, the assumption that the real driving forces are the markets suits many political leaders. Government officials will, Dr Makinda further argues, 'often try to blame globalisation for their policy failures. They will claim that they were powerless to do much for their countries in the face of globalising forces. But, as always, they will claim credit for any positive results from globalisation'.

Globalisation, no doubt, brings us into contact with one another, but it also strengthens profound divisions and fractures in terms of societies and income, and most importantly in our capacity to generate and utilize knowledge. There is a real risk of two civilizations emerging, with two ways of viewing and relating to the world: one based on the capacity to generate and utilize knowledge; the other passively receiving knowledge from abroad and deprived of the ability to modify it. The world now faces the prospect of this Knowledge Divide.

The huge income gap between rich and poor is now being exacerbated by a North-South 'digital divide' between those who have access to computers and the Internet and those who do not. Although there have been tremendous advances in science and technology over the last few decades, the developing world is still far behind in the technological race. The world has seen a revolution, the third industrial revolution in technological know-how during the last 30 years, which has raised people's expectations to new levels. This revolution based on the information age and the rapid introduction of new technology into all facets of human life, is changing the world into a global one.

Paradoxically, this globalisation, far from creating a homogeneous global society, is subjecting societies to a logic of disintegration. It has created growing gaps and antagonisms between the rich and poor, and dominant and oppressed ethnicities.

The British historian, Professor Paul Kennedy, in his contribution to the '21st Century Talks' in Paris on 6 November 1999 said:

If we want to work towards a knowledge-based society in the coming century, over at least the next 10 years, we need to make a concerted effort to bring poorer societies into the system of electronic communication. If we do nothing, then the growing gap between haves and have-nots will lead to widespread discontent and threaten any prospect of global harmony and international understanding. That is the most significant challenge we face.

The most obvious example is the wild scenes that erupted in Melbourne in mid-September this year during the World Economic Forum meetings. Anger was demonstrated by thousands of protesters. Similar ugly incidents also erupted in the Czech capital during the recent meetings by the G-7 ministers, the World Bank and the IMF.

The Internet gives users immediate and huge access to knowledge, and the knowledge explosion is at the heart of the modernization and globalisation of world society. The Internet may have more influence than any single medium upon global educational and cultural developments in this century.

According to a recent UN Human Development Report, industrialised countries, with only 15 per cent of the world's population, are home to 88 per cent of all Internet users. South Asia, with 23 per cent of the world's population, has less than 1 per cent of the world's Internet users. In Southeast Asia, only one person in 200 is linked to the Internet. In the Arab states, only one person in 500 has Internet access. The situation is even worse in Africa. With 739 million people, there are only 14 million phone lines. That's fewer than in places such as Manhattan or Tokyo. But moves are now underway to put high-tech to use for the world's poor. In July this year the world's wealthiest nations met in Tokyo and promised to support government efforts to bridge the digital divide.

Conclusions

This article identifies four challenges that we should face in the 21st century. The first is that of peace. Since the end of the Cold War, a fourth category of countries has appeared on the international stage, in addition to the industrialized and developing countries and those in transition. It comprises countries at war or emerging from conflict in which the state has been foundering in genocide and intercommunal massacres.

The second challenge: will this 21st century witness the onset of a new kind of poverty whose victims will live side by side with unprecedented wealth?

Sustainable development and the wise management of the global environment pose the third great challenge. Everywhere humanity is draining the resources which could have fed tomorrow's generation. We have to find our way towards another type of development. One that is more economic, more intelligent, more caring.

The fourth challenge is that of the 'erratic boat' syndrome. As a result of globalisation, many states appear to have mislaid their maps, compasses and direction-finding instruments, even the will to set a course. They are tossed about by the waves, who can no longer be controlled—financial markets, raw materials markets, statistics of all kinds.

Yet awareness of these problems has sharpened and solutions exist: hope remains. We need the international community to return to the basic principles of international co-operation and introduce the idea that a minimum level of science and technological capability, including access to the Internet, is an absolute necessity for developing countries, and should be the subject of international solidarity. And greater co-operation between nation states, multinational corporations, the NGOs and the global business community is needed in meeting these challenges.

From *Contemporary Review*, February 2001, Vol. 278, Issue 1621, pp. 82-86. © 2001 by Contemporary Review, Reprinted by permission.

THE RUSSIAN APPROACH TO HUMAN RIGHTS INTERVENTION

Dmitry Shlapentokh

THE end of the Cold War and the emergence of the United States as the only superpower raised several questions concerning the direction of the country's foreign policy. There is an assumption, at least among some representatives of the American elite, that the country should lead the world in a global implementation of 'human rights' (i.e. the liberal principles of the Western world). If needed, arms would be used for this very noble purpose. This option was favoured by, for example, R. Kaplan who elaborated on it in a recent issue of the New York Times. Yet these ideas are questioned. The new President Bush asserts that American foreign policy shall be shaped by national interests not by moral considerations. In this emphasis on pragmatism he, or at least his foreign policy advisers, acknowledges that it was not ideology but national interest which led America into confrontation with the USSR during the Cold War.

The post-Soviet Russians have become even more sceptical in regard to the moral underpinnings of 'humanitarian intervention'. Many of them have discarded not just the idea of humanitarian intervention but the idea of human rights, the liberal principles of Western capitalism in general. This decline in the interest in human rights in Russia has alarmed some observers who coined the expression 'Weimar Russia' implying that present-day Russians are similar to Germans who, upon disenchantment with Western liberalism, had installed a Nazi regime. Here the observers expressed similar concerns stating that nationalist-minded and cynical Russians would launch military intervention under the excuse of 'humanitarian intervention'. Based upon personal observations, I would argue that such a scenario would be unlikely precisely because of the deep cynicism as to any slogans which have marked present day Russia.

The end of the Soviet regime in 1991 instilled most Russians with great expectations regarding their future and a deep fascination with the West. A majority of Russians indeed believed not only that 'human rights' were the very foundation of Western policy but that the foreign policy of the Western nations was guided by no other principles but moral considerations. Indeed, the principles of 'humanitarian intervention' were the very reason why the Western governments sent their troops. As time progressed the vision of foreign policy became increasingly critical. NATO's war with Serbia was clearly a watershed. I was in Moscow at that time and saw the drastic change of the mood even among longtime staunch liberals who had admired the West for their entire life. At that point there was a public consensus that 'humanitarian intervention' is a code word similar to 'international duty' which was used by arrays of Soviet leaders, including Brezhnev, as a code for imperial aggrandizement such as the invasion of Afghanistan.

The Russians also bitterly complained that they were horribly deceived in their belief in the West's good will and gave up without a fight not just the Eastern European empire but the USSR itself just to see NATO divisions near Russia's almost sixteenth-century borders. They were genuinely afraid that the 'humanitarian intervention' could be used by the Western powers, which were now much stronger than Russia, to launch a war against Russia under the excuse of 'humanitarian intervention'. Assuming that all discussion on humanitarian aspects of intervention was nothing but a cover for geopolitical pragmatism and that the West was cynical to the marrow, the Russian elite started to use the same discussion on humanitarian aspects of intervention to cover the elite's interests. When Vladimir Putin was interviewed last year on American TV, he stated that one major reason to start the second war in Chechnya was the protection of Russian citizens from foreign invaders and mercenaries. It was a 'humanitarian intervention' of a sort. It is clear that Russians became thoroughly cynical and discarded human rights and the thought that nations were engaged in wars just because of pragmatic considerations.

Yet these very assumptions did not imply that they had been converted into new editions of Nazi Germans who, while masking their nationalism by moralizing considerations, would engage in foreign adventure or even purge ethnic groups which could be seen as dangerous. Paradoxically enough, it looks as though the Russians' deep cynicism led to a discarding not just of the idea of genuine humanitarian intervention but genuine nationalism as well. The public response to the terrorist attack in August of 2000 in Moscow could be a good illustration of this. I was returning from a library and decided to make a phone call to a friend. While I dialled I took note of a pretty girl who chatted with her lover on the phone: 'Honey I will be in your embrace in a moment. And by the way, there was a terrorist attack at Pushkin square. Quite a few people are hurt'. I forgot about my call and immediately rushed to the square. The place was surrounded by the police and the crowd of bystanders discussed the events. It was a consensus that all of this was the work of the Chechens who in such a way, 'commemorated' the first anniversary of the beginning of the second Chechen war.

Prudently concealing my American citizenship and taking advantage of my native Russian and casual outfit, I tried to provoke one of my bystanders into a politically sensitive conversation: 'You know we might need a dictatorship to save the country'. 'No, not at all. We already have such stuff, it just bled country white' he responded. 'Jews, not Chechens who are actually the source of all troubles. We need to look at Barkashov and his people for guidance. They are good people, whatever the other tell about them. That cause no harm'. Barkashov was, until recently, the leader of the odious Russian National Unity which openly used Nazi-type symbols in their public meetings. The man near Barkashov's admirer exploded: 'You are kike. This explains why you preach this'. The implication was that some of Zionist-minded Jews could provoke pogroms just to compel Russian Jews to move to Israel. The Barkashov supporter was absolutely dabbed by the fact somebody called him 'kike' and immediately retreated. 'We Russians are antisemitic. This is in our very blood' proclaimed the middle aged woman in a moment of national self-flagellation. The scene became increasingly animated, as though what unfolded was a theatrical performance rather than a place of national tragedy.

Vladimir Zhirinovsky, self-styled flamboyant Russian nationalist with Jewish roots, had appeared at the scene preaching the cleansing of Moscow from Jews and Chechens. He was greeted by the crowd. He immediately understood his role and started to give autographs as though he were a popular diva. The sense of theatricality was heightened by the emergence of TV crews of some Western companies; a female producer of the show, with a characteristic 'professional' smile, repeated cheerfully in English 'Moscow is in the stage of war'. Watching her, nearby Russian girls asserted that one 'needs to get out of this country' as soon as possible. Next to them, a rather good looking blond in her late thirties, started to discuss with me that she needed a lover for her husband paid little attention to her. 'He should be a smart man'.

Observing all of this, I remembered part of the movie Cabaret. Set on the eve of the Nazi takeover it presented the cabaret as the epitomy of the degenerated Weimar Germany. Yet all of a sudden a young Nazi with a swastika band around his arm rose. He called Germans to rise and avenge the humiliated motherland, and all of a sudden his appeal started to work. The patrons of the cabaret began to stand up. These had symbolized their transformation from perverts and drug addicts to patriotic Germans; as a matter of fact one of that movie's good points was that it demonstrated that the Nazi horrors were just another side of a deeply internalized patriotic feeling translated from words to deeds. Nothing of this sort could be imagined in present-day Russia whose citizens are mostly drenched in complete cynicism. This has definite implications for Russia's approach to problems of humanitarian intervention. Russians could well see any Western move as disguised imperialism. They might even envy the Western imperial virility. Yet they themselves would hardly engage in any actions of 'humanitarian' or any other justification, at least not in the near future.

Dmitry Shlapentokh is Associate Professor at Indiana University, South Bend. His book, Counter-Revolution in Revolution, *was published by Macmillan in 1999.*

From *Contemporary Review*, March 2001, Vol. 278, Issue 1622, pp. 156-158. © 2001 by Contemporary Review. Reprinted by permission.

Offshore shores up IT

Going overseas for tech help promises big savings, but companies shouldn't go overboard without considering the risks

By Andrew Dietderich

When a company like General Motors Corp. looked overseas, it used to be for things like assembly work or auto parts. But that's changed.

When it developed a Web site for car owners, the automaker used an offshore company to develop software, said Stu Dressler, global program manager for MyGMLink.com.

GM contracted with Cognizant Technology Solutions of Teaneck, N.J., to provide offshore out-sourcing of the applications used in the multimillion-dollar Web site. The automaker said it saved 50 percent and was able to launch the site sooner.

It was the first time that GM relied on an offshore company for software development, and it won't be the last, Dressler said. GM was able to save money without sacrificing quality because Cognizant assigned the work to skilled workers in India, he said.

Experts, including Dressler and others at local information-technology consulting companies, estimate that using offshore out-sourcing can cut costs by 25 percent to 50 percent.

Program analysts in the United States earn $70,000 to $90,000 annually, compared with $15,000 to $17,000 in India, said Anup Popat, president and CEO of Troy-based Systems Technology Group Inc., an information-technology business with workers in India and the United States. Similar rates are found in India's leading competitors: China, Russia and the Philippines.

Even with the potential for huge savings, those considering offshore out-sourcing need to be aware of what to look for, how they can benefit and the potential risks involved, said Christine Overby, an analyst at Cambridge, Mass.-based Forrester Research Inc.

"Business owners must consider the fact that this is not just about a question of costs," she said. "You can undoubtedly find workers who will work for $15 an hour, but are they going to be qualified enough to handle the type of project you're working on?"

Most offshore out-sourcing is limited to mundane tasks: programming, maintenance and conversion of mainframe systems to Web-based models, Overby said.

Users and providers say they can't ignore the benefits.

In February, Decision Consultants Inc. of Southfield announced a partnership to manage Indchem Software Technologies Ltd.'s center in Chennai, India. The deal allows Decision Consultants to have some work done at Indchem Software's office.

Decision Consultants provides application development and out-sourcing, installation and support.

The company needed to offer the offshore option to cut costs and respond to customer requests, said Nozer Buchia, vice president and general manager for application-management services.

"Offshore today is not an option; it's a way of doing business," he said. "Just the other day I was meeting with a potential client. A few minutes after I started my presentation, he jumped in and said, 'Tell me about your offshore options.'"

Farmington Hills–based Syntel Inc., also a provider of out-sourced information technology, signed deals with 45 new customers in 2001. Nearly all called for at least some amount of offshore work, said Bharat Desai, Syntel's co-founder, chairman, CEO and president.

About 2,000 of Syntel's nearly 3,000 employees work at two offices in India. Syntel has 1,500 employees at Mumbai and 500 in Channi, Desai said.

Syntel (Nasdaq: SYNT) plans to increase its employee count in India by 25 percent and plans to break ground on a $100 million office in Pune that eventually could house 9,000 employees, Desai said.

The story is similar for Farmington Hills–based Covansys Corp. (Nasdaq: CVNS). That company plans to increase its employees in India to 5,000 from 1,500 over the next two years and spend $10 million to expand.

India's attractiveness stems from being the home of the Carnegie Mellon University Software Engineering Institute and for having a large pool of information-technology workers that researchers estimate will reach 1 million by 2005.

Another benefit is the amount of time saved. Because of the 12-hour time difference, companies can work a 24-hour schedule, speeding up delivery of finished products, said Popat of Systems Technology Group.

Despite the benefits, companies using or considering offshore out-sourcing need to demand more than cost savings, experts said.

Savvy executives want to see plans for disaster recovery, said Venu Vaishya, executive vice president and COO of Covansys. Businesses also are asking their offshore service providers to have a presence in their domestic workplaces.

With GM's MyGMLink.com, for example, two people from Cognizant Technology worked in the Renaissance Center and about 25 in India.

Vaishya expects the ratio between employees working in the United States and those overseas eventually to be 50-50.

Forrester Research's Overby said a shortage of high-quality workers will be a challenge to those looking to out-source overseas. Her January report estimates that the number of information-technology workers in India will grow to more than 1 million by 2005, compared with 360,000 this year. But the supply will not meet the growing demand, she said.

"I liken it to finding a pristine, beautiful vacation spot that no one knows about," Overby said. "And then it becomes an extremely popular spot. The quality suffers."

Brent Snavely contributed to this report.

Andrew Dietderich: (313) 446-0315, adietderich@crain.com

From *Crain's Detroit Business*, April 15, 2002. © 2002 by Crain's Detroit Business.

Redefining the Business Case for Offshore Outsourcing

Insurers still see the benefits of outsourcing offshore, but post-9/11 more due diligence is occurring.

by Julie Gallagher

Until about six months ago, making a decision about whether or not to move development projects and even business processes and operations offshore was starting to look like a no-brainer for many insurance executives. The cost benefits alone appeared undeniable to a growing number of CIOs looking for ways to manage tighter-than-ever IT budgets and do more with less.

But the events of September 11 changed all that. Just as insurance carriers and the primarily India-based offshore service providers were beginning to master arcane details such as communications—key to the success of IT projects outsourced offshore—concerns about terrorism have left many US insurers asking a whole new set of questions.

Same Talent Shortage

It's not that the business drivers have receded—if anything, they're more pronounced than ever. "Shortage of talent is not as big a driver as it used to be," explains Jim Wood, vice president of global insurance, Satyam (Hyderabad, India). "A big driver now is cost." But, post-9/11, the "FUD factor"—the ability of fear, uncertainty and doubt (FUD) to overwhelm even the most objective quantitative analysis—has caused many executives to have second thoughts about the economic benefits of offshore project development and outsourcing.

Furthermore, at a time when Americans are concerned about boosting the economy and supporting the country, some insurers fear they may undergo criticism for not using American labor. "Many [insurance] companies are very sensitive to not wanting to be perceived as taking away [American] jobs," says Wood, However, he adds, "very seldom do [offshore providers] go in and replace American labor. Normally a provider will augment [an insurer's] staff because there are not enough people, or we will take over a legacy system so employees can be freed up to do new work."

Be that as it may, many of the most prominent of the India-based offshore technology services providers experienced a stall in new business immediately following September 11. However, a number of companies report they are starting to see a revival in business. It seems the FUD factor is no match for the "money talks" factor. Economic losses related to the September 11 attacks, on top of an already failing economy, have forced many carriers to reconsider the offshore option in order to remain competitive. Furthermore, points out Mike LaPorta, global director, insurance practice, Deloitte Consulting (New York), it's highly unlikely that any insurers already engage in outsourcing offshore prior to 9/11 will pull out of those arrangements.

But it's not totally business as usual. In addition to long-standing concerns about communications and deliverables, insurers now want guarantees about an offshore partner's security and business continuity plans. Additionally, they are looking for help in more specialized areas such as post-merger systems consolidation and business process outsourcing in areas such as call center operations.

"There had been a dramatic downswing [in business] post 9/11, and now it is back up," says Satyam's Wood. "There was a significant new customer slowdown for a number of reasons." In part, the slowdown reflected a paralysis of business in general. For instance, many compa-

Prudential Continues To Take Offshore Plans to New Levels

Prudential Financial, an early adopter of offshore IT outsourcing, is considering expanding its offshore strategy to include the outsourcing of business processes, such as call center management, according to Barbara Koster, senior vice president and chief information officer, individual life insurance and retail distribution, Prudential Financial ($371 billion in assets, Newark).

"I think that [all insurers] at this point, including Prudential, are thinking about the opportunity of [outsourcing] call centers or back-office processing," says Koster. Although she acknowledges there are some kinds of work that must be handled onshore, she also suggests that there are a number of processes in the life insurance area that could be suitable for outsourcing, including claims handling and small transactional processes such as name and address or beneficiary changes.

Adding that Prudential has just begun its investigation of the viability of outsourcing business processes offshore, Koster adds, "I am sure that there are cost advantages or efficiency advantages that are similar to [those gained on the] technology side."

Prudential currently splits its IT projects 50/50 between onshore and offshore. The company began outsourcing seven years ago to Tata Consultancy Services (Mumbai), four years before the practice gained popularity with insurers facing Y2K conversion. The original relationship—which involved the conversion of coding language from Prudential COBOL to a standard ANSI COBOL—eventually expanded into Tata's handling of Prudential's Y2K conversion. The outsourcing provider currently maintains Prudential Financial applications.

In the fourth quarter of 2000, facing a shortage of domestic IT talent, Prudential decided to build on its successful experience with Tata and try to leverage the opportunity to gain cost and quality advantages by sending projects offshore. It launched Prumerica Systems Ireland, Ltd. (Letterkenny, County Donegal), which develops and maintains new and existing technologies. At this point, according to Koster, Prudential's IT that is outsourced offshore to split 50/50 between Ireland and India.

jgallagher@cmp.com

offshore deals. And, because many carriers had to deal with disaster recovery, as well as an influx of claims, "the insurance industry became more inwardly focused," after 9/11, Wood explains.

Adding to FUD concerns—and causing a slowdown in business—were worries about a rise in political tensions and conflicts between India and neighboring Pakistan. Indian/Pakistani border conflicts heated up in late September while the US planned its attacks on terrorism, fueling new fears of doing any kind of business in that part of the world. "Insurers* are risk averse, and that is why the FUD factor is so important," says Wood.

Prospective customers need to put these developments into perspective, notes Venu Vaishva, executive vice president and chief operating officer, US operations, for Covansys (Farmington Hills, MI). "In the last 40 or 50 years both India and Pakistan have fought three different wars. If you go back even earlier to World Wars I and II, the southern part of India was never affected," he emphasizes. Vaishva also points out that many of the Indian tech development centers are located thousands of miles away from the fighting in Kashmir.

It is this kind of mix of political education and economic reality check that is causing existing offshore clients to stay the course, and convincing prospective offshore outsourcers to overcome their fears. A recent study from Cambridge, MA-based Forrester Research illustrates this trend. According to Christine Overby, analyst and author of "Offshore Outsourcing Restructures in 2002," this past October she and the study's other authors met with nine executives who had been interviewed for "The Coming Offshore Services Crunch," a Forrester study done before September 11. All but one of the nine interviewed said their firms planned to maintain and grow their offshore investments in 2002. "Surprisingly, the companies haven't scaled back efforts," says Overby. For example, one participant acknowledged that, while the risks of going offshore were great, he still needed to find ways to cut costs. Instead, "they have demanded business continuity plans from providers," Overby says.

> Meetings with US clients, since September, have included "a little education on the political situation [in India],"says Anant Krishnan, Tata Infotech.

This is the biggest change in the offshore equation, post-9/11. Insurers already working with tight IT budgets must now do all they can to manage the possible risks of outsourcing offshore. This has caused CIO concerns to be "shockingly different from what they were in the past," according to Deb Mukherjee, CTO at Cognizant Technologies Solutions (Teaneck, NJ). Mukherjee should

nies temporarily prohibited international business travel, which postponed the due diligence process for pending know—before joining Cognizant he was a top technology executive with Farmers Insurance.

He reports he is now having a lot more business contingency plan discussions with prospective clients. "[CIOs] are asking, 'If there is a terrorist attack, what will happen? What is the recourse and [which vendor] is better equipped?'" Mukherjee relates. Insurers are concerned not only with business contingency plans, but the physical security of Indian outsourcing centers, as well. "They are interested in facilities' security guards and if different departments are checking bags," says Mukherjee. "Also, they are watching closely to see how visitors and employees are treated."

According to Satyam's Wood, since 9/11 insurers have become very receptive to having back-ups for contingency management at offshore outsourcing provider locations in the US. "They are asking, 'If something happens in India, can [my company] use your US location as a back-up site?'" says Wood. "We didn't used to have that question."

Since September, meetings with prospective US clients have included "a little education on the political situation [in India]," according to Anant Krishnan, director of business development, Tata Infotech (Mumbai). Fears tend to be calmed when contingency plans are discussed. "Having more locations mitigates the risk perception," Krishnan points out. Tata Infotech, for instance, connects its Chicago and McLean, VA, development centers to its Indian centers with two high-speed data links. Customer locations are then linked to the US development centers. These connections, according to Krishnan, should give US-based insurers a greater sense of security.

> "The major Indian IT suppliers already have resilient networks, so no price increase is likely," says Jim Wood, Satyam.

Timing Is Everything

Although recent events have caused insurers to question the business continuity plans of their offshore providers, most of the major Indian suppliers already had such plans in place. Accordingly, the major players do not anticipate that pricing will be affected. "There should not be a significant price impact, [if any,] for a robust business continuity plan," contends Satyam's Wood. "The major Indian IT suppliers already have resilient networks, so no price increase is likely." Still, although most of its clients did not request reviews, Satyam has published its business contingency plan. Also, the provider has been certified by the information security management system (ISMS) as a BS 7799 security firm. BS 7799 is a British standard developed in response to demand for a common framework to en-

able companies to develop, implement and measure security management practices.

The business concerns that caused New York-based MetLife to begin outsourcing some of its legacy work to one of Cognizant Technologies' Indian locations six months ago have not changed in the post-9/11 world, observes Mukesh Mehta, vice president and leader of MetLife's offshore outsourcing strategy. The main driver was a desire to free up its IT personnel to work on "more exciting new technology," says Mehta, who previously led Aetna's offshore initiatives.

Coincidentally, according to Mehta, MetLife was in the process of reviewing Cognizant's contingency plans prior to September 11. Mehta also visited one of Cognizant's 10 Indian development centers in January to see the plans firsthand. "[Cognizant] had a lot of redundancy with communication links between its development centers, so if there is an issue with one center, people can be moved to another," says Mehta. "It has the resources and the space to handle that." MetLife has two communications links connecting it to a Cognizant development center in India, one of which is for primary use. The other is a back-up VPN link.

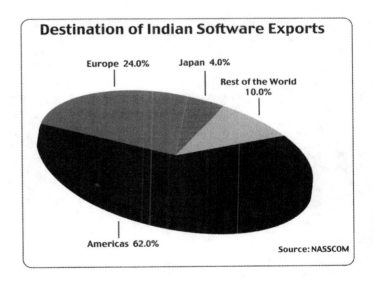

Destination of Indian Software Exports

Europe 24.0% Japan 4.0% Rest of the World 10.0% Americas 62.0%

Source: NASSCOM

Besides the long-standing motivation or redeploying internal and external resources, another trend that should convince hesitant insurers to take a second look at offshore is the expected acceleration of mergers and acquisitions in the industry. According to Shankar Krishnaswamy, Convansys' vice president of delivery for New England, carriers will be juggling consolidation along with general IT management post-merger and acquisition, which will convince them to outsource IT offshore. "Most companies that are post-merger have a five-year integration plan," says Krishnaswamy. "Usually when a CIO has to deal with consolidation while keeping operations going, outsourcing offshore fuels growth."

Because insurers are under greater pressure to be cost-effective, says Satyam's Wood, they also are looking at alternative processes to outsource. "Business process outsourcing [BPO], as a trend, is beginning now for insurers," says Wood. In fact, he says the move to outsource business processes, including call centers or back-office processing such as claims management or administrative functions, is "the next gold rush." Wood continues, "Call center valuation has already started and been proven. It's been going on for years, but not in insurance."

Despite all the proven benefits and likely opportunities, some companies conclude that while outsourcing makes sense, offshore just isn't for them. Allmerica Financial (Worcester, MA), which began its search for a provider in 1999, looked at US companies that had both offshore and nearshore facilities, says Greg Tranter, CIO, Allmerica Financial. "We wanted to [outsource to] a US-based business because of business continuity and because we wanted to deal with a provider locally," he says.

In the beginning of the process, says Tranter, Allmerica was more interested in sending IT functions offshore. "The more we looked at outsourcing offshore, the more discomfort the business units had with the idea because [India] was so far away," says Tranter. Allmerica recently decided to outsource property-and-casualty development and support of applications for its variable annuity business administration system nearshore to Keane, Inc.'s Halifax, Nova Scotia, location. "Halifax is an easy hour away by plane," says Tranter. "The cost savings just weren't worth [the distance of outsourcing offshore]."

jgallagher@cmp.com

From *Insurance & Technology*, April 2002, pp. A5, A8-A9. © 2002 by Miller Freeman Inc.

Comrades are on the march again

Even Honda, union-free for 16 years, has been forced to
recognise workers' rights. **John Kelly** on a union revival

Are the trade unions back in business? Or can we put the rail strikes down to the peculiar conditions created by the disaster of privatisation?

It is true that, since privatisation in 1994, the rail industry has become almost as strike-prone as Britain's badly managed postal service. Privatisation was supposed to cut the power of the national rail unions; competition between firms, it was said, would allow employers to play off one group of workers against another and drive down terms and conditions, freeing up profits for investors. In fact, recent labour shortages, coupled with union organisation and militancy, have allowed workers to play off one company against another and drive wages up.

But the more revealing evidence of union revival comes from firms that were formerly non-union. Within the past year, Euro-tunnel, a byword for sophisticated union avoidance, was compelled to sign a recognition agreement with the Transport and General Workers' Union. Within the past month, at the giant Honda car plant in Swindon, which has stood union-free for 16 years, nearly three-quarters of the workers voted to be represented by Amicus (the product of the merger between the AEEU, the engineering and electrical union, and the white-collar union MSF). The number of union victories of this kind has more than doubled since Labour's Employment Relations Act 1999 obliged employers to negotiate with a trade union if a majority of workers voted for recognition in a secret ballot.

Moreover, after falling from a peak of 13.2 million in 1979 to just above 7.5 million in 1998, total union membership is now rising annually and has recovered to about 7.7 million. And the unions—although they are still ignored over matters such as the private finance initiative and privatisation of air traffic control—have regained a measure of influence over government policy.

The British recovery is echoed widely, if unevenly, around the advanced capitalist world. American unions, which currently represent less than 10 per cent of the private sector workforce, have stepped up their efforts to organise non-union employees, with some notable successes. One example was the "Justice for Janitors" campaign, launched in Los Angeles in the early 1990s, and dramatically portrayed in Ken Loach's film *Bread and Roses*. The Italian union movement successfully exploited the collapse of the political system in 1993–94 to position itself as a stabilising force with which any government had

to deal if it wanted to enjoy legitimacy in the eyes of the electorate. Through a series of high-level negotiations, or "social pacts", the union confederations have exerted influence over a number of labour market, social security and pension reforms. It is a similar story in Spain, where despite a right-wing government coming to office in 1996, the unions have influenced several significant labour market reforms through high-level negotiations with government ministers.

How do we explain these signs of union revival? Politics is one factor. The advent of centre-left coalitions in countries such as the UK, Italy, France, Germany and New Zealand has created political opportunities for unions, even in countries where the union movement remains politically divided, as in Italy, France and Spain. These governments have had to face the harsh consequences of global competition and European deregulation but, unlike many of their right-wing predecessors, they have chosen not to exclude unions in the formation and implementation of state policy.

The same argument holds at company level. While there are still many employers, especially in the United States and the UK, who loathe and fear trade unionism, there are others who can see benefits in consulting and negotiating over change with independent worker representatives. Unions have also been adept at exploiting the growing volume of legal rights for the individual. Evidence shows that an individual who takes an employment claim to an industrial tribunal more than doubles his or her chance of success if represented by a union. This also affects compensation levels. The average tribunal award for sex discrimination is £2,515; the average figure for a union-backed claim is £17,082.

Such successes reflect some of the reasons that workers have given in recent years for joining trade unions, but the underlying factor is a general lack of trust in the willingness or ability of the employer to look after employees' interests. In the banking sector, for example, once renowned for its paternalistic management style, a typical 1990s press release would announce a substantial growth in profits, an imminent merger with another firm and a major round of job losses. Falling unemployment has also helped the unions, particularly when, as in Britain, it coincides with shortages of skilled labour arising because employers have been too foolish and short-sighted to invest sufficiently in training.

Finally, the unions themselves have played a part in shaping their own destiny. The increased resources going to organising non-union employees have had to be argued and fought for within the union movement by leaders such as John J Sweeney in the US and John Monks in the UK. Both realised that the unions had to recover their membership if they were to recover their power and influence. In Britain, the rhetoric of social partnership has also been used to allay the fears of employers and to refashion a softer union image, though many activists are rightly sceptical about the apparent conversion of some employers to a more co-operative union-management relationship.

Despite their recent successes, the unions still face many problems. The social pacts with centre-left government coalitions could disappear with electoral victories for the right (but it must be said that the weakening ties between union movements and their erstwhile social-democratic party allies could make it easier for unions to engage with administrations of the right, as has happened recently in Spain). And any return to very high levels of unemployment would seriously erode the power resources of most unions. That said, the outlook for the union movement today, in Britain and elsewhere, is probably better than it has been for 20 years.

John Kelly is professor of industrial relations at the London School of Economics

From *New Statesman,* January 28, 2002, pp. 18-19. © 2002 by New Statesman Ltd.

Article 45

Unions Forming Global Contract

By Roger Armbrust

Performers unions from North America and other continents are in the throes of developing a concrete international contract to globally protect actors in film, stage, and television productions.

The Alliance of Canadian Cinema, Television and Radio Artists (ACTRA) hosted a multi-national meeting of performers unions over last weekend in Toronto to discuss and charge up the global protection process. The meeting included representatives from Actors' Equity Association, Screen Actors Guild and the American Federation of Television and Radio Artists in the U.S.; British Actors Equity Association; Canadian Actors' Equity Association; the Media Entertainment and Arts Alliance in Australia; New Zealand Actors' Equity; and International Federation of Actors (FIA).

The group agreed to form a legal committee to begin drafting the international contract which the unions will eventually present to stage, film and television producers. It's too early to tell how the document might both protect actors globally while also insure individual unions' jurisdictions. For example, SAG has jurisdiction over filmmaking in the U.S., while ACTRA possesses that jurisdiction in Canada.

"We established a legal committee to examine the process of coming up with a model contract, and the legal implications of a model global production agreement that would attempt to establish the best rights, working conditions and uses possible for performers appearing in international productions," Stephen Waddell, ACTRA's national executive director, told *Back Stage* on Monday. "As you can imagine, there would be some significant opposition from producers where they see unions getting together to negotiate a production agreement which would be extraterritorial. This is our reaction to the globalizing of productions. We're now dealing with multinational and multibillion-dollar conglomerates. We can no longer sit in our own backyards and not be able to deal with them."

Greg Hessinger, AFTRA's national executive director, spoke with *Back Stage* last Friday, expressing both his union's overview of concern about media consolidation and hopes for finding some solutions at the Canadian confab. He noted that in

a recent meeting with Michael K. Powell, chairman of the Federal Communications Committee, "We expressed to him our experience has been that a diversity of voices and viewpoints in the marketplace is something that cannot exist in a massively consolidated industry; that ultimately the voices that emanate from those different consolidated TV and radio stations are coming from a single source which dictates that those voices are going to be singing the same tune. We do not believe that it's a healthy thing in terms of localism, which we believe is an important element of broadcasting; it certainly is not a good thing for an informed electorate of a democracy."

Waddell echoed that on Monday, saying, "multinational corporations are free to merge, consolidate, grow larger; but unions themselves, on one hand, are concerned about indigenous productions, and concerned about preservation of our culture; but with the global environment, we're still restricted by labor laws from exercising extraterritorial jurisdiction; for example, at ACTRA, we're confined to jurisdiction in Canada, and SAG and AFTRA in the U.S. We've got to be able to find legal means where we can get together, cooperate and eventually bargain together; to attempt to establish this kind of international production agreement."

Hessinger said at the time he was looking forward to the Canadian gathering as a meeting "intended to be a forum for us to explore strategies on how all of us, working together, can find a way to achieve the best terms for and protections for performers wherever they may work throughout the world."

The group seems to have begun positive pursuit of that goal, according to Waddell, who said, "We're giving ourselves a fairly short period of time in which to do this," i.e., come up with a draft of an international pact. "Such meetings in the past have been nothing but talk shops where we'd bring things to each other and nothing happens. In this case, we're giving ourselves a few months, and we'll get together and get firmer ideas about how to proceed. We have an ongoing relationship with SAG and AFTRA as unions in North America, and we're ready to advance this concept in a significant way. SAG's Rule One and its May 1 date gives us real need to move forward."

AFTRA Chief Seeks Global Solidarity

By Etan Vlessing

TORONTO—American Federation of Television & Radio Artists president John Connolly is calling for increased cooperation between international performer unions to protect members working on runaway film and TV productions by transnational media giants.

Connolly told Canadian actors gathering Friday in Toronto that footloose Hollywood studios and other global media giants should not be allowed to play national actor unions against one another as they seek out low-cost production centers worldwide.

"We need to grapple with the mechanics of creating equity for performers in different countries with different conditions," he told the annual general meeting of the Alliance of Canadian Cinema, Television and Radio Artists. Connolly's comments came as a prelude to this weekend's International Federation of Actors summit in Toronto, which will focus on protecting performers in the face of media globalization.

Connolly argued that bolstering the ability of unions to protect performers on international productions with minimum standards for fees and workplace conditions would act as a counterweight to the practice of major studios and other media giants jumping from market to market to find lower costs for their runaway productions.

Such union solidarity would aim to discourage studios from leaving their home market. Failing that, the initiative aims to ensure that unionized actors from the United States and elsewhere secure comparable fees and workplace conditions when they work on runaway film and TV shoots worldwide.

During his address Friday, Connolly criticized the Screen Actors Guild for wrongly opposing Canadian-shot runaway productions with "slogans, impressions and fancy."

In August, SAG's national board voted to support an initiative led by the Film and Television Action Committee, which is seeking a federal investigation into the legality of the subsidies offered by the Canadian government to lure American film and television producers. In endorsing the investigation, SAG's board assumed the controversial position of supporting the idea of countervailing tariffs, which FTAC is proposing as a remedy for runaway production, if the Canadian subsidies are found to be illegal. AFTRA, along with nearly every other entertainment guild, opposes the idea of tariffs, fearing it could spark a trade war.

"Is it all about singing 'Blame Canada' and not realizing the song is a satire?" Connolly told his ACTRA audience. "When satire loses its sense of humor, only demagoguery remains."

Connolly's call for union solidarity was echoed by ACTRA national president Thor Bishopric, who urged national actor unions to go beyond protecting their own back yards and work together to protect performers in an increasingly global industry.

"When working for the same mega-corporations, we need to be certain we are approaching them with the same objectives," Bishopric said.

Connolly and other union executives caution that talks aimed at forging union solidarity are at an early stage. The weekend summit will seek to identify respective interests to ensure that jurisdictional wars do not break out between international unions.

Stephen Waddell, ACTRA's national executive director, said SAG proposing an extension of Rule One on U.S. productions abroad, and urging countervailing duties as a remedy to runaway productions, underlined how the asserted rights of one domestic union can intrude on the rights of other domestic unions.

Waddell added that a consensus was developing that SAG was rethinking its stance on countervailing tariffs. What's more, SAG agreed on the weekend, according to Waddell, that its committee currently implementing the union's global Rule One extension will provide an FIA group with an initial draft of the SAG guidelines. It's important for SAG to gain the support from the international unions because they will be calling on them to help enforce global Rule One.

The weekend summit also resolved to look at removing legal obstacles in the way of further coordinating collective bargaining processes in different jurisdictions.

Besides AFTRA and SAG, FIA member unions taking part in the Toronto summit include the British Actors Equity Assn., the New Zealand Actors Equity and the Media Entertainment and Arts Alliance in Australia.

Etan Vlessing writes for The Hollywood Reporter.

Rule One Specifies

SAG has announced that its Global Rule One, the provision which states that every member of SAG shall work under a guild signatory agreement anywhere in the world, will become enforceable as of May 1. Traditionally the guild has enforced Rule One only on productions shot in the U.S.

"We appreciate that we're in a global production environment, but how SAG's extension of Rule One might impact our respective jurisdictions is a concern," Waddell explained. "To that end, SAG has waited until this meeting to go further through their committee on defining the rules. So it was useful that we had this discussion. SAG will go back to the Rule One committee and put together some draft rules and will circulate them to our English-speaking union group and get feedback before Rule One is extended on May 1."

Waddell indicated that, while the other unions agree with SAG's efforts, they needed to see the specific wording that the U.S. guild will include in the rules.

"We think it's very positive that they're focusing on Rule One," Waddell stressed, "but our membership and memberships of the other unions who have dual members—we have ACTRA-SAG members, and British Equity has SAG members—we need to know how the rules will impact them when working in their own countries. For example, a Canadian performer who's a resident of Canada and happens to be a SAG member, what will be the impact? Or what's the impact with respect to productions they're involved in Canada, for the CBC for instance, or other domestic companies? Or does it only im-

pact performers who go to the States during pilot season? Questions like that."

John McGuire, SAG's senior adviser, represented the guild at the Toronto talks. "We had very strong indications of understanding and support of what we're trying to do," McGuire said regarding SAG's extension of Rule One. He agreed with Waddell's assessment that SAG's Rule One committee would review the other unions' concerns which they presented to McGuire at the meeting.

McGuire also emphasized the meeting's chief purpose "to fully explore how best to coordinate all FIA unions and the English-speaking unions and maximize protection of performers everywhere." He indicated he and SAG staff would be preparing the first draft of the unions' model international contract.

From *Back State*, February 22-28, 2002, pp. 1, 58. © 2002 by Billboard Publications, Inc.

The Incredible Shrinking World

Virtual meeting rooms are on the rise, and are being used to replace face-to-face meetings—saving time and money

By Julie Demers

The increasing globalization of business has triggered the emergence of new technologies that are helping to "shrink" the world. The need for executives to travel to finalize business deals, make major decisions, and take part in crucial meetings will soon be a thing of the past. The potential for organizing visual conferencing and the tools needed to conduct such meetings are on the rise. Companies now have the option of eliminating the expense of global air travel and hotel accommodation, and the costs associated with lost time and opportunity.

Teliris, a UK company, recently launched Global-Table, a system for convening and holding meetings at different venues across the world. GlobalTable is based on the Interactive Telepresence™ framework, which is the result of extensive research into the physical and psychological aspects of meeting environments. This research investigated in detail how the human mind reacts to visual and audio cues under different circumstances. The variables include image stability, clarity and colour, transmission delay, signal compression and audio bandwidth. For example, Teliris has modelled many different camera angles and sight lines to achieve the level of eye contact and directional consistency required for a natural meeting environment.

GlobalTable delivers meeting rooms across the world that can be instantly connected using DVD-quality video and full duplex sound with undetectable loss or delay. According to Teliris, the technology allows natural eye contact and across-the-table interaction between participants who may be on opposite sides of the world— creating the sense that they are actually in the same room.

David Bell, chairman of the *Financial Times* and director of international media company Pearson Group plc, says: "It's the first time we have seen the creation of a real 'meeting environment' in which people—many thousands of miles apart—can have conversations that are completely normal in every sense. The system represents a major breakthrough in global communications. Pearson is using GlobalTable to link up offices in London and the United States."

Webex

Other types of conferencing services accessible via the Internet have also emerged. Webex Meeting Center is one of the most popular forms of Web conferencing services. All you need is a browser and a phone. This user-friendly system accommodates current software such as Excel, PowerPoint and PhotoShop, and most other software that the host of the meeting might have for delivering presentations. Workgroups can collaborate on any project, any time, from anywhere.

For more information on virtual meetings, visit the following Web sites:

- www.teliris.com
- www.webex.com
- www.placeware.com
- www.astound.com
- www.sneakerlabs.com

Participants can view, annotate and edit documents online. Up to 500 people can participate in Webex meetings, although some believe that Webex is more suited to groups of under 20 individuals in distant sites, who may be in either their hotel room or office. Communication is by telephone or instant messaging. A special feature allows you to have a private conversation with one of the participants while the group conversation continues. However, total costs, calculated by the minute per user, can be high, although less costly than bringing everyone to the same location for a meeting, or investing in the additional equipment needed to set up such a system customized to the specific needs of the company.

PlaceWare

PlaceWare also operates a Web site that allows you to organize virtual meetings using the Internet. PlaceWare's "Meeting Center" is essentially the same as the Webex system, running on the same operating principles and requiring as few elements as Webex. PlaceWare meetings can be programmed from anywhere, and can include up to 2,500 individuals. PlaceWare's Meeting Center services are designed for small groups, whereas larger groups are accommodated using its "Conference Center." As with regular meetings, question periods and voting are also possible. The cost of this service varies depending on the number of users.

Both Web sites offer demonstrations that will give you an idea of the capabilities of the systems. Most Web conferencing services offer administration, registration, evaluation, archiving and scheduling capabilities for large meetings and special events. Other portals, such as Astound and SneakerLabs, also offer Web conferencing. For business meetings in the 21st century, instead of flying across the world, all you need to do is compare prices and capabilities of Web conferencing services and find the one that meets your needs.

Julie Demers (jdemers@managementmag.com) is the associate French editor of *CMA Management*.

From *CMA Management*, November 2001, p. 58. © 2001 by CMA Management. Reprinted by permission.

Has Strategy Changed?

The powerful forces of globalization are fundamentally changing the nature and dimensions of strategy.

Kathleen M. Eisenhardt

Has strategy changed in the wake of the recent economic frenzy and subsequent downturn? Is the New Economy finished? Has the Old Economy returned? At this point, most managers understand what the advent of the Internet implies—operating efficiency for most companies, a terrific channel for some and a fundamentally new business opportunity for only a few. So is it back to "strategy as usual"?

The answer is no. While many executives were focused on the implications of the Internet, a more powerful force was quietly transforming the economic playing field. Globalization. Massive in scope, deep in impact—and ironically, almost unmanaged—globalization is the increasingly deep interrelationship among countries, companies and individuals. The connections may be cultural, as in the case of global brands like Sony, or environmental, as in global climate change and overfishing of the oceans. The connections may be technical, as in the case of the Web and wireless communication, or financial, as in the linking of major stock exchanges and the proliferation of NAFTA-like trade agreements. Globalization, not the Internet, is the fundamental driver of the real New Economy.

Instability

Density of connections throughout the world affects corporations by amplifying instability. Even small events in one location can affect events in another, in often oblique and nonlinear fashion. Cold weather means increased coal usage in England that can trigger acid rain in Ukraine. Economies of scale at a smattering of Australian wineries can affect life in rural France. AIDS activists in South Africa can threaten the profits of the pharmaceuticals industry. The scale and pace of change are particularly challenging to predict. Wall Street expected that a correction would follow dot-com mania, but no one anticipated the correction's magnitude and speed.

The international power structure, or lack of one, further amplifies instability. For almost five decades, the geopolitics of the post-World War II era were shaped by the two principal Cold War combatants. Today, although the United States is dominant and the European Union is asserting a more unified point of view, free trade and transparent markets are the forces shaping commerce, not any one nation. The Internet speeds communication. Invention spreads almost overnight. Yet no one is in charge. In the era of globalization, it is not obvious whether major political leaders, such as British Prime Minister Tony Blair, or business leaders, such as AOL Time Warner's Steve Case, have much economic clout. Perhaps both types will take a back seat to some single-issue global crusader. Adding to the instability is a strong and often thoughtful backlash to globalization among an unlikely coalition of trade unionists, environmentalists and cultural nationalists.

At the same time, industries with strong network effects (for example, telecommunications), in which standards can take hold rapidly, and industries such as software, which depend on the economics of information rather than the economics of things, have further destabilized the predictable world of business. Globalization, together with those forces, has created a new economic playing field. The play on that field is high-velocity with strikingly nonlinear instability, unpredictability and ambiguity. No wonder that the principal theme of the January 2002 gathering of the economic and political elite at the World Economic Forum in New York City is designated as "coping with fragility."

New Economics, New Strategy

Does the new economic playing field imply throwing out traditional economics? No, but it does suggest that the belief in equilibrium and the naïve understanding of (or perhaps lack of interest in) the internal workings of corporations that characterize traditional economics render its paradigms less germane. Rather, a new economics—or more accurately, an *old* new economics pioneered by Frank Knight, Friedrich Hayek and Joseph Schumpeter—is coming into its own. This latter form of economics is entrepreneurial in its riveted focus on disequilibrium, the capture of fleeting opportunities and the relentless cycle of wealth creation and destruction.

The new economic playing field also suggests a fresh view of strategy. During conversations on our collective work, Donald N. Sull of Harvard Business School struck upon a military analogy that graphically conveys the point. Military leaders often fight traditional wars in the map room by locating defensible positions and then fortifying them. In the same way, executives plan their strategic positions and defend them with carefully intertwined activity systems.

Sometimes a traditional war is fought in the storeroom, with leaders amassing stockpiles of specific weapons such as tanks and then deploying them wherever the battle may be. Similarly, executives may formulate resource-based strategy and then leverage their related core competencies in many markets.

But as we know, there are wars in which the enemy is difficult to engage, battle dynamics fluctuate, and the terrain is treacherous and unknown. Here, the strategy of choice is guerilla warfare—moving quickly, taking advantage of opportunity and rapidly cutting losses. That kind of entrepreneurial strategy always makes sense for underdog companies because they lack resources and position. But in unstable, unpredictable and ambiguous terrain like the new economic playing field, entrepreneurial strategy is attractive for large companies as well. The fundamental precept that "strategy is about being different" continues to be true. But what constitutes that strategy has changed. The new strategic watchwords are simplicity, organization and timing.

Strategy Is Simple

First and foremost, strategy on the new economic playing field has to be simple. Complicated, intertwined activity systems or elaborately planned leveraging of core competencies make sense in slower and more-linear situations. On the new high-velocity playing field, they are cumbersome and glacially slow. Managers now must jump into uncertain situations because that is where the opportunities are most abundant. They must capture and exploit promising opportunities or drop them rapidly if they fail to develop. Counterintuitively, complicated markets demand simple, back-to-basics strategy.

Simple strategy means using one or two critical strategic processes and the handful of unique rules that guide them. The critical processes are those that put the corporation into the flow of the most promising opportunities and therefore will differ company to company. For con-

sumer-products giant Colgate-Palmolive, global product management is a key strategic process. Product managers follow a few simple precepts, such as "maintain the brand" and "keep relative product positioning stable." But within those rules, Colgate managers around the globe have considerable freedom. For example, while maintaining the defined brand image of toothpaste and its relative positioning against other Colgate dental-care products, managers can alter the flavor, change the packaging, create locally tailored advertising, tinker with the ingredients, shift prices and more. Within a few parameters, managers move as they see fit.

Another example is Netherlands-based Ispat International, one of the fastest-growing steel companies in the world. Throughout the 1990s, the Ispat strategy was centered on the acquisition process and a few simple guidelines for two aspects of that process: first, which acquisition opportunities to pick (state-owned companies, companies in which costs could be reduced, companies with direct-reduction or electric-arc technologies); second, how to integrate the acquisitions (always retain existing top managers, insist on daily meetings and reporting). But within the guidelines, Ispat managers could buy companies from Germany to Kazakhstan and run them in accordance with the changing flow of opportunities.

In contrast, complicated and richly resourced strategies often do not work. Take Pandesic, the joint venture for e-commerce services that Intel and SAP launched in 1997 and that folded in 2000. Too much effort went into a strategic plan that was overly complex and difficult to revise. Too many people were assigned to execute the plan. Pandesic executives had too many resources and an overly defined strategic position. What they did not have was simplicity. As the real market opportunity unfolded, they needed a simple focus in order to adjust flexibly.

Strategy Is Organizational

Programming the strategy from the top and then figuring out an organization to implement it may work in slow-moving markets. It's the signature approach of strategists who simplistically think of organizations in terms of control and alignment of management incentives. In high-velocity markets, that approach won't work. In such circumstances, strategy consists of choosing an excellent team, picking the right roles for team members and then letting their moves emerge. It's like basketball. Los Angeles Lakers' coach Phil Jackson does not mastermind the moves of Kobe Bryant and Shaquille O'Neal. Rather, he puts the right personnel in a triangle offense and lets them play. To the uninformed, the moves seem to flow from an elaborate playbook, but the astute fan understands that the organization itself is the strategy.

For companies, organizational strategy is the unique mapping (often termed patching) of modular businesses onto specific market opportunities. Think Velcro. Organizational strategy is firm and clear at any point in time but also is able to change quickly. A prime example: Hewlett-Packard's wildly successful strategy in the mid-1980s to mid-1990s, which led to domination of the global printer industry.

H-P executives focused their business-unit teams—whether in Spain, Italy, Idaho, Colorado or Singapore—on clearly defined product and market targets. The teams' assignment was to "take the hill." They were guided by a few simple rules—for example, never spend money on an activity if someone else can do it. But the real key to the strategy was organizational. The quarterly realignment of the businesses against the shifting pattern of emerging, colliding, splitting and declining market and product opportunities defined the H-P strategy. As the markets changed, H-P executives added businesses, such as scanners and printer cartridges. They split off businesses, including removing the deskjet business from LaserJets. Sometimes they combined businesses (the dot-matrix and network-printing businesses). Occasionally, they exited a business. The repatching of businesses was rarely reported in the media, because the moves were usually small and even routine. Nonetheless, the frequent realignment of business units was the central feature of H-P's enormously successful printer strategy.

More subtly, organizational strategy involves choosing the business scale, not just the focus, that is uniquely suited to the velocity of each market. Dell managers operate their businesses at the scale of about $1 billion. As businesses grow beyond that size, they are broken into smaller modules. Microsoft managers often operate their businesses at the scale of about 200 programmers.

The Economist magazine embodies a particularly strategic use of modularity and scale. From the outside, the weekly publication's strategy seems to be to leverage a core competence in writing and to position itself as a magazine for the sophisticated reader. From the inside, the strategy is the organization. Editors at The Economist give their writers unusually large swaths of territory and considerable freedom in choosing what to cover. The organizational strategy not only gives writers greater scope to develop stories, it enables senior editors to hire fewer (and, presumably better) writers and compensate them more, both with money and with unfettered, interesting work. The resulting product is more creative than that of other news magazines and has the greater depth that appeals particularly to the upmarket reader.

Strategy Is Temporal

Finally, strategy is temporal. In traditional strategy, time is not part of the strategic equation. After all, markets are assumed to move slowly and predictably, if at all. In contrast, time is crucial on the new high-velocity playing field. The easiest way to think about temporal strategy is through understanding the concept of corporate genes. A corporation's unique mix of genes is its combined products, brand, technology, manufacturing capabilities, geo-graphic locations and so on. Managers using temporal strategy conduct a kind of genetic engineering, pursuing a series of unique strategic moves in which one or more genes are changed. They may introduce a new technology, change a brand, enter a new country or drop a manufacturing competence. They are constantly splicing in new genes or cutting out others to engineer genetic evolution.

The best temporal strategies also exhibit a pattern that occurs in the natural world of earthquakes and tropical storms: the inverse power law. That is, small events are common, midsize events occur occasionally, and large events are rare. Good temporal strategies are unique combinations of small, incremental changes plus midsize changes and large, radical changes. Most of the time, temporal strategy should feature safe, small changes that elaborate on aspects of the core business. But temporal strategy needs to include medium-scale moves occasionally and, even more occasionally, large-scale moves that reinvent significant portions of the corporation. This also means that the dichotomy of "stick to the core" versus "creative destruction" is a false one. Effective managers pursue both approaches.

> **Although most executives would like sustained advantage, they are forced to operate as if it does not exist. The challenge is coping with not knowing whether such an advantage actually exists—except in retrospect.**

EBay offers an excellent example of temporal strategy. The Internet star was launched as a Web site where traders of collectibles could congregate and trade. It morphed into an auction, added other kinds of merchandise (such as cars and fine art), branched beyond the auction format to fixed-price markets and expanded into numerous countries. It became what the business-to-business exchange was to have been. Most often, eBay's changes were small. Occasionally they were large. There was always a mix of large and small changes, with varying emphasis on changing the genes of country, merchandise, business model or auction format. EBay managers also sometimes added rhythm to their temporal strategy by pacing the evolution more rapidly or more slowly as the opportunity for advantage dictates. As a result, eBay managers evolved their businesses through varying moves—and created the Internet's most durable star.

Sustainable Competitive Advantage?

Is sustained competitive advantage still relevant? Sometimes long-term competitive advantage and its attendant creation of wealth can occur on the new economic playing field. More often, they cannot. The more salient point is, however, that the duration of competitive advantage is unpredictable. It may last 10 minutes, 10 months or 10 years. So although most executives would like sustained advantage, they are forced to operate as if it does not exist. The challenge is, therefore, not so much achieving sustainable advantage as it is coping with not knowing whether such an advantage actually exists—except in retrospect.

Strategy is still about being different. But today, the way in which strategy is different is itself different. Globalization is rearranging the turf. The speed of play on the field is lightning fast. The scale and pace of change are unpredictable. The economics of disequilibrium and information have moved to center stage. As a result, the recipe for effective strategy must now focus on unique strategic processes with simple rules, on the modular patching of businesses to fleeting market opportunities and on evolutionary timing for ongoing strategic moves. In other words, we are not back to "strategy as usual." Whether we like it or not, strategy has changed.

ACKNOWLEDGMENTS

The author is grateful for the wisdom, counsel and creativity of Chris Bingham, Shona Brown, Charlie Galunic, Jeff Martin, Filipe Santos and Don Sull in helping to shape the ideas expressed.

Kathleen M. Eisenhardt is a professor of strategy and organization in the Department of Management Science and Engineering at Stanford University. Contact her at kme@at@;leland.stanford.edu.

From *MIT Sloan Management Review,* Winter 2002, pp. 88-91 by permission of the publisher. © 2002 by Massachusetts Institute of Technology. All rights reserved.

Personnel Demands Attention Overseas

NEW YORK--Human resource considerations should be paramount when investment companies consider going global, and yet usually, they are given the lowest priority, according to Sheryl Colyer, global head of human resources at Citigroup Asset Management of New York. Colyer spoke at the National Investment Company Service Association east coast regional meeting held here earlier this month. The priority given human resources could be decisive in a company's success or failure abroad, she said.

Staffing is one of the critical issues for a company when entering new markets, according to Colyer. A company's approach depends on whether it is expanding overseas by acquiring an existing company or by building ones own, new operation, she said. Citigroup has both formed several joint ventures and made acquisitions in Latin America while it has created its own operations in Asia.

Regardless of whether a company chooses to build its own or acquire existing operations, companies must decide if they are going to hire locally or send workers from existing offices and pay expatriate costs, according to Colyer.

"We really need to think about this hard and fast and consider it up front," said Colyer. When going into other markets, there are certain skills needed, she said. In some cases, those skills will not be found locally. If some people have the necessary skills, there can be stiff competition for them and a company will probably pay a premium for the skills.

Companies should have specific plans with regard to expatriate issues, she said. When Citigroup reviewed its expatriate costs, it found that many people were "career expatriates," meaning they and their families lived abroad permanently, according to Colyer. That is not the best system because it does not make the best use of workers' experiences and because expatriate employees are, in general, more expensive than people hired locally, she said.

"What we've learned from this is to certainly have an exit strategy in terms of sending someone over to do specific things," said Colyer. "The plan is to train and transfer the skill and knowledge to someone in the other country or [to] rotate them out. We now look at the expatriate situation to be something not more than a 3-year assignment."

When a company buys an existing overseas operation, retention of the existing employees is a key concern. When doing a cost/benefit analysis and determining whether it is advantageous to go into another country, companies must figure in the cost of retention packages, according to Colyer. "Often we don't [do this] and we have found that it is a significant cost to retain," she said. "We try to phase that in over time." Usually, it can be paid out over a two-year period, she said.

"What we have found is that if you're not careful with your comp and benefit packages and how you staff your leadership in these countries, you become the recruiting ground or training ground for other firms," Colyer said. "It's important to note that, if a company is entering that country, they will pay a premium for that skill that you have spent many hours and dollars training."

Furthermore, with regard to compensation, companies need to determine which jobs are global, meaning they require certain compensation regardless of location, according to Colyer. The majority of jobs are not like that."A one-size-fits all philosophy won't work," she said. "A pay scale out of New York may not be appropriate in Taiwan. Complications around a global pay scale severely disrupts the pay practices when you have other businesses in those countries."

Understanding what resources are available and at what cost, specifically with regard to human capital, is critical before moving into new markets, according to Sanjay Vatsa, vice president of global operations and business strategies and solutions at Merill Lynch Investment Managers of New York."In some countries, people are less expensive than gas and water," said Vatsa.

"You have to understand the data mix in that country before you can adopt a process and implement a system."

While it is always important for companies to be explicit with regard to how they measure performance, it is particularly important when working globally because of the independence global offices are given, according to Colyer."

It is so important to be clear on the success criteria in terms of how you are going to measure the employee that you have across the world," said Colyer. "I can't overemphasize this. We don't do a good job, in general, of being clear with the success criteria—how will you be measured? What are the goals? We [at Citigroup] don't do it well when they're sitting in the same office, never mind when operating around the globe. This becomes critical because of the way compensation is perceived [and regulated] differently around the world."

For example, Citigroup has encountered situations in Latin America in which an employee's pay and title are associated with what type of car they can receive, and in Japan, where regulations impede a company from offering stock options at the same time as salary. It is imperative to make it absolutely clear what benefits come with any given position, she said.

Having a clearly defined organizational strategy is also important when going into new markets, said Colyer. Companies can either have a functional structure, where employees report back to the central office, a regional structure, where they report to a regional business manager, or a combination of both, said Colyer. Citigroup uses a combination of the two. In Asia, Latin America and Europe, it has regional business managers to whom wholesalers and people with other functions report, but these people have a direct connection with and report back to the home office as well. Having that dual approach can be complicated, she said.

"There can be a lot of misunderstanding around who makes final decisions about things," she said. "In our structure, because we do this combination, it appears as if we are decentralized, when in essence we are very centralized because a lot of our decisions are really out of New York. We like to think we are making them in a decentralized fashion, but… the regions around the globe really are not as strong in decision-making as we would like them to be."

The goal is to make decision-making regional, but this has to be achieved gradually, she said."

You want to get the decision-making to where the work is actually being done because you can certainly find yourself in this U.S.- centric thinking that does not hold true across the world," she said.

Culture is another critical factor, but is often overlooked because it is not tangible, according to Colyer. For example, when Citigroup Asset Management merged with an insurance company in Taiwan and got a part of its asset management business, the local Citigroup office was changed to the local name. That caused unexpected problems, according to Colyer.

"It was perceived [by employees] that it was better to work for a non-local entity and so the Citigroup name was important and [local workers] joined because of that," said Colyer. "When the name was going away and the local entity name would now be the name of the company, we ran into some severe retention issues because the employees identified with the name Citigroup as opposed to the local company, and they did not want to work for that local entity even though we would still be part of it. Don't underestimate or over-estimate the brand name of your entity around what that means from an organizational cultural standpoint. And certainly when you're doing marketing to your customers, understand the implications to your employees."

Employees and resources need to be specifically dedicated to human resources when expanding globally, said Colyer.

Andrew Brent

From *Mutual Fund Market News*, March 19, 2001, p. 1. © 2001 by Mutual Fund Market News. Reprinted by permission.

Safe Haven

Accommodating the needs of employees and families in hostile environments can increase expenses and alter tax liability.

*By Barbara Hanrehan
and Donald R. Bentivoglio*

Family members accompanying employees assigned to foreign work sites always have been a major focus of international HR (IHR) programs, and the Sept. 11 terrorist attacks and the conflict in Afghanistan have increased concerns for their safety. Anecdotal evidence indicates that assignees in at-risk areas are not requesting an early return home, but some workers are asking employers to send their family members home or move them to a more secure environment.

Many employers are trying to accommodate these requests, but such a change in the family's residence raises a number of human resources and international assignment program (IAP) issues, some of which have a potential tax impact.

If the assignee's family is relocated from the international work location to their home or another location, the organization must decide whether to allow increased home leave for the assignee. This may appear to be strictly an IHR issue, but the organization and the assigree also face tax implications of more frequent trips home, as well as the costs of maintaining dual households.

Home Is Where the Work Is

Under the Internal Revenue Code (IRC), the tax home of a taxpayer is the primary business location, although that may not be where the family lives. That means that if the assignee's family returns to the United States, and the assignee is eligible for increased home leave trips, the costs of those visits are equivalent to taxable home leave. However, if the trips are coordinated with business meetings near the family location, they may not be considered taxable home leave, so HR should consider this cost-savings strategy.

Regardless of the tax implications, HR managers must determine the number and duration of reimbursable home leave tips they will provide. Prior to Sept. 11, most North American-based companies allowed one trip home per year, but that policy generally assumed that the family would be traveling together.

Paying for additional home trips may be significantly more costly to the company if the assignee is tax-equalized i.e., the company would generally assume the assignee's additional tax costs of the reimbursed extra trips in addition to the actual costs of the trip. If the assignee is not tax-equalized, the company could deduct these travel expenses as a normal compensation expense, but any travel reimbursements to the assignee would be considered taxable income to them. A third alternative would be for the assignee to absorb all expenses related to the additional home leave with the company simply providing the additional time away from the assignment. In this case, there are no taxable events to either party.

On another note, if an employee had been on a long-term assignment and the family moved back home prior to the end of the assignment, which had less than one year to run, the assignment is still considered long-term. But home leave trips do not qualify as deductible business trips if the assignment is for less than one year.

Middle Ground

Alternatively, some families may not return to the United States but instead may relocate to a country that is considered safer than the work site. Normally, if the assignee maintains a second household, only the expenses related to the household nearest the work assignment can be used in computing the housing cost allowance. However, in certain situations (for example, when the second foreign home is necessary due to dangerous or adverse conditions) individuals may include these doubled housing expenses (i.e., the expenses of maintaining a second home for a spouse and dependents) in computing the housing cost exclusion, according to Section 911 of the IRC.

U.S.-based assignees sometimes feel threatened by events near the work site and choose to relocate their families to areas that are more pro-American. Such adverse conditions could include war or civil insurrection. For example, if the assignee was originally in Pakistan and the family has relocated to Hong Kong for safety, the IRS would allow the housing cost exclusion to include the costs of both households. However, that would not change the tax home for the assignee, and the company's reimbursements for the assignee's travel expenses for trips to the second household would be taxable as compensation.

HR also must consider the taxability of moving expenses when the family relocates but the employee remains. Are costs of relocating the family a deductible (i.e., non-taxable) moving expense? For moving expenses to be deductible, the primary business location must change. If only the family moves, the primary business location has not changed, so the expenses are not deductible. If the employer pays moving costs, that would be considered taxable income to the assignee.

Protecting Employees

If the assignee (and family) remains in a potentially unsafe work location, the company may be required to re-evaluate and upgrade security arrangements, which could increase expenses. For example, providing a car and driver to certain employees would normally be taxed as ordinary income, because employees cannot normally deduct commuting expenses. However, under the IRC section that governs working condition fringe provisions, an employer may provide specialized tax-free transportation for employees whose security is threatened. Because many businesses have legitimate safety concerns when employees commute in certain foreign locations (including traveling to and from business meetings and business sites), employers may provide a driver and a specially equipped vehicle (for example, bulletproof), with the value being excluded from the assignee's gross income. However, the normal cost of commuting still remains nondeductible, and, if provided to an employee, it would be a taxable benefit.

A company must meet the following conditions to deduct the costs of improving employees' security:

- The company must establish a formal security program for its employees. The 24-hour plan must apply to the work location, the commute and the home environment.

- The company must provide a chauffeur or driver trained in evasive driving techniques. If the driver is not a professionally trained security driver, then no part is excluded from income.

- The overall security plan must apply to all aspects of the employee's daily life. If the workplace has been secured and the home has not been secured, the program fails to meet the overall security plan requirement. In addition, the plan must cover not only the assignee but also his or her spouse and dependents.

Similar rules apply to employer-provided aircraft if the assignee uses it in remote and/or large geographic areas.

Barbara Hanrehan is a tax partner with Deloitte & Touche's International Assignment Services. Donald R. Bentivoglio is a senior manager with Deloitte & Touche's International Assignment Services specializing in international human resources.

From *HR Magazine*, February 2002, pp. 52-53 by Barbara Hanrehan and Donald R. Bentivoglio. © 2002 by Society for Human Resource Management, Alexandria, VA. Reprinted by permission.

International HR manager

The Christmas festivities are but a dim memory and you're battling your way to work through the snow and ice, coping with cancelled trains and equally grim commuters.

Suddenly the thought of being an international HR manager—landing, Tony Blair-like, to sort out a little local difficulty, preferably somewhere hot—seems positively attractive.

The role of international HR manager can indeed be some of this, but the reality is that in an increasingly global business community it is a pivotal position, often acting as a springboard to greater things—as well as giving you an intimate knowledge of airport departure lounges.

"In my last year, I think I spent the equivalent of two whole weeks, 24 hours a day, sitting in airline seats. It was grindingly awful," laments Ian Mann, who until 1997 was international HR manager at NatWest Bank. Now chief executive of ECA International, a firm specialising in providing data for international assignments, Mann says being a successful international HR manager requires two key elements: a broad knowledge base and a sharp awareness of cultural mores.

By its very nature, an international HR manager role will be less parochial than its domestic equivalent. Being able to make sense of the different employment legislation between countries and making sure the international operations have seamless international HR policies in place are central elements of the job.

"You don't have to have all the answers, but you do need to know where to access those answers. A good address book is a big help," says Mann. A decent international HR manager will also be expected to spread the organisation's culture across borders, argues Frances Wilson, international manager at the CIPD.

Being aware of cultural differences is a must, adds Mann. For instance, attitudes towards the family—and hence legislation regarding provision for old age—vary widely from the Far East to Europe and the US.

The role is likely to encompass dealing with regional offices and involve co-ordinating with local staff as well as expats who may not necessarily be British. Key tasks might include the deployment of staff, both expat and local,

Case study: Mark Davies

Mark Davies has been international HR manager for Europe, the Middle East and Africa with Dow Jones Newswires since September.

Based in London, he joined the newswire service of the global financial news organisation—home to the Wall Street Journal—from Dutch chemicals firm Royal Vopak.

With a team of two, he oversees the HR for 425 reporters, IT, sales and marketing staff across the EMEA region.

Davies got his CIPD qualification in 1985/86, working his way up through Racal Electronics and BP Chemicals, part of oil giant BP, before joining Vopak in 1994 in an international HR role, primarily in Europe.

His last 18 months there saw him co-ordinating a pan-European management change project as the company merged a number of separate organisations into one.

At Dow Jones, inevitably there is more of a US bias. For instance, despite being a stand-alone department, Davies reports directly to the New York head office. A key challenge of this year will be the introduction of an appraisal system across the EMEA region.

"Other challenges will include general support and coaching of managers and staff from long range, managing local expectations and taking cultural considerations into account from long range," he says.

An ability to see the big picture and ensuring you have sound advice on local employment law are vital attributes to succeeding in international HR management, he argues.

"You have to be able to concentrate on the big issues. It is about dealing with issues and managers who are not just down the corridor, so that is an additional challenge," he says.

transfer of knowledge from expats, international recruitment and assessment and psychometric testing.

Other minefields can be competency assessment (of which both attitudes and practices can vary immensely from country to country) and compensation and benefits. The introduction of the euro as a tangible currency within the eurozone countries on 1 January has put this issue firmly in the spotlight at the moment.

The international manager role will be a fairly senior one, probably at board level or just below. The manager may answer to a global director or similarly titled position or report directly to the board.

The position will normally command a salary of not much less than £45,000 although there may also be substantial foreign subsidies, relocation allowances, schooling payments and so forth.

An international HR manager, Wilson says, normally needs to have proved his or her mettle on the domestic stage, probably for about two years. A CIPD module on international HR, a university qualification or an MBA can all help.

"A lot of companies are sending out younger people to take on their international roles. It gives them some valuable management and development experience.

"It is seen as a good role for high-fliers. It is becoming quite necessary on your CV to have had an international role if you are going to make it to the higher echelons," she says.

There may also be fewer issues surrounding family, mortgages and so on with younger staff.

Languages can be useful, but as English is the language of business across the world, not essential.

Nevertheless, being prepared to learn at least enough to make polite chitchat will inevitably earn you Brownie points.

In the rapidly changing business environment, one of the difficulties with an international role is that, once posted, there may be a sense of feeling out of the loop. E-mail and videoconferencing have, to some extent, made this less of an issue in recent years.

But, after a few years out, even if a position has been guaranteed back at HQ, head office may seem like a very different place. Indeed, if the organisation has merged in that time, it may actually be a different place.

And with so much travelling involved, being an international HR manager can play havoc with your family or private life, warns Wilson. "It is not like going for a holiday. Once you are there you are stuck in an office."

You may also find yourself working early or late in the office to fit in with other people's time zones.

But, on the plus side, you will be doing something different and will be exposed to different cultures and working practices that will probably be fascinating, challenging, infuriating and stimulating.

"I can genuinely say no two days were alike. It is a job of infinite variety, best served by a wealth of common sense," says Mann.

From *Personnel Today,* January 15, 2002, p. 2. © 2002 by Reed Business Information.

Reforming Globalization

Multinational firms have contributed to economic growth in the developing world. But the risk of growing corporate power is that it abuses this power. How does one balance the two concerns? Merely returning these countries to "localism" will not work, argues this economist. He offers his own reforms.

Jay Mandle

THE PURSUIT OF A JUST SOCIETY involves carefully balancing two contradictory necessities with regard to the corporate sector. Since corporations are responsible for much of the wealth and many of the jobs in a modern economy, they must be nurtured. At the same time, however, even as the corporate sector is fostered, justice and fairness require that these firms not be permitted to exercise disproportionate power.

The corporate sector must at once be economically encouraged and politically constrained. A careful balancing is needed in which excessive corporate power is curbed, but doing so does not put in jeopardy the prosperity that large firms help to create.

The need to encourage the corporate sector is rooted in the fact that corporate-driven economic development dramatically raises living standards and thereby reduces the injustices associated with deprivation. The increased volume and array of goods and services to which even moderate-income people in developed societies have access is a prized advance that they will not and should not be expected to concede. Similarly, the people who live in poor countries legitimately seek the broadly

distributed improved levels of health, education, and material comfort that are promised by a future of economic development. But even as corporations and financial institutions contribute to material advances, the risk is that they will promote their own interests in ways antagonistic to the well-being of the society as a whole. Democratic norms therefore require that the corporate sector not be permitted to dominate other segments of society in determining the rules governing its behavior.

An anticorporate politics will not be able to attract extensive support if it requires economic retrenchment in the developed world or impedes the emergence of improved living conditions in poor countries. But at the same time, the left's egalitarian commitments necessitate reducing disproportionate corporate power. The corporate sector must at once be economically encouraged and politically constrained. A careful balancing is needed in which excessive corporate power is curbed, but doing so does not put in jeopardy the prosperity that large firms help to create.

With globalization, this problem of balance has become an international one. In the past, individual nations were able to pursue their own balance without giving much consideration to how that same process was evolving in other societies. With the increased integration of global markets, however, this ability to pursue insular strategies with regard to corporate governance has become attenuated. Advances in the technology of information processing, communications, and transportation mean firms increasingly are able to locate production wherever they choose. This new corporate mobility means that if a country attempts to curb corporations

by, for example, increasing business taxation or reducing their ability to retrench workers, it could be exposed to a loss of corporate investment. As Robert Kuttner has written, globalization "influences the domestic political balance" toward one in which "the global market trumps the domestic mixed economy" (Kuttner 2000, 155).

The objective of reining in corporate power nevertheless remains a goal that attracts large numbers of adherents all over the world. Indeed, globalization itself has provided a renewed impetus in this direction. As multinational firms extend the geographic sphere of their activities across nations and continents, their enhanced leverage over social and economic policymaking has been placed in bold and forbidding relief. Thus it is that in recent years anticorporate activism has intensified, even as corporate global ascendancy has been extended.

Though far from agreeing on a specific agenda of reform, the anticorporate activists share the pervasive sensibility that globalization should be slowed if not reversed. The geographic scale of production, investment, and distribution should be reduced from global to smaller geographic units. Localism is seen as the antidote to domination by multinational corporations. As Naomi Klein, a sympathetic observer of the antiglobalization movement, puts it, "There is an emerging consensus that building community-based decision-making power... is essential to countering the might of multinational corporations" (Klein 2000, 2). It is not hard to find evidence that Klein is right. For example, the Green Party platform on which Ralph Nader based his presidential candidacy called for a "community-based eco-

Table 1

Data Related to Economic Defelopment for Selected Country Groups

Country Group	1998 GNP per capita[1]	1997 HDI[1]	1998 FDI per capita[1]
High income countries	$23,420	0.919	$506.0
Group I: Mexico, Thailand, Turkey, Brazil	6,580	0.751	$140.6
Group II: Philippines, China, Indonesia, Egypt	$3,133	0.697	$24.7
Group III: India, Pakistan, Bangladesh, Nigeria, Ethiopia	$1,787	0.514	$3.5

Source: PPP gross national product per capita: *World Development Indicators 2000* (Washington DC: World Bank, 2000), table 1.1; Human Development Index: *Human Development Report 1999* (New York: Oxford University Press, 1999), table 1; Foreign Direct Investment per capita computed from *World Devlopment Indicators 2000*, tables 1 and 6.7.
1. Population-weighted mean.

nomics." It advocated an agricultural system "that moves as rapidly as possible towards regional/bioregional self-reliance" and support for enterprises engaged in local production and consumption. The platform not only explicitly opposed the North American Free Trade Agreement (NAFTA), the General Agreement on Trade and Tariffs (GATT), and the World Trade Organization (WTO). In addition, it declared, "We reject any agreement which threatens the authority of states and local communities to establish more stringent health, safety and environmental standards" (Green Party Platform 2000, 26, 27, 31, 28, 32).

This same theme of support for localism is adopted by a task force assembled by the International Forum on Globalization, which includes prominent activists Lori Wallach, Walden Bello, Helena Norberg-Hodge, John Cavanagh, Edward Goldsmith, Martin Khor, David Korten, and Jerry Mander. The group's draft document is quite explicit in explaining that it opposes "corporate-led economic globalization" because it "entails, first, and foremost, de-localization and disempowerment of communities and local economies." Its position is that it is "necessary to reverse directions and create new rules and structures that consciously favor the local and follow the principle of subsidiarity, i.e., whatever activities can be undertaken locally should be" (International Forum on Globalization 1999, 3).

Unacknowledged in the argument for localism, however, are the costs that would be associated with it. By definition, that strategy would bar firms from taking advantage of the cost-reducing characteristics of advanced technologies in international communications and transportation. Lost, therefore, would be the efficiencies achieved when large multinational firms participate in international trade and global production networks. Favoring relatively small firms that are confined to local markets, as the advocates of localization would do, involves choosing to confine pro-

duction to lower amounts of a smaller range of goods at higher prices than would be the case in a globally integrated economy. The upshot would be a diminution in international living standards. Because localization involves abandoning an important mechanism of contemporary economic development, there cannot be much doubt that it would put downward pressure on the well-being of the poor in the wealthy nations and on those who are seeking to escape poverty in the underdeveloped world.

While it is easy to show that FDI has an important role in economic development, there is virtually no track record of success.

Insight into the process by which multinational firms have contributed to growth and improved welfare is provided in Table 1, which mobilizes information for the world's high-income nations and the thirteen largest poor nations. The three measures reported on for these countries are gross national product (GNP) per capita, adjusted for purchasing power parity (PPP), an indicator of economic development; the United Nations Human Development Index (HDI), a statistic designed to measure human well-being; and direct foreign investment (FDI) per capita, a measure of the productive capacity created by foreign firms. The goal is to find whether there is evidence that development, human welfare, and foreign direct investment are positively related to each other. In other words, where there is a high level of development and high scores in the HDI, does there tend also to be a high level of FDI? If such a pattern is observed, it would support the view that multinational firms help

to advance both economic development and human welfare.

The pattern revealed in Table 1 is quite straightforward. Both the level of economic development and the level of human welfare are closely associated with direct foreign investment. This relationship prevails not only in a comparison of the developed with the poor nations, but also when the members of the latter group are ranked by their level of development. Thus, among the thirteen largest underdeveloped countries in the world, the human development index is lowest where direct foreign investment is least. Conversely, that measure of well-being stands at a relatively high level in the countries in the developing world where foreign investment is relatively high. To be sure, these relationships do not suggest that FDI is the only or even the most important determinant of development and well-being. Domestic economic policies clearly play the principle role in determining success in development. Nevertheless, the fact remains that foreign investment does play a role in the process, a role that is forgone to the extent that a society shuts itself off from such capital flows.

While it is easy to show that FDI has an important role in economic development, there is virtually no track record of success with which to defend localization. Even William Greider, himself a critic of globalization, acknowledges that "the concept of development directed at the internal fundamentals has been advocated for many years, but the truth is that there are still not many living examples of success" (Greider 2000, 15). Decoupling and disengagement from the world economy have been attempted by a variety of third-world countries over the years. But in no case have economic modernization and rising standards of living been the outcome, and in a large majority of such countries the effort was ultimately abandoned in favor of greater global economic integration.

Thus the anticorporate movement, in endorsing localism, offers a model of growth that has substantial grounds for skepticism. It seems to be willing to put at risk the contributions made by multinational firms to global development. With that the case, the best that the movement can hope for is nuisance-value politics. There is enough hostility to multinational corporations to fuel disruptive demonstrations. But because the movement's economic strategy threatens economic well-being, it will not attract enough supporters to impose a political discipline on international firms.

At this relatively early stage in the globalization process, success at constraining multinational firms while still promoting development is not an unrealistic possibility. The institutional structures associated with the global economy are still under construction. Because this is so, their shape is subject to influence.

In all market systems, laws defining acceptable and unacceptable behavior are required. A system to adjudicate conflicting claims is needed. To function effectively, markets also need mechanisms to facilitate the adjustments they require. Needed as well are systems to protect against damaging disruptions emerging from market failures. It is not, therefore, surprising that the integration of the global economy has been accompanied by the emergence of supportive institutions. Emblematic in this regard is the WTO. Established in 1995 as the culminating achievement of the Uruguay Round of trade negotiations, the WTO was created to provide a means by which to enforce rules of global trade.

A wide array of possibilities exists concerning the future content of the rules and administering institutions that will govern globalization. That array ranges from procedures that will tightly regulate the flow of goods and services between countries, to essentially a laissez-faire regime where such controls are maintained at minimal levels. The choice made with regard to the extent of market regulation is a political determination, in this case the outcome of negotiations among sovereign states.

The rules governing the global economy emerge from multilateral talks that reflect the bargaining power of the negotiating countries, power that in turn broadly corresponds to the size of each country's economy. The larger the economy, the greater the damage that it could inflict by its withdrawal from the process of rules codification, and thereby the greater the ability to shape those rules. What this means specifically is that the United States, far more than any other country has had a decisive voice in determining the content of the rules and procedures that have accompanied globalization. Its voice is dominant in multilateral organizations such as the World Bank and the International Monetary Fund, and it was the most powerful influence in shaping the content of the rules that the WTO enforces.

The U.S. position with regard to the shape of the global economy has been remarkably consistent over the years. The transition from Republican administrations in the 1980s to Democratic ones in the 1990s caused no substantial change in its content. John Williamson is given credit for first labeling as "the Washington consensus" the package of policies the United States endorsed in trade negotiations and insisted upon in the councils of the World Bank and International Monetary Fund. With the Washington consensus, the United States unreservedly insisted on unregulated markets and a reduced role for governments in economic activity. In Williamson's original formulation (1999, 2), the Washington consensus was composed of ten elements:

1. Fiscal discipline in government spending.
2. A redirection of public expenditure away from subsidies.
3. A reduction of marginal tax rates.
4. Decontrolling interest rates.
5. Moving away from fixed exchange rates to more market-determined ones.
6. Trade liberalization.
7. Liberalizing foreign direct-investment inflows.
8. Privatization of public enterprises.
9. Deregulation of output markets.
10. Securing private property rights.

The policy orientation of the Washington consensus is unmistakable. Its intention is to advance the role of markets at the expense of other social institutions. In providing a high level of freedom to market participants—most particularly to multinational corporations and financial institutions—it clearly reflects the preferences of those firms themselves.

In some respects the Washington consensus has worked well. Policies to free FDI do seem to have helped at least some countries to accelerate economic growth. And the liberalizing of trade has advanced the interests of consumers throughout the world as flows of imports and exports have increased dramatically in recent years. But the reduction in the role of government that the consensus calls for does not work equally well in all contexts. This weakness is particularly dramatic in the case of labor and financial markets. It is in these areas that the Washington consensus is most in need of reversal.

In the first place, globalization, to be fair, requires a strengthened, not a weakened, social safety net. The very act of engaging in cross-border trade initiates a process of change that, though socially beneficial, imposes costs on specific sectors of the economy. Trade encourages nations to shift their production to those sectors in which they have a comparative advantage. What this means in a more negative sense is that, with trade, those industries in which a country does not have a comparative advantage face their demise. Global trade results in productivity advances raising living standards generally. But the industries that go bankrupt and their displaced

employees become innocent victims of the process.

All this is well known to international trade economists and so, too, is the appropriate policy response. The standard remedy to the inequities caused by international trade, in the words of a recent publication of the Brookings Institution, "is to require that the winners share some of their gains with the losers through some form of compensation." The authors add, "We take this seriously as a political requirement and a moral obligation" (Burtless et al. 1998, 131–32). Programs such as job retraining, temporary income supports, stipends or tax benefits for relocations associated with employment, and portable health care insurance all would reduce the burdens unfairly borne by individuals as a result of the changes created by international market integration. The problem is that there is precious little room in the Washington consensus for this kind of social safety net.

A second area where there is a need for governmental intervention concerns financial capital flows. These movements of finance are distinct from the FDI undertaken by multinational firms. Financial flows represent the speculative placement of funds in capital markets. The movement of such funds by financial institutions can now be undertaken with lightning speed. As a result, cross-border and short-term flows of such funds have skyrocketed in recent years, and the fragility of global capital markets has increased as well. Investors engage in herdlike behavior: The movement into or out of markets occurs at a massive level as they take their cues from each other and act in lockstep. The result is very large swings in market prices, with little or no relationship to changes in output or product sales. Because transactions in overseas financial markets require the purchase of foreign currencies, these capital movements result in correspondingly large swings in exchange rates as well. The result is the risk of crises, as capital flows into a country and then is followed by a flight that leaves in its wake indebtedness and bankruptcy for both firms and banks. The 1997 financial crisis in Asia was only the most recent of an epidemic of such events, disruptions that have set back precisely the growth that is globalization's promise to the world.

Jagdish Bhagwati, a preeminent trade theorist, argues that the desirability of "full capital mobility" is a myth. Bhagwati complains that "none of the proponents of free capital mobility have estimated the size of gains they expect to materialize, even leaving out the losses from crises that can ensue." On the contrary, Bhagwati cites the economic historian Charles Kindleberger as teaching that capital flows are characterized by "panics and manias" (Bhagwati 1998, 7, 9, 8). Bhagwati is joined by Joseph Stiglitz in this skepticism about the desirability of unregulated short-term capital flows. Even during his tenure as the chief economist at the World Bank, Stiglitz was critical of the Washington consensus, arguing that "all too often the dogma of liberalization became an end in itself, not a means of achieving a better financial system." Indeed, he writes that "the focus on freeing up markets may have had the perverse effect of contributing to macroeconomic instability by weakening the financial sector" (Stiglitz 1998, 8,3).

If the Washington consensus were rejected and instead extensive support systems for dislocated workers were made available and hyper market mobility in financial flows were constrained, globalization would be both more stable and more equitable. Destructive economic downturns would become less likely. At the same time the costs associated with economic restructuring would be lifted from the shoulders of the innocent victims of the process and would be more widely shared. Indeed, it is easy to envision combining the two: If a policy were adopted to reduce speculative capital flows such as a tax on such transactions (the Tobin tax), the proceeds of the tax could be used to help workers in poor countries adjust to changed circumstances. Thus, for example, such tax revenues could be channeled to the Windward Islands banana farmers who are losing their preferential access to the British market in the name of the antidiscrimination rules of the WTO. At the same time, the provision of income and job supports to dislocated workers in the developed world would help to reduce working-class protectionist pressures created by anxiety over the disruptions associated with increased global trade.

There is very little risk that either of these reversals of the Washington consensus would materially slow globalization. Avoidance of the lost production caused by financial panics would more than compensate for whatever reduction in investment might occur because of constrained short-term capital flows. And, while support systems will be costly, they earn goodwill for the globalization process where now there is suspicion and hostility. The laissez-faire content of the Washington consensus, in short, not only is not fundamental to globalization, but also probably acts as a brake to it. It contributes to the system's instability and fuels its political opposition.

Globalization does not require unregulated markets, and the reduction of poverty is not advanced by localism. But because the anticorporate left ignores the costs of localism, it has adopted a politics inconsistent with the interests of the world's poor. A more stable and more just globalization is what the poor need, not its wholesale rejection. In turning its back on a nuanced globalization as its goal in favor of an ill-defined localism, the movement has doomed itself to political marginality. The left's message, obviously unacceptable to

elites, is also unlikely to gain adherence from the very large numbers necessary to overcome official hostility because that message ignores the issue of economic development.

An alternative opposition politics to secure greater justice in the global economy is, however, feasible. Rather than regarding the international integration of markets as a process to oppose, such a politics would seek the adoption of policies that would stabilize globalization, ensure that its victims are protected, and make certain that its benefits are widely shared. The Washington consensus, the policy framework emerging from a corporate-dominated decision-making process, would be the obvious target of such a movement. Rather than opposing a process that raises standards of living, as the localism movement does, a new opposition could argue that it is the Washington consensus, not globalization, that limits its improvements in well-being. In that way, it could endorse a position that values the wealth corporations create but at the same time develops interventionist policies that would bring greater justice and stability to the system.

A politics in opposition to the Washington consensus would have to focus most of its attention on policy formation in the United States. In this it would have to take on what Bhagwati describes as "the exceptional clout" that Wall Street possesses in Washington in defense of its "obvious self-interest in a world of free capital markets." Bhagwati argues that Wall Street's efforts at persuasion are particularly effective because there is "in the sense of a power elite à la C. Wright Mills, a definite networking of like-minded luminaries among the powerful institutions—Wall Street, the Treasury Department, the State Department, the IMF and the World Bank" (Bhagwati 1998, 11).

Cast in this light, the Washington consensus is but one manifestation of a more pervasive problem in American politics: the power of private wealth to shape the agenda and outcomes of policy debates. Our economic policies are excessively pro-corporate, not because corporations are economic agents, but because of their disproportionate influence on the political process. They set, to a great extent, the rules governing their own behavior. What is needed to correct the biases in policy created by such an obvious conflict of interest is a political rules-making context that is independent of the influence of the corporate and financial sectors. If that were in place, business firms could continue in their role of wealth creation, but they would do so in an environment reflecting the democratic will of the country.

In opposing excessive corporate influence in policy-making, a movement that is pro-globalization but anti-Washington consensus would call for the reform of American politics

and in particular a reduction in the role of private wealth in our political processes. This approach would have considerable overlap with the localist movement that also calls for such reforms as the public funding of elections and the control over "soft money" political donations. But a new movement in favor of a just globalization would possess a much greater long-term potential than the localist one. A movement that endorses globalization, but seeks to control financial speculation and protect dislocated workers would identify with the hopes of both Americans and the people of the third world for improved living conditions. It thus might be attractive enough to serve as a vehicle to reform and humanize globalization.

For Further Reading

Bhagwati, Jagdish. 1998. "The Capital Myth." *Foreign Affairs* 77, no. 3 (May–June 1998).

Burtless, Gary; Robert Z. Lawrence; Robert E. Litan; and Robert J. Shapiro. 1998. *Globaphobia: Confronting Fears About Open Trade.* Washington, DC: Brookings Institution.

Green Party Platform 2000. As ratified at the Green Party National Convention, Washington DC, June 2000. Available at www.gp.org/platform/ gpp2000.html.

Greider, William. 2000. "Shopping Till We Drop." *Nation,* April 10.

International Forum on Globalization. 1999. "Beyond the WTO: Alternatives to Economic Globalization: A Preliminary Report." Available at www.ifg.org/ beyondwto.html.

Klein, Naomi. 2000. "The Vision Thing." *Nation,* July 10. Available at www.thenation.com/issue/ 000710/07l0klein.shtml.

Kuttner, Robert. 2000. "The Role of Governments in the Global Economy." In *Global Capitalism,* ed. Will Hutton and Anthony Giddens. New York: New Press.

Stiglitz, Joseph. 1998. "More Instruments and Broader Goals: Moving Toward the Post-Washington Consensus." 1998 World Institute for Development Economic Research Annual Lecture, January 7. Available at www.worldbank. org/ html/extdr.extme/js-010798/ wider.htm.

Williamson, John. 1999. "What Should the Bank Think About the Washington Consensus?" Institute for International Economics. Available at www.iie.com/ TESTMONY/Bankwc.htm.

JAY MANDLE is W. Bradford Wiley Professor of Economics at Colgate University.

From *Challenge,* March/April 2001, pp. 24–38. © 2001 by M. E. Sharpe, Inc., Armonk, NY 10504. Reprinted by permission.

The Core of the Global Economy

The combined U.S.–EU gross domestic product is
$18 trillion, dwarfing all other economic relationships in the world.

WILLIAM RICHARD SMYSER

The European Union and the United States form the core of the global economy. America has the world's largest single GDP, about $9.5 trillion. The 15 states of the European Union jointly have the next largest, $8.5 trillion, and will have a larger one when all the prospective new members join by the second decade of this century. Japan, at about $3.2 trillion, is a distant third.

The United States and the EU are also the most important members of the World Trade Organization, which governs the international trading system, as well as of the World Bank and the International Monetary Fund.

Moreover, the United States and four EU members—France, Germany, Italy, and the United Kingdom—form the preponderant majority of the Group of Seven (G–7), in which they try to coordinate global economic policy with each other and with Japan and Canada.

Most of the cooperation between the EU and the United States moves so smoothly that it escapes notice. Goods and individuals travel across the Atlantic as easily and naturally as people used to cross a river a hundred years ago.

American trade with the EU exceeds every other bilateral trading relationship. American exports of goods to the EU have averaged $150 billion per year over the last several years, whereas U.S. imports have averaged $185 billion, leaving an EU trade surplus of about $25 billion. Annual U.S. exports of services to the EU have averaged $90 billion, giving a surplus of $20 billion over U.S. imports of $70 billion.

America's main exports to the EU are aircraft, computers, engines, and precision instruments. Its main imports are cars and trucks, engines, specialty chemicals, and aircraft. Thus, the two exchange over a billion dollars in goods and services ev-ery day as well as trillions of dollars of currency a week.

Mutual investments

American and EU companies also invest massively in each other. European direct investment in the United States amounts to $500 billion, with the main investors being British, Dutch, and German. American direct investment in the EU amounts to $450 billion, with most of it being in the United Kingdom, the Netherlands, and Germany.

Almost one-half of U.S. direct investment abroad is in EU states, while 60 percent of EU direct investment abroad is in the United States. General Motors and Ford produce cars in Europe, while Intel and Microsoft produce computer chips and software. In return, Daimler-Chrysler and BMW produce cars and trucks in the United States. The two exchange over 1,000 mergers and acquisitions a year.

THE WORLD & I

Various currencies from the early 1990s: Implementation of the euro has helped the EU become a single market, with goods and people traveling freely across borders.

Even as European-American economic relations have grown, EU integration has proceeded at an ever-accelerating pace. During the 1990s, the European Union became a single market, as goods and people traveled freely across its borders and common industrial and service standards developed. The EU also made organizational changes to speed up its decision-making processes and give more power to institutions like the European Parliament.

The EU expanded during that decade to include Sweden, Finland, and Austria, attaining a population 100 million larger than America's 280 million. The EU hopes to expand across almost all of Europe by 2012, integrating 12 more states from central and eastern Europe and the Mediterranean.

In a step toward full economic integration, the EU has launched a new European currency, the euro, administered by the new European Central Bank. The ECB, whose governing board includes 12 of the 15 EU states (only Denmark, Sweden, and the United Kingdom have not joined), makes decisions that affect the entire European economy as well as the economies of each EU state.

A Growing Entity

- During the 1990s, the EU became a single market as goods and people traveled freely across its borders and common industrial and service standards developed.
- The EU made organizational changes to speed up its decision-making processes and give more power to institutions like the European Parliament.
- It expanded to include Sweden, Finland, and Austria, attaining a population 100 million larger than America's 280 million.
- The EU hopes to expand across most of Europe by 2012, integrating 12 more states from central and eastern Europe and the Mediterranean.

The euro will become a daily reality in the lives of Europeans on January 1, 2002, when euro coins and bills will replace such national currencies as the German deutsche mark, the French franc, and the Spanish peseta. It could also become a competitor to the dollar as an international reserve and transaction currency.

Slow-moving economy

But the EU economy as a whole, while increasingly integrated, still moves more slowly than the American. In some areas of fundamental financial importance, like stock exchanges and investment services, Europeans often find it hard to act quickly and jointly. A mix of national and continental regulations impedes new enterprises, as do relatively conservative management cultures. And workers do not like to move from one country to another in search of jobs.

An American inventor can easily find investors ready to finance new ideas and workers willing to move across the country for new jobs. All this has yet to come to Europe.

The European economy therefore grew more slowly during the 1990s. As Americans moved aggressively into the new world of computers, the Internet, e-commerce, and globalization, Europe (like Japan) lagged behind. In the EU states, on average, GDPs grew at under 3 percent while unemployment rates lingered above 9 percent, whereas the United States enjoyed growth rates above 4 percent and unemployment rates below 5 percent.

Despite the differences in economic cultures, American-European economic relations generally work smoothly. Managers, traders, and workers on both sides of the Atlantic understand each other. They can coordinate production schedules and trade efficiently. Many have gone to the same management schools, mainly in the United States, and can communicate fluently in the common jargon of their trade.

Nonetheless, various bitter disputes have roiled trade relations for several years. The following show no sign of easing soon:

- Bananas, perhaps the longest-running and bitterest of all European-American disputes. The EU, which has generally followed a restrictive policy for agricultural imports to protect European farmers, has particularly blocked banana imports. It produces no bananas but wants to buy them from former European—mainly French—colonies. Led by France, the EU has kept out competing (and cheaper) bananas grown by such American firms as Chiquita in Central and South America. The WTO has agreed with an American complaint that EU banana policy violates international trading rules. It has instructed the EU to permit open entry of American bananas, but the EU has not complied. Washington has retaliated by placing prohibitive tariffs on several kinds of European imports to the United States. Chiquita has also sued the EU.
- Commercial jets, with the new European Airbus firm competing against the U.S. airframe manufacturer Boeing. The Americans complain that the EU has arranged low-interest guaranteed loans and subsidies to help Airbus compete against Boeing, whereas the EU complains that Washington subsidizes Boeing by military research and production contracts. The dispute has become particularly bitter because a new double-decker Airbus superjumbo, the A-380, threatens the dominance of the Boeing 747.
- Beef, with the EU preventing the import of American gene-modified beef, which the WTO has pronounced safe. The EU contends that the beef could constitute a health hazard and has insisted on labeling it with a warning (most Europeans are still leery of gene-modified products). The whole argument may become moot, for the Europeans face a much more sobering threat in the form of European beef tainted by mad-cow disease.

These disputes cannot be easily resolved. They exist against a background of several other trade complaints, such as EU charges that the United States unfairly subsidizes exports by tax preferences for export firms. But one should not make too much of them, because 99 percent of European-American trade moves without impediment, to the benefit of both sides.

As the EU gradually expands from 15 to 27 nations, many new members will need large infusions of aid and protection for years.

Future EU expansion

The impending expansion of the European Union may have an important if indirect impact on European-American relations. Most of the new countries that are expected to join the EU between 2004 and 2012 are very poor states that may need a great deal of support.

Even now, the EU is not a union of true equals. It contains large economies such as France, Germany, Italy, and the United Kingdom as well as small economies like Belgium, Finland, Ireland, and the Netherlands. It contains highly developed, rich economies such as Austria, Denmark, and Sweden as well as relatively less developed and poorer economies such as Greece, Portugal, and Spain. Each economy has its own needs and characteristics, so the EU must try to reconcile all those factors into a common policy.

As the EU gradually expands from 15 to 27 nations, many new members will need large infusions of aid and protection for years. Some potential members, such as Cyprus, Malta, or Slovenia, have economies as developed as the lower level of current EU states. But others, such as Poland, Romania, Bulgaria, or Lithuania, have much lower per capita income than any EU state and may require decades of development to catch up.

The EU already spends almost half its budget on special funds, known as cohesion and structural funds, to bring the less-developed economies up to the average EU level. With the new members, it will have to spend even more on such funds. It may also have to offer more support to farmers, both in its older economies and the new ones, unless it wants to give up its farm support system. Under those circumstances, the EU may be even less inclined to permit large influxes of farm goods from the United States.

Thus, the EU may have to concentrate on managing its own enlargement and be unable to attend to its economic relationship with the United States.

The EU must also decide whether it wishes to open its markets to help boost the global economy. With Japan in recession for most of the 1990s and European growth at relatively low levels, the United States became the most open market for EU members selling goods. If America enters a recession in 2001, as some experts now predict, Europe may need to become the engine of global growth. If European exports to the United States decline, Europe may have to take more imports from the United States to help sustain world prosperity.

Although the European economy shows signs of picking up speed during the new millennium, no EU leader has yet announced that the EU will deliberately try to become a global growth engine. The European Central Bank is still pursuing a relatively cautious monetary policy instead of stimulating growth. Europe thus might join the United States and Japan in recession, risking a major deflationary cycle for the world as a whole.

Even as they face these difficulties, Europe and America must prepare for the next round of trade talks, originally planned for launch during the year 2000 at a WTO meeting in Seattle but now scheduled to begin during 2001 or 2002. These talks, termed the Millennium Round, will address such controversial topics as trade in agriculture and services, about which Washington and Brussels have had major disagreements in the past.

As the EU evolves and the global economy turns, Europe and America face daunting difficulties. They need to coordinate their economic policies more closely than they have in the past.

They have a joint responsibility to keep the long economic boom on track, and they need to make sure that they meet that responsibility together. To do that, they must eliminate old problems and prevent new ones from arising, concentrating on the positive totality of their economic cooperation.

William Richard Smyser teaches the political economy of European integration at Georgetown University. His books on European and German issues include *From Yalta to Berlin* (2000) and *The German Economy* (1994).

This article appeared in the April 2001 issue and is reprinted with permission from *The World & I*, p. 27, a publication of The Washington Times Corporation, © 2001.

Globalisation's misguided assumptions

Markets, competition and free trade are all essential for healthy globalisation to take place. Or are they? Critics argue that while globalisation has the potential to become a positive force for economic growth, too many of the benefits go to well-off countries, while the costs of adjusting markets and institutions are being borne by millions of already poor workers worldwide. Others go further still and blame free trade for many of the woes of the poor everywhere, and farmers in particular. **José Bové** of France's Confédération Paysanne (Small Farmers' Federation) is one such anti-globalisation activist. In this article he explains what he considers to be the "false assumptions" underlying the arguments of the free-market camp. The article originally appeared in the French newspaper *Le Monde*[*].

Humanity is grappling with a formidable creed, which, like so many others, is totalitarian and planetary in scope, namely free trade. The gurus and zealous servants of this doctrine ("responsible" people) are saying that the Market is the only god, and that those who want to combat it are heretics ("irresponsible" people). So we find ourselves faced with a modern-day obscurantism—a new opium on which the high priests and traffickers are sure they can make populations dependent. Recent articles in the international press supporting new trade rounds and the like are quite clear on the dogma that some people would like to impose on the men and women of this planet.

More and more people are coming out against the free market credo advocated by the WTO, the damage inflicted by it being so plain to see, and the falsehoods on which it is based so blatant.

The first falsehood is the market's self-regulating virtues, which form the basis of the dogma, but this ideological mystification is belied by the facts. In the field of agriculture, for example, since 1992 the major industrialised countries have embraced global markets with open arms—the United States enacted the FAIR (Federal Agriculture Improvement and Reform) Act, a policy instrument that did away with direct production subsidies, instead "decoupling" aid and allowing farmers to produce with no restrictions whatsoever—but this has done nothing to calm the wild swings in the markets.

It has, in fact, done quite the opposite, since markets have experienced unprecedented instability since the trade agreements signed in Marrakech in 1995. The most spectacular effect of this American "decoupling" has been the explosion of emergency direct subsidies to offset declining prices. These subsidies reached a record high of more than $23 billion in 2000 (four times more than the amount budgeted in the 1996 Farm Act).

So, contrary to free-marketers' assertions, markets are inherently unstable and chaotic. Government intervention is needed to regulate markets and adjust price trends, to guarantee producers' incomes and thus ensure that farming activity is sustained.

The second blatant untruth is that competition generates wealth for everyone. Competition is meaningful only if competitors are able to survive. This is especially true for agriculture, where labour productivity varies by a factor of a thousand to one between a grain farmer on the plains of the Middle West and a spade-wielding peasant in the heart of the Sahel.

To claim that the terms of competition will be healthy and fair, and thus tend towards equilibrium if farm policy does not interfere with the workings of a free market, is hypocritical. How can there be a level playing field in the same market between a majority of 1.3 billion farm workers who harvest the land with their hands or with harnessed animals, and a tiny minority of 28 million mechanised farmers formidably equipped for export? How can there be "fair" competition when the most productive farmers of rich countries receive emergency subsidies and multiple guarantees against falling prices on top of their direct and indirect export bonuses?

The third falsehood is that world market prices are a relevant criterion for guiding output. But these prices apply to only a very small fraction of global production and consumption. The world wheat market accounts for only 12% of overall output and international trade takes place at prices that are determined not by aggregate trade, but by the prices of the most competitive exporting country.

The world price of milk and dairy products is determined by production costs in New Zealand, while New Zealand's share of global milk production averaged only 1.63% between 1985 and

1998. The world price of wheat itself is pegged to the price in the United States, which accounted for only 5.84% of aggregate world output from 1985 to 1998.

The proponents of free trade cannot bear the idea that life can reproduce on its own, free of charge, whence the race for patents, licences, profits and forcible expropriation.

What is more, these prices are nearly always tantamount to dumping (i.e., to selling below production costs in the producing and importing countries) and are only economically viable for the exporters thanks to the substantial aid they receive in return.

The fourth falsehood is that free trade is the engine of economic development. For free marketers, customs protection schemes are the root of all evil: they claim that such systems stifle trade and economic prosperity, and even hinder cultural exchanges and vital dialogue between peoples. Yet who would dare to claim that decades of massive northbound coffee, cocoa, rice and banana exports have enriched or improved the living standards of farmers in the south? Who would dare to make such a claim, looking these poverty-stricken farmers straight in the eyes? And who would dare to tell African breeders, bankrupted by competition from subsidised meat from Europe, that it is for their own good that customs barriers are falling?

To achieve their ends, the proponents of free trade exploit science in the name of so-called "modernism", asserting that the development of any scientific discovery constitutes progress—as long as it is economically profitable. They cannot bear the idea that life can reproduce on its own, free of charge, whence the race for patents, licences, profits and forcible expropriation.

Obviously, when talking about agriculture, it is impossible not to evoke the farce of GMOs. Nobody is asking for them, yet they must be the answer to everyone's dreams! There is pressure on us to concede that genetically modified rice (cynically dubbed "golden rice") is going to nourish people who are dying of hunger and protect them from all sorts of diseases, thanks to its new Vitamin A-enriched formula. But this will not solve the problems of vitamin deficiencies, because a person would have to eat three kilograms of dry rice every day, whereas the normal ration is no more than 100 grams.

The way to fight malnutrition, which affects nearly a third of humanity, is to diversify people's diets. This entails rethinking the appalling state of society, underpinned by free market economics which strives to keep wages in southern countries as low as possible in order to maximise profits. It is therefore a good idea to throw some vitamins into the rice that is sold to poor people, so that they don't die too quickly and can continue working for low wages, rather than helping them build a freer and fairer society.

Jacques Diouf, Director-General of FAO, recently pointed out that "to feed the 8 003 million people who are hungry, there is no need for GMOs" (*Le Monde,* 10 May). No wonder the Indian farmers of Via Campesina, an international small farmers' movement, destroy fields of genetically modified rice.

The FAO is not the only international institution to question some of the certainties and radical WTO positions regarding the benefits of free markets. The highly free-market OECD acknowledges in a recent report entitled *The Well-being of Nations* that the preservation and improvement of government services (healthcare, education) are a key factor underlying the economic success of nations.

We therefore have every reason to oppose the dangerous myth of free trade. Judging by the substantial social and environmental damage free trade has inflicted, before anything else, it is necessary for all of us—farmers and non-farmers alike—to make it subject to three fundamental principles: food sovereignty—the right of peoples and of countries to produce their food freely, and to protect their agriculture from the ravages of global "competition"; food safety—the right to protect oneself from any threat to one's health; and the preservation of bio-diversity.

Between the absolute sovereign attitude of nationalists and the proponents of free trade, there are other roads.

Along with adherence to these principles must come a goal of solidarity-based development, via the institution of economic partnership areas among neighbouring countries, including import protection for such groups of countries having uniform structures and levels of development.

The WTO wants to take its free-market logic even further. Next November, in the seclusion of a monarchy that outlaws political parties and demonstrations—Qatar—it will attempt to attain its goals. But if major international institutions are becoming increasingly critical and are casting doubt on these certainties, then mobilised citizens can bring their own laws to bear on trade.

Between the absolute sovereign attitude of nationalists and the proponents of free trade, there are other roads. To echo the theme of the World Social Forum that took place in Porto Alegre last January, "another world is possible!"—a world that respects different cultures and the particularities of each, in a spirit of openness and understanding. We are happy and proud to be part of its emergence.

*José Bové's article originally appeared (in French) in *Le Monde,* 12 June 2001; see http://www.lemonde.fr/

From *Observer,* September 2001, pp. 17-19. © 2001 by OECD Observer.

Heavy surf & tsunamis

Ellen Frank explains why reform of the world financial system is in the interests even of the globalizers.

Another world IS possible

Keeping the world's financiers and speculators under control would be like King Canute trying to turn back the tide, according to standard thinking. But would it? Couldn't we come up with alternative proposals that would foster stability and thereby benefit everybody concerned?

INTERNATIONAL financial markets, as any self-respecting critic of globalization can tell you, move some $1.5 trillion round the world on a daily basis—$10 trillion a week, $45 trillion a month, $550 trillion a year; an amount 10 times greater than total world income and 25 times greater than total world trade. As this sea of cash sloshes from shore to shore, it generates heavy surf for the major countries and tsunamis in lesser economies. For the G7 nations, the financial markets are a source of continual instability as exchange rates and asset prices bounce back and forth, threatening profits, wealth and living standards. For hundreds of other nations, the financial seas carry threats of mounting debt, capital flight and currency collapse.

The deregulation of global financial flows—by which national governments lifted restrictions on cross-border borrowing and lending and allowed exchange rates to be mostly set by the market—began in the 1960s with the US, Britain and Can-ada, not surprisingly, taking the lead. European economies deregulated in the 1970s and 1980s, Asia and the larger 'emerging markets' in the 1990s. Financial deregulation served the broader purposes of international businesses as they sought markets, materials and workers abroad. It allowed businesses to borrow abroad in foreign currencies, enabled firms to repatriate foreign earnings with few restrictions, simplified accounting practices for globally minded businesses. Of course, wherever money is moving about, speculators soon step in, looking to make money on the movement of money itself. By the 1970s, the trickle of international monetary flows had become a river. By the 1980s the river had become a sea and in the 1990s the sea became a flood. By the turn of the 21st century, the sheer size and scope of the financial markets and the havoc they wrought in Asia, Africa and South America seemed to epitomize the problems of corporate-led economic globalization.

But if the international financial markets are a symbol of globalization, they are also globalization's bane, perhaps even its Achilles' heel. If by globalization we mean the determined efforts of international businesses to build markets and production networks that are truly global in scope, then the current monetary system is in many ways an endless headache whose costs are rapidly outstripping its benefits.

When a wave of financial crises struck in 1997, US, Japanese and European banks stood to lose over $100 billion dollars in bad loans to Asia. The IMF stepped in, reorganized the debt, pressured the affected governments to take over the foreign-currency obligations of their private businesses, oversaw the economic 'restructuring' required to ensure repayment and unleashed torrents of criticism and recrimination. The bailouts, progressive critics contended, turned previously debt-free nations like Korea overnight into wards of the international financial

Time for Tobin

Take three good ideas. Taxing the rich; giving the proceeds to poor countries to allow them to pull themselves out of poverty; and regulating markets that fail. In 1972 US Nobel Prize-winning economist James Tobin came up with a simple proposal incorporating all three: a small tax on damaging currency speculation, the proceeds of which could be spent on development.

A tax set as low as a tenth of one per cent could raise $390 billion a year—seven times the current level of development aid.

Anti-poverty charity War on Want has been campaigning for the tax since 1998. Together with other European charities and campaign groups we have met with considerable success in recent months.

British finance minister Gordon Brown, Belgian Prime Minister Guy Verhofstadt, French Prime Minister Lionel Jospin and German Chancellor Gerhard Schroeder have all recently announced that they want to see the tax given serious consideration by European leaders over the next few months. Canada, Finland, India and Brazil have expressed various levels of support.

Some economists have argued that the tax is unfeasible because every major government would have to sign up to it, and currency transactions would be driven offshore. However, the recent terrorist attacks in the US have prompted the Bush administration to prop up the country's stock exchange and consider closing down tax havens to block money laundering by terrorist groups. This ability to intervene in the markets for the sake of a noble cause proves that there is no insurmountable barrier to introducing measures to control currency speculation.

Anti-poverty and development campaigners demand a world where people come before profits, but we have been criticized for lacking practical proposals. The Tobin Tax is the most practical of solutions.

Carolyne Culver, War on Want

institutions, driven to sell resources and assets at deep discounts to Western corporations in order to service unjust debts. In the ensuing few years, a number of South American economies suffered a similar plight. Brazil, the world's ninth-largest economy, lost most of its foreign-exchange reserves to speculators and piled on more debt as part of an IMF agreement. A number of governments, including New Zealand, Argentina and Ecuador, announced plans to 'dollarize' or 'euroize' their economies, to avoid the ceaseless attacks of financial speculators and damaging volatility in exchange rates. The parallels with European colonialism seemed self-evident—destroying a colony's monetary system and installing the colonizer's currency in its stead was a hallmark of imperialism, a practice that allowed the French to strip Algeria and the British to plunder India, exchanging resources for francs and sterling printed on the imperial press. Debt and currency crisis were the postmodern version of imperialism, serving the long-term interests of the G7 economies and relegating developing countries forever to the periphery of the global economy.

But globalization today is driven less by the imperatives of nation-building than by the imperatives of corporation-building. National governments, to be sure, press the case and pave the way, but the beneficiaries and promoters of globalization are international businesses positioning themselves in a world market.

Money scrambles around the globe in quest of the banker's holy grail—sound money of stable value—while undermining every attempt by cash-strapped governments to provide the very stability the wealthy crave. Governments of developing countries try to peg their currencies, only to have the peg undone by capital flight. They offer to dollarize or euroize, only to find themselves so short of dollars that they are forced to cut off growth. They raise interest rates to extraordinary levels to protect investors against currency losses, only to topple their economies and the source of investor profits.

IMF bailouts provide a brief respite for international investors but they are, even from the perspective of the wealthy, a short-term solution at best. Not only are bailouts a public-relations disaster, they leave countries with more debt and fewer options.

The current crisis in Argentina testifies to the fact that the globalizers are fresh out of ideas on how to resolve this mess. There is simply no policy or set of policies that would allow Argentina to make payments on a $132-billion foreign debt, maintain enough dollar reserves to satisfy investors as to the stability of its pesos, and promote sufficient internal growth and stability to make doing business worthwhile. The Argentinas of the world economy are in an awful bind and that bind is not good for business.

In the immediate wake of the Asian financial crisis, many officials called for a new international financial 'architecture'. It was fairly clear that the crises were due not to the shortcomings of specific governments, but were systemic failures of the financial markets that required multilateral solutions. A global economy requires a global monetary system and that requires a public body of some sort to regulate it. The question is: what sort of system is required and who should run it?

Progressive NGOs and officials in developing countries have their own ideas—some sort of democratically managed central bank or payments institution that could settle debts between sovereign states, help countries manage exchange rates and institute widespread debt cancellation. Such an institution would certainly stabilize the world financial system. To work, it would almost certainly give governments of smaller countries enhanced powers to re-regulate cross-border money flows without going begging to the IMF or to international investors.

The G7 governments and their corporate sponsors have kept their own counsel. This is not because they are satisfied with the *status quo*. All these little individual countries—all with their own currencies and crises—are an impediment to building an economy of genuinely global businesses. Money doesn't travel very well, when all is said and done. But the sort of reform they desire would provide greater stability without removing the privileges, perquisites and lack of accountability of the

current system. Their ideal, I suspect, would be a global currency issued by an institution akin to the European Central Bank, but less democratic and with Alan Greenspan, rather than Wim Duisenberg, at the helm—someone more seasoned at managing the occasional crisis and bailing out the banks.

Unfortunately for the corporate globalizers, they have overplayed their hand too often to float such a proposal. Even if the proposal is concocted in secrecy, they risk the embarrassment of leaked documents creating another public-relations disaster like the Multilateral Agreement on Investment. That was run into the sand by concerted worldwide resistance that even predated

the protests on the streets of Seattle. The globalizers are being watched, and they know it.

Contact

ATTAC
Association for the Taxation of Financial Transactions for the Aid of Citizens www.attac.org

Tobin Tax Initiative
CEED/IIRP, PO Box 4167, Arcata, CA 95518–4167, US Tel: +1 707 822 8347 www.tobintax.org

War on Want
37–39 Great Guildford St, London SW1 OES, England Tel: +44 (0) 20 7620 1111 www.tobintax.org.uk

Halifax Initiative
153 rue Chapel St, Suite 104, Ottawa, ON K1N 1H5, Canada Tel: +1 613 789 4447 www.halifaxinitiative.org

From *New Internationalist,* January/February 2002, pp. 28-29. © 2002 by New Internationalist. Reprinted by permission.

Index

Index

Test Your Knowledge Form

We encourage you to photocopy and use this page as a tool to assess how the articles in *Annual Editions* expand on the information in your textbook. By reflecting on the articles you will gain enhanced text information. You can also access this useful form on a product's book support Web site at *http://www.dushkin.com/online/*.

NAME: _____ DATE: _____

TITLE AND NUMBER OF ARTICLE: _____

BRIEFLY STATE THE MAIN IDEA OF THIS ARTICLE: _____

_____

LIST THREE IMPORTANT FACTS THAT THE AUTHOR USES TO SUPPORT THE MAIN IDEA:

_____

WHAT INFORMATION OR IDEAS DISCUSSED IN THIS ARTICLE ARE ALSO DISCUSSED IN YOUR TEXTBOOK OR OTHER READINGS THAT YOU HAVE DONE? LIST THE TEXTBOOK CHAPTERS AND PAGE NUMBERS:

_____

LIST ANY EXAMPLES OF BIAS OR FAULTY REASONING THAT YOU FOUND IN THE ARTICLE:

_____

LIST ANY NEW TERMS/CONCEPTS THAT WERE DISCUSSED IN THE ARTICLE, AND WRITE A SHORT DEFINITION:

We Want Your Advice

ANNUAL EDITIONS revisions depend on two major opinion sources: one is our Advisory Board, listed in the front of this volume, which works with us in scanning the thousands of articles published in the public press each year; the other is you—the person actually using the book. Please help us and the users of the next edition by completing the prepaid article rating form on this page and returning it to us. Thank you for your help!

ANNUAL EDITIONS: International Business 03/04

ARTICLE RATING FORM

Here is an opportunity for you to have direct input into the next revision of this volume.
We would like you to rate each of the articles listed below, using the following scale:

1. **Excellent: should definitely be retained**
2. **Above average: should probably be retained**
3. **Below average: should probably be deleted**
4. **Poor: should definitely be deleted**

Your ratings will play a vital part in the next revision.
Please mail this prepaid form to us as soon as possible.
Thanks for your help!

RATING	ARTICLE	RATING	ARTICLE
	1. New Realities of Globalization		34. International Alliance Negotiations: Legal Issues for General Managers
	2. Rebuilding Afghanistan: A Multi-Billion Dollar Plan		35. Putting Branding on the Map: Branding a Country Has Outgrown its Corporate Roots to Develop Positioning Insights That are World Class
	3. Money's Costing More		
	4. Going Global Can Bring on a World of Challenges		
	5. International Trade: Globalization vs. Protectionism		36. Does Globalization Have Staying Power?
	6. American Corporations: The New Sovereigns		37. International Growth Patterns Remain Strong
	7. 2001's Most Influencial People in World Trade		38. The Role of International Trade and Investment
	8. Europeans Covet U.S.		39. AAEI Conference Highlights: What Does China's Entry Into the WTO Mean for U.S. Exporters?
	9. Free Trade Bush's Way		
	10. Smart Globalization		40. Post–Cold War International Relations: Trends and Portents
	11. Integrating Multinational Firms into International Economics		
	12. Where the Elite Preens Itself		41. The Russian Approach to Human Rights Intervention
	13. Free Trade Area of the Americas: NAFTA Marches South		
			42. Offshore Shores Up IT: Going Overseas for Tech Help Promises Big Savings, but Companies Shouldn't Go Overboard Without Considering the Risk
	14. The Deficit That Just About Everyone Overlooks		
	15. The Sacking of Argentina: The IMF Deserves to be Blamed, but So Does the Country's Willing Political Class		
			43. Redefining the Business Case for Offshore Outsourcing
	16. Failure of the Fund: Rethinking the IMF Response		44. Comrades Are on the March Again
	17. Accounting Challenges Overseas		45. Unions Forming Global Contract
	18. What the New Currency Means to the European Economy		46. The Incredible Shrinking World
			47. Has Strategy Changed?
	19. Economics Focus: Big MacCurrencies		48. Personnel Demands Attention Overseas
	20. Nike's Voice Looms Large		49. Safe Haven
	21. Social Accountability in Central America: Not Just Ethical, But Economical		50. International HR Manager
			51. Reforming Globalization
	22. Ascension Years		52. The Core of the Global Economy
	23. The Non-Performing Country		53. Globalisation's Misguided Assumptions
	24. The Gains and Pains of Free Trade		54. Heavy Surf and Tsunamis
	25. Free Markets and Poverty		
	26. Empires Without Umpires		
	27. Hype at the End of the Tunnel		
	28. Chile's Democratic Challenge		
	29. Government: Progress Against Corruption		
	30. Serving Up the Commons: A Guest Essay		
	31. Analyzing and Managing Country Risks		
	32. The Highest Court You've Never Heard Of		
	33. The World According to Monti		

(Continued on next page)

BUSINESS REPLY MAIL
FIRST-CLASS MAIL PERMIT NO. 84 GUILFORD CT

POSTAGE WILL BE PAID BY ADDRESSEE

McGraw-Hill/Dushkin
530 Old Whitfield Street
Guilford, Ct 06437-9989

NO POSTAGE
NECESSARY
IF MAILED
IN THE
UNITED STATES

ABOUT YOU

Name

Date

Are you a teacher? ☐   A student? ☐
Your school's name

Department

Address   City   State   Zip

School telephone #

YOUR COMMENTS ARE IMPORTANT TO US!

Please fill in the following information:
For which course did you use this book?

Did you use a text with this ANNUAL EDITION?   ☐   yes ☐   no
What was the title of the text?

What are your general reactions to the *Annual Editions* concept?

Have you read any pertinent articles recently that you think should be included in the next edition? Explain.

Are there any articles that you feel should be replaced in the next edition? Why?

Are there any World Wide Web sites that you feel should be included in the next edition? Please annotate.

May we contact you for editorial input?   ☐   yes ☐   no
May we quote your comments?   ☐   yes ☐   no